Letters on India; with etchings and a map.

Maria Graham

Letters on India; with etchings and a map.
Graham, Maria
British Library, Historical Print Editions
British Library
1814
8°.
T 11190

The BiblioLife Network

This project was made possible in part by the BiblioLife Network (BLN), a project aimed at addressing some of the huge challenges facing book preservationists around the world. The BLN includes libraries, library networks, archives, subject matter experts, online communities and library service providers. We believe every book ever published should be available as a high-quality print reproduction; printed on- demand anywhere in the world. This insures the ongoing accessibility of the content and helps generate sustainable revenue for the libraries and organizations that work to preserve these important materials.

The following book is in the "public domain" and represents an authentic reproduction of the text as printed by the original publisher. While we have attempted to accurately maintain the integrity of the original work, there are sometimes problems with the original book or micro-film from which the books were digitized. This can result in minor errors in reproduction. Possible imperfections include missing and blurred pages, poor pictures, markings and other reproduction issues beyond our control. Because this work is culturally important, we have made it available as part of our commitment to protecting, preserving, and promoting the world's literature.

GUIDE TO FOLD-OUTS, MAPS and OVERSIZED IMAGES

In an online database, page images do not need to conform to the size restrictions found in a printed book. When converting these images back into a printed bound book, the page sizes are standardized in ways that maintain the detail of the original. For large images, such as fold-out maps, the original page image is split into two or more pages.

Guidelines used to determine the split of oversize pages:

• Some images are split vertically; large images require vertical and horizontal splits.
• For horizontal splits, the content is split left to right.
• For vertical splits, the content is split from top to bottom.
• For both vertical and horizontal splits, the image is processed from top left to bottom right.

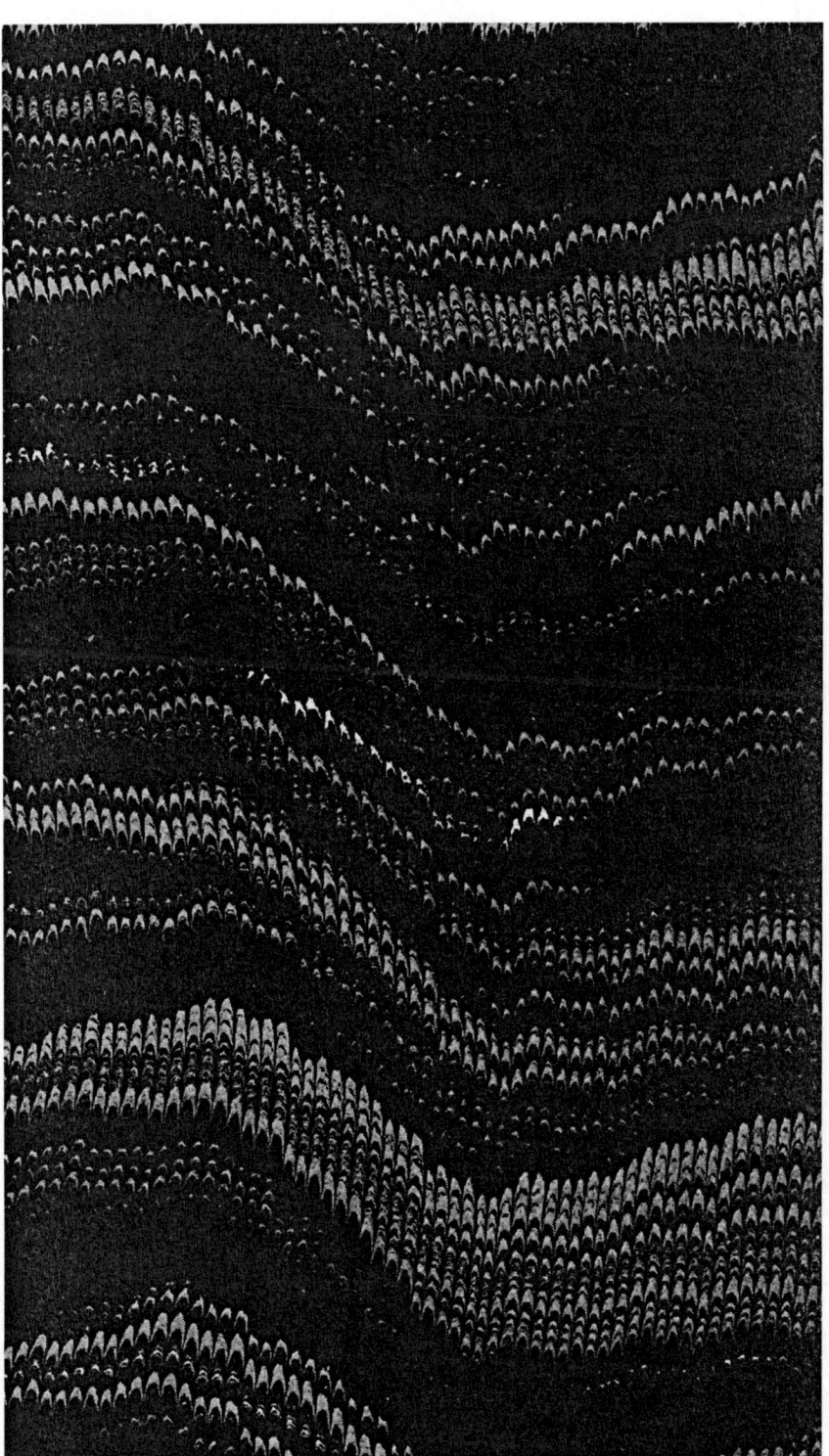

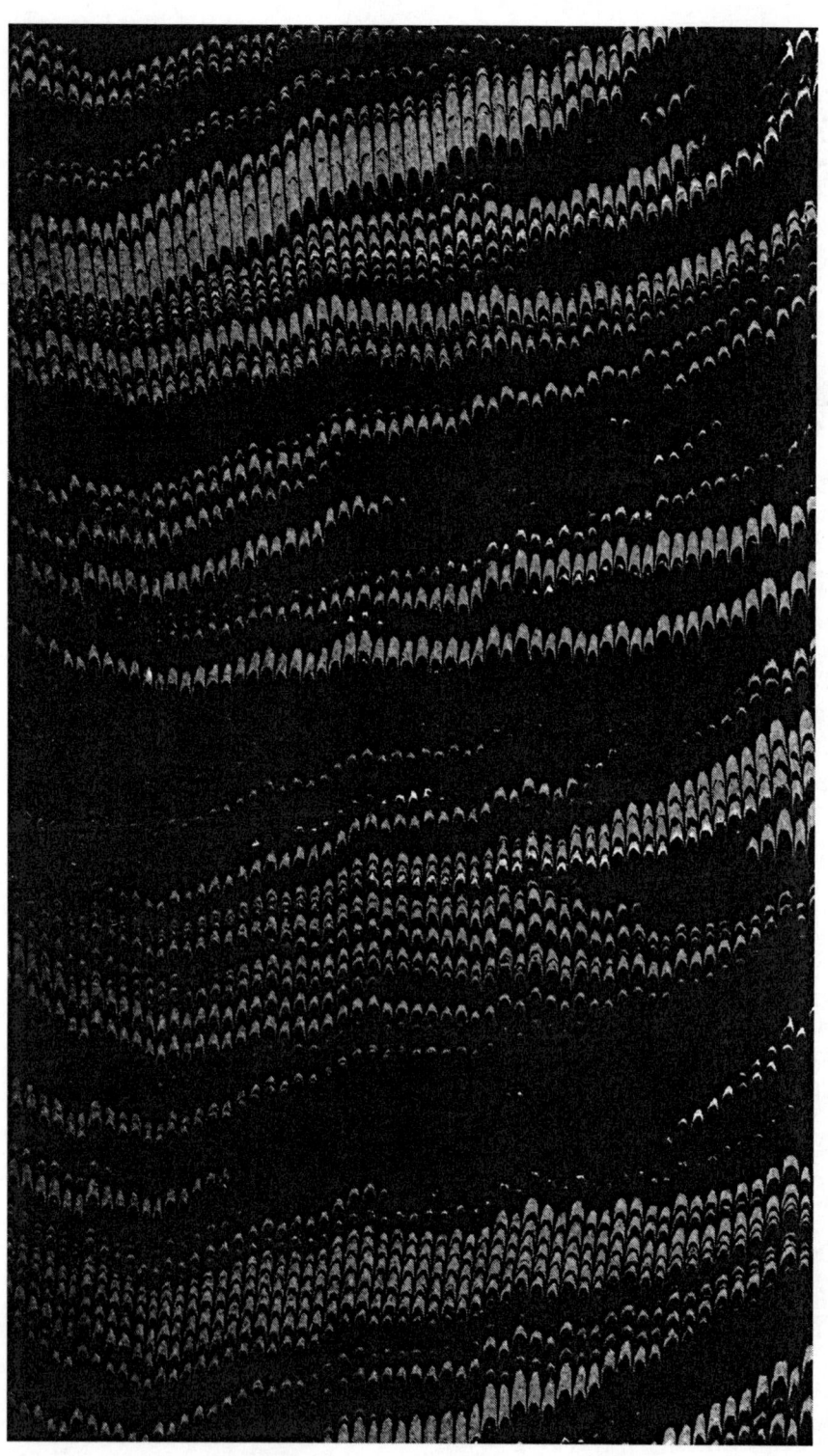

1846. e. 1.

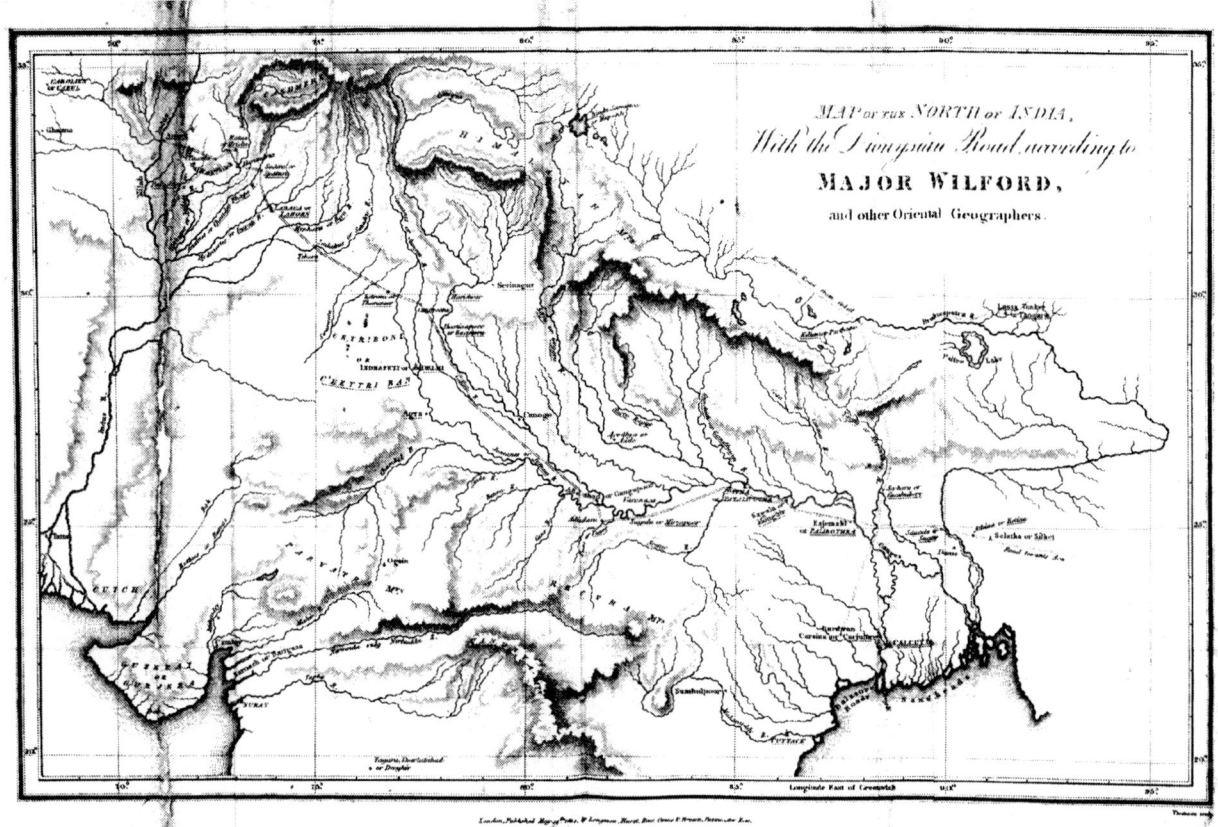

MAP of the NORTH of INDIA,
With the Dionysian Road according to
MAJOR WILFORD,
and other Oriental Geographers.

London, Published May 1 1816, by Longman, Hurst, Rees, Orme & Brown, Paternoster Row.

LETTERS

ON

INDIA;

BY

MARIA GRAHAM,

AUTHOR OF " JOURNAL OF A RESIDENCE IN INDIA."

With Etchings and a Map.

LONDON:

PRINTED FOR LONGMAN, HURST, REES, ORME, AND BROWN,
PATERNOSTER-ROW;
AND A. CONSTABLE AND CO. EDINBURGH.

1814.

G. WOODFALL, Printer, Angel-court, Skinner-street, London.

PREFACE.

THE indulgence with which the Public received the "Journal of a Residence in India," induced the writer to hope, that the curiosity concerning our oriental possessions was still sufficiently alive to promise a favourable reception to the following little work. It is written solely with the design of being useful to such as are called upon to go at an early period of life, to India, and who therefore cannot have had time to make themselves acquainted with even the general outline of the history, religion, or science of that country; and though the execution must necessarily have fallen far short of the design, yet it is hoped that the general

sketch here presented may not be found
uninteresting or uninstructive. The sources
from which the information contained in
the following pages is chiefly drawn, are,
the papers of Sir W. Jones, Mr. Colebrooke, and Major Wilford in the Asiatic
Researches; and where these guides have
failed, those who could, in the writer's
humble judgment, be best relied on, were
chosen. Colonel Wilks's admirable History of Mysore, Orme, Scott, Dow, Malcolm, Buchanan, have all been referred
to; and if on every occasion where the author has made use of their works she has
neglected to name them, it is because such
references would have been too numerous
at the bottom of her pages.

For the etchings which accompany the
letters, the writer is indebted to her ingenious young friend and relation Mr. J.
D. Glennie, of Dulwich, who kindly in-
terrupted his higher and more interesting

pursuits to give her the advantage of presenting, without embellishment or caricature, the subjects of the Hindû chissel, which she had been fortunate enough to preserve, when many other drawings were lost on her passage homeward from the East.

With much diffidence she takes leave of her little book to send it forth to the world, certain that it requires much indulgence, but trusting that the motives of the undertaking will cancel some of its many faults.

CONTENTS.

LETTERS ON INDIA.

MY DEAR SIR,

ALLOW me to congratulate you on your recent appointment; and on the accomplishment of the wish you have so often expressed to visit the East. I feel highly flattered by your applying to me for information concerning the country you are so soon to see, and to judge of for yourself; but conscious of my inability to satisfy you as I could wish, on many subjects relating to it, I had once thoughts of referring you to such books as contain the best accounts of the country, its customs, and its inhabitants. However, on reflecting that your time must be too fully occupied in preparations for your voyage, to allow you to engage in the perusal of very voluminous works, I have, though with considerable diffidence, determined to send you the abstract you request, of the notes made for my own use.

I perfectly agree with you that many of the evils complained of in the intercourse between the European residents and the native inhabitants of India, are owing to the want of mutual understanding, and of mutual knowledge. The happiness of so many millions of our fellow-creatures, now brought still nearer as our fellow-subjects, cannot be a matter of indifference. But we can scarcely be interested for those whom we do not know, and I have, therefore, always thought, that it would be an acceptable service to collect from the more elaborate works on India such a popular view of the history, literature, science and manners of that country, as should excite an interest in its inhabitants; and by exhibiting a sketch of its former grandeur and refinement, restore it to that place in the scale of ancient nations, which European historians have in general unaccountably neglected to assign to it.

This idea induced me to collect the notes in question; I shall send you a portion of them from time to time, and if you have not leisure to read them before your departure, they may, perhaps, serve to amuse you in your passage to " India and the Golden Chersonese and farthest Indian Isle Taprobane."

On looking over the map of modern India, one is astonished at the immense tract of country contained within the lines which mark the British possessions, nor is the wonder lessened by the consideration, that the territory nominally under the government of the Nizam ul Muluc, or Soubadar of the Deccan, and that subject to the Peishwa of Poonah, are guarded and garrisoned by British subsidiary forces, while these princes, not less than the shadow of the Great Mogul, are prisoners in their palaces, to troops paid by themselves. Thus the whole of the immense region from the frontiers of Cabul to Cape Comorin north and south, and from the Indus to the Ganges east and west, is virtually under the British dominion; while the very few really independant chiefs and princes preserve that independance merely by sufferance, as you may convince yourself by an inspection of their geographical positions relatively to the British territory. But after all, it is chiefly the empire of opinion that supports us in our possessions, for the natives outnumber us in such a proportion as must make us tremble, if ever injuries offered to them, or interference in those points of religion or custom to which they are attached, shall rouse them to the exercise of the physical superiority they undoubtedly possess, and to shake off the timid and humble peacefulness which has hitherto distinguished them.

Long before the Mahomedan conquest of Hindostan the great monarchies of that country had been torn by internal commotions, and divided into many smaller kingdoms, which like their parent states contained in themselves the seeds of destruction, from the vicious principles on which they were founded. Though it might be true, that if angels could descend to rule over men, absolute monarchy would be the best form of government, yet as we are constituted, such a government can scarcely possess stability. And the slight traces of Indian history which remain to us, would confirm, if it were needful, this well known truth. If in one picture we are presented with a Hindoo monarch reigning with justice, or extending his conquests over the whole Peninsula, in the next we see an insignificant race of successors at first governed, and afterwards dethroned, by their more enterprising servants, who, in founding new dynasties, only prepared for their descendants the same train of miseries they had themselves inflicted on their unfortunate masters.

The better authenticated history of the Mahomedan kingdoms of Hindostan presents us with the same scenes; and as the Mussulman sovereigns and usurpers were even more absolute than those of the Hindûs, on whom the sacerdotal class was always a considerable check, the changes were still more sudden and violent; so that, before the arrival of the Europeans in India, the Mahomedan monarchy was already weakened by the detachment of some of its richest provinces. And although Aureng Zebe succeeded in re-uniting them to the crown of Dehli, and even in extending his dominions beyond the former conquests, his successors were gradually spoiled of province after province, till his throne was filled by a mere shadow of royalty, placed and upheld there by the army of a company of western merchants.

But I must defer entering into the history of Mussulman India at present, as I think I should but ill perform your wishes if I neglected to preface it with that of the most ancient possessors of the soil that we are acquainted with, and there are besides some interesting topics on which it would not perhaps be amiss previously to enter.

Nature seems to have taken pleasure in embellishing and enriching the favoured country of Hindostan with every choicest gift. Under a pure sky and brilliant sun the soil produces the most exquisite fruits, and the most abundant harvests; the rocks are rich in gems, the mountains teem with gold, and the fleecy pod of the cotton furnishes in profusion the light garment fitted to the climate. In travelling in the interior your eyes will often be enchanted with the most delicious landscapes. Amidst stupendous forests you will not unfrequently be charmed with a cultivated spot, where, if ever, you might realize the dreams of the poets, and indulge in that impassioned indolence which is the parent of poetry and of the fine arts.

One would imagine Milton had mused in oriental groves when he describes

" Insuperable heights of loftiest shade,
Cedar and pine, and fir, and branching palm,
A sylvan scene——

* * * * * * * * * * * *

Groves whose rich trees wept odorous gums and balm,
Others whose fruit burnished with golden rind
Hung amiable, Hesperian fables true,
If true, here only, and of delicious taste:
Betwixt them lawns, or level downs, and flocks
Grazing the tender herb were interposed
On palmy hillock; or the flowery lap
Of some irriguous valley spread her store,
Flow'rs of all hues, and without thorn the rose.

I might go on to quote all his descriptions of Paradise and all its bowers, before I could exhaust the resemblances.

But, alas! it is not the natural riches of the country, nor the exquisite beauty of its sylvan scenery, that will most attract your attention. Vast cities now too large for their diminished inhabitants, towns embellished with temples and with tombs now falling to decay, and absolutely unpeopled, and stupendous monuments of art, which have not served to transmit even the names of their founders down to our times, will frequently arrest your steps ; but while these are hastening to decay, the customs and habits of the natives seem immortal, and present us now with the same traits under which they are painted by the Greeks who visited them two thousand years ago.

Perhaps in their moral character the Hindûs are worse than their ancestors, but before we absolutely condemn them we shall do well to consider the causes of their depravity. The poet has said, " Whatever day, makes man a slave, takes half his worth away," and in our measure of censure against the falsehood and perjury we meet with in India, we should re-member that for many centuries they have been slaves to hard masters, and that if by subterfuge they could not conceal their property, they had only to expect robbery and violence ; thus falsehood became the only defence of the weak against the strong, and lost something, at least, of its criminal character.

Yet that it is not the peculiar character of the Hindûs, or encouraged by their laws or their faith, we may convince ourselves by referring to those sublime passages in their Sastras, where truth is identified with the Almighty mind, and described at once in the most awful and the most enchanting colours; and though in the modern Hindûs every generous feeling seems broken down, and replaced by an almost brute apathy, yet the spark though smothered is not extinguished, but ready to blaze forth if properly awakened, into all that genius and fancy can hope; or, if aroused by ill timed or ill directed interference with principles, which through loss of liberty, of empire, of riches, have clung closely round every heart and entwined themselves with every fibre, into vengeance, before which, ordinary means of safety will be vain, and ordinary courage subdued.

But I trust, that as we have hitherto used our power soberly, and on the whole, have made our government beneficial to the inhabitants of India, so we shall continue in the same wise moderation, and conduct the innovations necessary for their permanent improvement and our own security, in such a manner as that the hand of authority be never seen, but in the punishment of crimes, and her voice never heard, but in the dispensing of justice.

Into whatever part of the country you travel, or wherever you may be stationed, you will find much to examine; and if it be your good fortune to see various and distant parts of India, you will find a considerable variety of character, and sufficient difference of customs·and of faith, to interest you; but in order to derive every possible advantage from your change of situation, you should seriously apply yourself to the study of some of the native languages. The Hindostanee is the most widely diffused, though should you be stationed in Bengal, the Bengalee or ancient language of Gaur will be most useful, as it is spoken over a pretty extensive district. However if you wish to travel much, learn Persian, which may be called the French of the East; for you will not find a village where at least one person cannot speak it. Besides, it will gain respect from the natives, who consider a knowledge of various languages as the mark of a superior education, not to mention the great importance it must be of to an officer to understand the language of those whom he is to command. It was not perhaps the least part of the policy of the Romans, to plant their language in every conquest, in order to attach their new subjects; and the emperor Akbar increased the number of schools in Hindostan, and caused the Persian and Hindostanee to be publicly taught, together with the Sanscrit, and encouraged the translation of poems and scientific works from the ancient language of the Bramins into the vernacular tongues, by which means they became more popular. Perhaps if something of the same kind were done by the English;

if translations of their own books were given to them, it would induce them to learn the language more generally, and thus open to them the road to all those improvements of which we hear so much said, but which I fear our countrymen do not go the right way to introduce. I think if I were a powerful person, I should propose a reward to the little Hindû boys who should read or repeat most fluently a tale from Mr. Wilkins's Heetopadesa. I am sure the boy would read English much sooner by giving him the ideas he was accustomed to in his own country, clothed in our language, than by imposing upon him the double difficulty of a new language and new ideas also; and I am equally sure, that when the boy grew up and found that by his knowledge of English, he could carry on his trade without the intervention of an interpreting clerk to make out his English accounts, he would prize the language the more, and be the more anxious that his children should be instructed in it; thus interest would tend to diffuse knowledge if it were once put within the reach of the people.

But I must have already tired you with this long letter, and I dare say we shall have occasion to return to this very important subject in our future correspondence. Mean time adieu, and receive my best wishes.

M. G.

LETTER II.

I THANK you for your very kind though very short letter, and in reply to your question about the Sanscrit, I have only to say that I do not think it would be worth your while to begin to study it, unless you had a prospect of a much longer residence in the East, than I trust you look forward to. But that your curiosity respecting it may not be wholly unsatisfied, I shall give you a short account of that venerable tongue, and of some of the languages derived from it, which I have taken from Mr. Colebrooke's interesting essay on the subject.

Were all other monuments swept away from the face of Hindostan, were its inhabitants destroyed, and its name forgotten, the existence of the Sanscrit language would prove that it once contained a race who had reached a high degree of refinement, and who must have been blest with many rare advantages before such a language could have been formed and polished. Amidst the wreck of the nations where it flourished, and superior to the havoc of war and of conquest, it remains a venerable monument of the splendor of other times, as the solid pyramid in the deserts of Egypt attests, that where now the whirlwind drives the overwhelming sand-wave, and plows up the loose and barren dust, a numerous population once enlivened the plain, and the voice of industry once gladdened the woods.

The languages of India are usually reckoned to be four.

The Sanscrit or language of the gods.

The Prácrit or spoken language.

The Paisachi or language of the demons.

The Magad'hi.

Some writers however substitute for the two latter the Apabhransa or Jargon, and the Misra or mixed language.

The word *Sanscrit* literally means *adorned*, and that language is indeed highly polished; it is cultivated throughout India as the language of science and literature, of laws and religion; and of its great antiquity some comparative idea may be formed from the time in which most of the elegant poets flourished, which was about the century preceding the Christian æra. Now, many ages must have elapsed, before so rich, so perfect a language could have been framed, and its rules so accurately fixed. " It evidently draws its origin (says Mr. Colebrooke) from a primeval tongue which was gradually refined in different climates, and became Sanscrit in India, Pelavi in Persia, and Greek on the shores of the Mediterranean."

Although the Sanscrit is now a dead language, it was probably at one period the spoken language of most parts of India, and the objections which might be made to this opinion, such as the inordinate length of the compound words, and the strict rules for the permutation of letters in these compounds, are obviated by the fluency with which those persons deliver themselves who still speak the language.

I think that, from the fragments of the history and literature of the Bramins which have been translated—and from these only I can judge—we are authorized to conclude, that excepting in times of great civil commotion or religious wars, the Bramins lived a life of retired indolence; not, indeed, like the western monks, withdrawn from domestic cares within the walls of a monastery, but in sacred groves and caverned rocks, where, surrounded by their pupils and their slaves, they cultivated poetry, music, and astronomy; and only deigned to appear in the active world to receive the homage of a court, and direct its monarchs; or sometimes to pronounce on them the malediction, which was almost sure to be followed by the desertion of their servants and the rebellion of their subjects.

It was in these retirements that, given up to study, the Bramins perfected their sacred language, and composed those numerous and profound treatises of grammar, which have since employed so many commentators, whose works have been considered as of such high consequence, that the writers are said to have been inspired. Of the original treatises, the grammar of Panini is the most ancient that remains to us, and of the highest authority: but its great antiquity and studied brevity have required and received numerous scholiæ, all esteemed divine. The Amera-cosha, the most esteemed of all the vocabularies, was composed by Amera Sinha, one of the nine poets who adorned the court of Vrcramaditya*, and who was either a Jaina or a Baud'ha: his work has passed through the hands of numerous commentators, and many vocabularies have been formed to supply its deficiences, besides various nomenclatures, and the Nighanti of the Vedas, which explains obsolete words and unusual acceptations.

The *Prácrit* language formerly included all the written dialects used in the common intercourse of life, and cultivated by men of letters; but the term Prácrit is now commonly restricted to the language spoken on the banks of the Seraswattee.

There appear to have been ten polished dia-

* It is doubted whether this is the Vrcramaditya, King of Onjein, who gave name to the chronological æra, and who flourished 56 years before Christ, or a later monarch, sometimes called Raja Bhoja.

lects in India, prevailing in as many different civilized nations, who occupied the provinces of Hindoostan and the Deckan.

The *Saraswati* was a people which occupied the banks of the river *Seraswattee*, and the Bramins of that nation now inhabit the Panjāb. Their language may have prevailed over the southern and western parts of Hindoostan Proper, and is probably the idiom called Prácrit. It is a cultivated language, and great part of most dramas, and many poems, are written in it.

The *Canyacubjas* possessed a great empire, the capital of which was Cannoge. Their language seems to be the groundwork of the modern Hindustani or Hindwi, of which there are two dialects, in the most refined of which there are numerous poems, and both abound in songs, or rather ballads, and odes. Well educated people in Hindustan and the Deckan, use this language, and there is scarcely a village where some of the inhabitants do not understand it; which I beg you to observe, is the reason I particularly advised you to study it, that you may not be among those speakers of jargon, whom one hears violating all the rules of grammar and good sense, at our settlements in India, till they have actually produced a tongue that I am persuaded no Hindû, fresh from the interior, would understand.

The *Gaura*, or *Bengali*, is spoken in the provinces of which the ancient city of Gaur was once the capital, and of which nothing remains but widely spread ruins. The language contains some original poems, besides many translations from the Sanscrit: it appeared to me, when I heard it spoken, to be a soft agreeable language, though less pleasing to the ear than the Hindustani.

The *Mait'hila*, or *Tirhuctya*, is used in the Circar of Tirhut and the adjoining districts, and appears not to have been much cultivated.

The language and alphabet called Uriga are used in the Suba of Orissa, whose ancient names are *Utcala* and *Odradesa*.

These five countries are called the five Gaurs, and occupy the northern and eastern parts of India, though Orissa seems more properly to belong to the five Draviras which occupy the Peninsula as far as Cape Comorin; and Guzerat, which is sometimes reckoned among the Draviras, would find a more natural place among the Gaurs.

The language of Guzerat or Gurjera is nearly allied to the Hindwi, and, like it, is commonly written in an imperfect form of the

Devanagari character, in which the Sanscrit is expressed.

Dravira is the southern extremity of India, and extends from Cape Comorin to twelve or thirteen degrees of north latitude. The language is the *Tamel,* called by the Europeans Malabars. I have seen translations from some Tamel songs, both of love and of war : and one I recollect of a humourous description, purporting to be the quarrel between a man's two wives, one of whom was a Tamel and the other a Tailinga lady; but as it appeared that one was much younger and handsomer than the other, the quarrel was naturally enough decided in her favour; though I own that, to me, the other seemed to have the right side of the argument.

The *Maharashtra,* or *Mahratta,* is a nation which has in the two last centuries greatly enlarged its boundaries ; but it anciently comprehended only a mountainous district south of the Nermada, and extending to the Cocan. The language boasts of some treatises of logic and philosophy, besides many original poems, chiefly in honour of Rama and Crishna, and some translations from the Sanscrit.

Carnata, or *Canara,* is the ancient language of Carnataca, a province which has given names to districts on both coasts of the Peninsula ; the dialect still prevails in the intermediate mountainous tract.

Tailangana must formerly have comprehended not only the province of that name, but those on the banks of the Crishna and Godavery. Its language (Telinga) has been cultivated by poets, if not by prose writers.

Besides these ten polished dialects, there are some others, derived, like them, from the Sanscrit, and, like them, written in a character more or less corrupted from the Deva Nagari. There are also some spoken by the mountaineers, who are probably the aborigines of India, and which have certainly no affinity with the Sanscrit.

Some of these tongues are divided into local and provincial dialects, and many beautiful pastorals are written in the two most remarkable—the Panjābi, spoken in the Panjāb or country of the five rivers, and the Vraja Bhasha, spoken in the neighbourhood of Mathura, which derives its name from the cow-pens, *Vraja*, of the forests of Vrindha.

Translations of at least part of two Sanscrit Grammars appeared in English in the year 1808; the first from Saraswata, by Mr. Colebrooke, and the second, by Mr. Carey, is partly a translation, partly original, from the Grammars used in Bengal, where the teachers have unfortunately accommodated the sacred language to the vernacular idiom and pronunciation. A Sanscrit Grammar, by Mr. Wilkins, appeared in the same year, which has the character, among the learned, of accuracy, preciseness, and perspicuity, notwithstanding its great length, which the multitude of rules and exceptions in the language has swelled to 656 pages.

The author of the able article upon this Grammar, in the thirteenth volume of the Edinburgh Review, has given a very interesting table of the analogy of the Sanscrit with some other languages, which certainly goes far to confirm the opinion of Mr. Colebrooke and of Sir William Jones, concerning the primeval tongue from which these languages may have been derived, and which I quoted in the early part of this Letter. The first part of the analogy consists of words expressing the names of different parts of the body, and the relations of consanguinity, thus—

Sanscrit.	Latin.	Persian.	German.	English:
pitara	pater	pider	vater	father
matara	mater	mader	muder	mother
bhratara	frater	brader	bruder	brother

In this last word, there is an example of the manner in which the Sanscrit double letters are changed into letters of the West,—a transposition not accidental but constant, the bh into f, the ch into qu, as in chator, quator (four), and many others.

The second point is the analogy in the structure of some of these languages, perceived in the distinctions of the feminine and neuter genders; the declensions of nouns; the signs of comparison; the infinitives and declensions of verbs, which goes so far as the irregularity and defectiveness of the substantive verb.

The eight cases render the use of prepositions superfluous; they are, therefore, exclusively prefixed to verbs, being without signification alone. But I shall venture no farther on this subject, which, I fear, I can hardly render as interesting as I should wish; for I intend, in my next Letter, to notice some of the principal writers in the languages I have been mentioning: and I hope to present you with rather an agreeable picture of ancient Hindostan, when I lay before you the amusements of King Vicramaditya's court, and introduce you—if you have not already introduced yourself—to the elegant Calidas, and the pious and venerable Valmiki.

The Indian poetry is rich, high, and varied, abounding in luxuriant descriptions, and occasionally displaying both grandeur and tenderness: but it must be confessed, that it is often rendered dull by repetition and bombast, and deformed by an indelicacy unknown to European writers.

> " They loudest sing
> " The vices of their deities, and their own
> " In fable, hymn, or song, so personating
> " Their gods ridiculous, themselves past shame!
>
> PARADISE REGAINED.

You will, nevertheless, find something to please, and more to interest you. India, it is probable, if not certain, is the parent of all the western gods; and, consequently, of that beautiful body of poetry which has the Grecian mythology for its basis: and though the child be grown up to a beauty and strength, of which the mother could never boast, we cannot behold without reverence, the origin of all that has delighted and instructed us, of those heavenly strains which have soothed our griefs or quieted our passions, and in a manner given us a new moral existence. How often in our evening walks on the banks of the Thames, or amid the woody glens of Scotland, has the spring of life, the breathing flood of existence around us, seemed to realize the fables of the poets, and to people every tree and every wave with a tutelary deity! And believe me, that in the forests of

6

Hindostan, and on its caverned mountains, the same divinities have been adored, for the same feelings and passions have filled the hearts of their votaries.

***

LETTER III.

DEAR SIR,

SINCE the Bramins were almost exclusively the lettered men of India, it will not appear extraordinary that the literature of that country should be so intimately blended with its religion, that it seems impossible to separate them : however, I shall put off to another time the history of the Vedas, or four sacred books of the Hindoos, and content myself at present with profaner poems. But, before I proceed, I must say one word of the Sanscrit prosody, which is said to be richer in variations of metre than any other known language.

Sanscrit and Prácrit poetry is regulated by the number, length, and disposition of syllables, and is disposed into several classes, each of which is again subdivided. Some of the metres admit any number of syllables, from twenty-seven to nine hundred and ninety-nine ; and others are equally remarkable for their brevity :

but the most common Sanscrit metre, is the stanza of four verses, containing eight syllables each.

Sanscrit poetry admits both of rhyme and blank verse, and is in some instances subject to very rigid rules, although, in others, there is scarcely any restraint.

The rules of prosody are contained in brief aphorisms, called *Sutras*, the reputed author of which is PINGALANA, a fabulous being, in the shape of a serpent, and who, under the name of PATANJALI, is the author of the *Maha Bhashya*, or great commentary on grammar. The *Sutras* have been commented on by a great variety of authors; and there are also some other original treatises on the subject, the most remarkable of which, is that by the poet CALIDASA, who teaches the laws of versification in the very metres to which they relate.

Every kind of ornament seems to be admissible in the Indian poetry, and some embellishments which we should look upon as burlesque, are admitted even in the most pathetic poems. Calidasa himself, in the Nalodáya, gives an example of a series of puns on a pathetic subject, and employs both rhyme and alliteration in the termination of his verses.

When you have time, I advise you, if you wish to know all the varieties of metre, and their rules, to look into Mr. Colebrooke's Essay on the Sanscrit and Prácrit Poetry, in the tenth volume of the Asiatic Researches, from which I take the greater part of the substance of this Letter, and perhaps, occasionally, his very words.

I will now proceed to mention the books of the Hindoos, on which Sir William Jones and Mr. Colebrooke will be our guides. There are eighteen orthodox *Vedyas*, or parts of knowledge. The first four are the *Vedas*, of which I propose hereafter to give you a particular account. The four following are the *Upavedas*, or treatises on medicine, music, war, and mechanical arts. The six *Angas* treat of *pronunciation*, religious ceremonies, grammar, prosody, astronomy, and the explanation of the difficult words and phrases in the Vedas. Lastly, the four *Upangas* contain—first, eighteen Puranas, for the instruction and entertainment of man; second, books on apprehension, reason, and judgment: third, moral and religious duties and laws; and fourthly, the books of law and justice*.

* The names of the eighteen *Vedyas* are as follow, the *Rich*, Yajush, Saman, and Athervan Vedas; the Ayush, Gándharva, Dhanush, and St'hapaya Upavedas; the Sirsha, Calpa, Vyacarana, Ch'handas, Jyotish, and Nirueti Angas; and the Purana, Nyáya, Mimansa, and Dherma Sastra, Upangas.

The Maha Bharata, and the Ramayuna are the most ancient historical books, and for the information of the lower classes there are some works adapted for them, as none but the *twice born*, that is the three highest castes are permitted to read either the eighteen Vedyas or the two great poems.

There are besides these works of the heterodox sects upon almost all the subjects above enumerated.

The most ancient Indian poem is the Ramayuna, of Valmiki. Three volumes of it have been printed at Serampore, in the Devanagari character, accompanied by a literal translation by the missionaries Cary and Marshman. I do not know whether it was wise to translate literally so long a poem, especially as it abounds in those repetitions and tedious details which deform the eastern writings, and as the closeness of the translation to the original, naturally makes it obscure to persons accustomed to the English idiom, and takes from it, to me at least, the character of poetry*.

The first section of the first book may be

* Three hundred rupees per month are allowed to the translators by the Asiatic Society and the College of Fort William, and it is proposed to translate and publish a series of the oriental poems.

considered as the argument of the whole poem.
It opens with a salutation to Rama, the
hero of the poem, and to Valmiki the author,
who is denominated a Kokila, (a singing-bird)
mounted on the branch of poetry chanting the
delightful note Rama, Rama, Rama! Valmiki
is then introduced consulting Nareda, the deity
of song, upon a fit hero for the subject of a
poem, and is accordingly directed to Rama,
the son of Dusharuthra, king of Ayodhya or
Oude.

The pious Dusharuthra, in order to obtain
children, performed an Aswa-medha or the sacrifice of a horse to the gods, and soon afterwards were born to him four sons—Rama, whose
mother was Kooshulya; Bharata, whose mother was Kikeeya, and Lukshmana and his twin
brother, sons of Soomitra. The old king designed Rama for his heir, and had already
prepared all the ceremonies for his inauguration, when Kikeeya, the mother of Bharata,
claimed a promise that her son should reign,
upon which, " To preserve inviolate the promise, made through affection to Kikeeya, the
hero at his father's command, departed into the
forest. He departing into exile the wise, heroic
Lukshmana, his younger brother, through affection, accompanied him. His beloved spouse,

always dear as his own soul, the Videhan Sita, of Januka's race, formed by the illusion of the Deva, amiable, adorned with every charm, obedient to her lord followed him into exile. Endued with beauty, youth, sweetness, goodness, and prudence, she was inseparably attendant on her lord as light on the moon. Accompanied by the people and his sire Dusharuthra, he dismissed his charioteer at Shringuvera, on the banks of the Ganges."

The three illustrious exiles built themselves a pleasant bower on the mountain Chitrakoota, and shortly afterwards Dusharuthra " departed to heaven lamenting his son." Bharata who was called to the succession, immediately sought Rama, and intreated him to reign, but the hero, respecting his father's promise, gave his sandals to Bharata, and commanded him as his elder brother to return and govern the kingdom.

Rama and his companions retired into the forest of Dundacca, whence after some adventures he departed and fixed his residence in the country of Panchwattee, where he carried on an exterminating war against the Rakshusas, and while absent on one of his warlike expeditions, Ravuna, the king of Lanka, entered his bower and carried off Sita. Rama and his brother then turned their arms to the South, and in their way towards Lanca met with many singular adventures, and performed deeds of arms which would have graced the knights of Ariosto, and like them they also met with enchantresses and wizards, who alternately assisted and distressed them. At length, however, they met with the monkey Hanumân who became their constant and most useful attendant. Hanumân introduced them to his king Soogriva, who, delighted with Rama's prowess, became his friend, on condition that he should aid him in his war with Bali, a rival baboon monarch.

" The chiefs of monkeys and of men, Rama and Soogriva entered the cave of Kishkindhya. There the mighty ape roared like thunder. At this terrible sound Bali, lord of the monkeys, came forth. Having comforted Tara, he went out to meet Soogriva, and was there slain by an arrow of Rama's."

The monkeys then went to the different quarters of the earth in search of Sita; and Hanumân being directed by the vulture Sumpati, having leaped across the ocean, obtained a sight of her in the gardens of Lanca, and was even able to deliver to her a pledge from Rama, and to receive one in return, with which he hastened back to the impatient hero.

Rama having conquered and slain Ravuna, suspected Sita of infidelity towards him, but she, indignant at the accusation, went through the fiery ordeal, and having thus established her innocence, she was received by Rama, while heavenly music sounded in the air, and showers of flowers fell upon the earth.

Rama and his companions then took leave of the sylvan nations, and returned to Ayodhya, where he reigned happily and honoured.

Valmiki lived at the court of the monarch whose actions he has immortalized, and whose reign Major Wilford places at least fifteen centuries before Christ.

Besides the mere subject of the poem, there are many curious topics treated of in the Ramayuna, particularly details of religious sacrifices and ceremonies, descriptions of cities, and of the pomp of royalty and of the priesthood. But I am particularly pleased with the picture it gives of the amusements of the court of Rama. After a great and pompous sacrifice, accompanied by games and exercises, the two disciples of Valmiki, the sons of Rama and Sita, Kooshee, and Luva, with voices by nature melodious, and skilled in music, rehearsed the actions of their father in the assembly, when the surrounding sages united in a joyful burst of applause, saying, " Excellent ! excellent ! The poem, the very expression of nature, the song, the air!" And each bestowed a gift upon the young minstrels.

I am sure you will immediately recollect the songs of Demodocus and the plaudits of his hearers in the eighth book of the Odyssey, and if it be true that Homer meant the blind poet as a picture of himself, Valmiki's recording the homage paid to his own strains will not appear to be any extraordinary degree of vanity, though I confess to our taste they may not be so well deserved as those that even to these times are almost piously bestowed upon the blind Melesigenes.

The other great historical poem entitled the Mahabharut contains the adventures of the hero Crishna, and the great wars which distracted India in the fourteenth century before Christ, and which introduced some very important changes in the religion of the Hindûs. It is written by Vyasa, who is the reputed compiler of the Puranas. I shall probably have to notice more particularly the events which form the subject of the Mahabharut in a future letter, and as I have never seen any translation of any part of it, or of the Bhagavat, though I know that a portion of the latter has been translated by the elegant pen of Mr. Wilkins, I shall proceed to mention other works.

Next to these great poems which are held sacred, the epic poem of Megha may be ranked. It is called Sisupala bad'ha and describes the death of Sisupala, slain in war by Crishna. In the first Canto, Nareda commissioned by Indra, like the evil dream sent by Jupiter to Agamemnon, incites Crishna to war with his cousin and enemy Sisupala, king of the Chédis. Accordingly on the first occasion which presented itself, namely, contempt shewn by Sisupala and his followers for Crishna, by withdrawing from a solemn sacrifice performed by the Rajah Yudishthera, where divine honours were paid to Crishna, the hero assembles his troops, and the armies of the rivals meet, when that of Sisupala being destroyed, the two chiefs engage in single combat contending with supernatural weapons, Sisupala employing arms of fire which are overcome by the watery trisool of Crishna, who finally slays his foe with an arrow, which ends the twentieth Canto. This poem is one of the six excellent compositions in Sanscrit, which I shall name together.

The second is the Ciratarjuníya of Bharavi, and contains the history of the hero Arjuna's journey and penance on the mountain of India Keiladree, in order to obtain celestial weapons from the gods, to be employed against king Duryod'hana. That part of his adventures which gives the title to the poem is his wrestling with Siva, who appeared to him in the form of a Kerata or sylvan king.

The third is the Naishadhíya of Sriharsha, by some esteemed the most beautiful poem in the language. It is founded on an interesting story, which however is not related at length, but is to be found in the Nalodaya of Calidasa. It describes the marriage of Nala king of Nishada, and Damayanti daughter of Bhima king of Viderbha, and the loss of his kingdom by gambling, through the artifices of Cali in a human shape. After that misfortune he deserts his wife, and suffers a transformation, under which, after many wanderings and much distress, Damayanti discovers him; which, like the conclusion of the Fairy Tales, seems to have broken the spell which bound him to his monstrous form, for he immediately recovered, and they were restored to their kingdom.

The three other excellent works are by the poet Calidasa, and are the Cumara, Raghu, and Meghadata. Of the first of these three only a part remains; the subject is the birth or origin of Cumara the son of Parvati, but the fragment closes with the marriage of the goddess. In it all the personages not excepting her father, the snowy mountain Hymalaya, are described with the human form and human manners.

The Raghu contains the history of Rama and his predecessors, from Dilpa the father of Raghu and his successors to Agniverna. It is impossible to enumerate the poets who have celebrated Rama, both in the Sanscrit and Prácrit languages, and indeed in every Indian dialect.

The Megha-duta consists of no more than a hundred and sixteen stanzas. It supposes a Yacsha or attendant of Cuvera, to have been separated from a beloved wife by an imprecation of the god Cuvera, who was irritated by the Yacsha's negligence in suffering the heavenly garden to be trodden down by India's elephant. The distracted demigod, banished from heaven to earth, takes his abode on a hill, and intreats a passing cloud to convey an affectionate message to his wife. The great elegance and tenderness of this little poem have entitled it, notwithstanding its brevity, to a place among the six *chef d'œuvres* of the Hindû poets. Its author Calidasa appears to have been a most voluminous writer, for besides the three masterpieces I have just named, he has left other poems, besides a work on prosody and some dramas, one of which you are probably already acquainted with from the translations of Sir William Jones and Mr. Wilkins. The drama of Sacontala is founded on the marriage of Dushmanta, one of the ancestors of Vicramaditya, whose court Calidasa adorned, and before whom the prologue gives us to understand it was played. The scene opens with a hunting party of the youthful monarch, where he appears chasing the deer in a chariot drawn by horses, and guided by a young charioteer to the confines of a sacred grove. Dushmanta, in order not to violate the holy place, dismisses his charioteer and advances alone in the direction of some female voices, and discovers Sacontala, a young princess under the guardianship of the high priest of the grove, with her attendants. The Bramin being absent, the young damsels perform the rites of hospitality, and the prince and Sacontala mutually fall in love and contract a marriage unknown to any but the attendants of the latter; a few days afterwards the king being called to his capital, departs, and gives Sacontala a ring as a token of their marriage. On the return of the Bramin to the grove, he is informed by inspiration of all that has happened in his absence, and sends Sacontala to the court of Dushmanta, accompanied by proper persons to deliver her to her husband; but in the mean time Sacontala having, in the first moments of her grief for the departure of the king, neglected to perform the rites of hospitality towards a Bramin, the irritable priest pronounces a malediction upon her, by which, he on whom she was then thinking should forget her. However her companions who alone heard the curse, rely on the ring for recalling her to his mind, but in bathing for the last time before she quits the grove of her foster-father, she drops the ring into the water, and thus loses the talisman. When she presents herself at court, the young king, though charmed with her beauty, refuses to accept her, alleging he knows her not, and that she must be the wife of some other man. On this Sacontala faints and is conveyed to the heavenly court of Casyapa the father of the gods, where her son Bharata is born. Meantime the fatal ring is found by some fishermen in the belly of a fish, and on its being restored to Dushmanta, he remembers Sacontala and bitterly laments her loss, weeping over her picture and forgetting his pleasures and his business, till his assistance is required by the gods in quelling the demons. After having relieved the divinities from their distress, he goes to the court of Casyapa, and there meets a beautiful child dragging along a lion's whelp; this child he proves to be his own by handling a magic bracelet, which only the parents of the young prince could touch with impunity; Sacontala then appears in a widow's garb, and being recognized by her lord, all the mysteries are explained and they return happily to earth.

Such is the outline of Sacontala; but my

D 2

description, short as it must be, can convey no idea of the beauty of the sentiments, and the native tenderness which the poet has bestowed on the young recluse, and which even in translation must charm. This drama presents us with a picture curious in itself, and interesting as it regards the ancient braminical Hindûs. It pourtrays the simple and austere manners of the priesthood, their proud dominion over their monarchs, their constant vigilance, which induced them even to condescend to act the part of court buffoons, and the prodigious influence they must have possessed, as they appear to have been charged with the education of the royal children of both sexes, to whom they performed the part of guardians as well as tutors, and into whom they were thus at liberty to inculcate their own maxims and instil their own sentiments. But to me the most interesting part is the pleasing light in which it places the early condition of the Hindû women, before the jealous Mahomedan maxims had shut them up in zenanas, and reduced them to the degrading situation in which they are now placed. Here we see the king's mother charged with the care of the royal city and council during her son's absence. The young women of the forest practising the rights of hospitality, and exercising all the functions of rational creatures, admitted to a considerable share of the religious learning of their preceptors, and skilled in the fine arts, as we see in the young paintress whom Dushmanta employs to paint the portrait of Sacontala after he had lost her, and who by the description of the poet was not content with the cold delineation of the features, but represented the princess as the hero first beheld her in the forest, surrounded by her young companions at their pastoral occupations.

In short, if we may judge by this specimen, I should think the dramatic part of the Hindú literature would be the most pleasing to Europeans were it better known, and this opinion is confirmed by Mr. Colebrooke, to whom we are indebted for a sketch of the subject of another drama, and for a translation of some of the scenes.

The plot, setting aside the supernatural part, which, however, the firm belief of the Hindûs in magic and necromancy rendered pleasing to them, is such as would do no discredit to an European pen. It is called Malati-Mad'hava, written by the poet Bhavabhuti, and is in ten acts, the five first of which are the most interesting, and seem to form the natural developement of the story. Bhurivasu, minister of the king of Padmavati, and Devarata, in the service of the king of Vidherba, had agreed, while their children were yet infants to crown their long friendship by the marriage of Malati daughter of the first with Mad'hava son of the latter. Meantime the king having hinted an intention to propose a match between Malati and his favourite Nandana, who was old and ugly, the two fathers concert a plan for throwing their children in each other's way, and conniving at a clandestine marriage, in pursuance of which Mad'hava is sent to finish his studies in the city of Padmavati under the care of the old priestess Camandaci, by whose contrivance, aided by Lavangica the foster-sister of Malati, the young people meet and become mutually enamoured. At this period the play opens with a dialogue between the old priestess and a female pupil, in which all the preceding events are naturally mentioned, and we are prepared for the appearance of the other characters of the piece, and particularly of Saudamini a former pupil of the priestess, who has arrived at supernatural power by religious austerities, and of Aghoraghanta a tremendous magician, and his female pupil Capalacundala, who both frequent the temple of Carala the dreadful goddess, near the cemetery of the city.

Mad'hava, his companion Macaranda and servant Calapansa then appear upon the scene, and Mad'hava discloses his meeting with Malati and his love for her. His attendant then shews him his own picture drawn by Malati, which he had obtained from one of her damsels, and in return Mad'hava draws the features of the young heroine on the same tablet, and writes under it a passionate stanza. The tablet is conveyed by the attendants alternately to the lovers, whose affection is thus fostered and increased. Meantime the king sends to Bhurivasa, to make the projected proposal for the marriage of his daughter with the favourite Nandana, and the minister having answered that the king may dispose of his daughter as he pleases, the lovers are thrown into great agitation. Camandaci then contrives another interview between them in a public garden, but at the same moment a cry of terror announces that a tremendous tyger had rushed from the temple of Siva, and the youthful Madayantica sister of Nandana is in great danger, when Mad'hava's companion Macaranda is seen rushing to her rescue. He kills the tyger, is himself wounded behind the scenes, and is brought in insensible, but revives by the care of the women, and Madayantica whom he has saved falls in love with him.

The preparations for the marriage of Malati with Nandana are then announced, and Mad'-hava takes a resolution which none but a Hindû lover could have imagined, namely, that of going to the cemetery and selling his living flesh to the ghosts and malignant spirits, in order to obtain the accomplishment of his wishes. While he is wandering by night for this purpose among the tombs, where in a soliloquy he thus describes the cemetery, " the river that bounds it, and tremendous is the roaring of the stream breaking away the bank, while its waters are embarrassed among fragments of skulls, and its shores resound horribly with the howling of shakals and the cry of owls screeching amidst the contiguous woods," he is alarmed by the voice of a female in distress, and recognises the voice of Malati.

The scene opens and discovers the enchanter and sorceress above named, with Malati adorned as a victim, the inhuman wizard having stolen her while sleeping for the purpose of a sacrifice to the dreadful goddess. While he is preparing the horrid rites, Mad'hava rushes forward and Malati flies to his arms for protection, when voices are heard without in search of her; Mad'hava places her in safety and encounters the magician, when they quit the stage fighting. The event of the combat is told by the sorceress, who vows vengeance against the hero for slaying her preceptor. And here an European writer would have finished his piece with his fifth act; but a Hindû, whose story can never be too long, continues it through five other acts, and relates

the contrivance of the priestess to dress Macaranda in the habit of Malati, and thus to disgust
Nanda and obtain an interview for the disguised
lover with Nanda's sister, who agrees to accompany him to the place of Malati's concealment,
where however they do not find her; for the
sorceress has carried her off in a flying car. The
lover and friends are now in the utmost despair,
till the arrival of Saudamini the pupil of the
priestess, who by her preternatural power re-
leases Malati, and the play concludes with a
double wedding.

This story you perceive has considerable interest, and, bating the preternatural part, is
really dramatic. But I have already said so
much of it that I fear I shall have tired you,
and therefore I shall say adieu.

P. S. I had forgotten while on the subject of
dramatic writing, that as we have had our mysteries and moralities in Europe, the Hindûs are
not without a sort of mystic drama, the only
specimen of which that I have seen is entitled
" The Rise of the Moon of Intellect," and its
subject is the war between king Reason and king
Passion, wherein all the orthodox virtues and
follies fight for the first, and the poor heretics
are all turned over to the service of king Passion, who is not overcome till the birth of young

Intellect, I forget whether male or female, when the play ends*.

———

LETTER IV.

YOUR enquiry concerning the lyric and amatory poetry of the Hindûs, encourages me to hope that my last letter was more interesting to you than I had dared to believe when I dispatched it. There certainly can be no difference of opinion concerning the puerile taste that could tolerate Hanumàn and his baboon associates in an epic poem; yet we must not forget that one of our best poets in the present age has his Gylbin Horner.

As the belief of necromancy and magic was general in India, I cannot see the impropriety of introducing it in poems of every description. The magic of Medea and the incantations of the Weird Sisters are great examples of the sublime use that may be made of this supernatural, and I had almost said, picturesque machinery; and though my knowledge of the classics is only a kind of secondhand acquaintance

* Since these Letters went to press, a particular account of Dr. Taylor's Translation of the " Rise of the Moon of Intellect," has appeared in the forty-fourth number of the Edinburgh Review.

through the medium of translation, like the man who fancied himself intimate with the village lord, because he had crossed the ferry in the same boat with his lordship's horses, I will venture to ask you, if the sorceress of Bhava-bhuti be not at least as poetical a personage as Lucan's old witch? The fatal effects of the hasty curse pronounced by the choleric Brahmin in Sacontala, shocks you, but you forget how many Greeks fell sacrifices to the vengeful imprecations of Chryses, or how Ajax perished and Ulysses wandered, the victims of supernatural curses.

I know you will laugh at all this, but remember I am not saying that the luxuriant shoots of the Oriental palm-tree surpass in beauty or in flavour the purple clusters of the European vine, but only that there is a beauty, inferior indeed, but striking and characteristic in these monuments of eastern civilization and literature.

I believe that there are many lyric poets among the Hindû writers, but I can only name Jayadeva, whose odes the Hindûs are fond of explaining in a moral and religious sense, as the Persians do those of Hafiz, but I believe that the poets certainly mean what they say, and not what their countrymen choose to attribute to them, and I think you will be of the same opi-

nion unless you discover a spiritual sense in such
lines as

> When in the goblet's ruddy dies
> I see the sun of bliss arise,
> In her bright cheek who hands the wine
> A thousand mantling blushes shine.

Or,

> If in the breeze thy sighing breath
> Should pass where Hafiz sleeps in death,
> Quick should the flow'rets fragrant bloom,
> And gaudy tulips deck his tomb.

The amatory poetry of India is said not to
be deficient of tenderness of expression and
thought, but the passion it sings is too little
refined for our western taste, though its language is highly polished. There is, however,
a serious kind of love poem, the description of
which is exceedingly laughable, though it be
written in sober earnest. In it, various descriptions of lovers and mistresses distinguished by
age, temper, and circumstances, are systematically classed and logically defined, with the utmost seriousness and precision, as if they were
intended for the *bureau de mariages*, which
I hear has lately been opened at Paris. Nor is
this the only childishness the venerable Bramins have tolerated; for though I cannot learn
that they ever hit upon the pretty conceit of
writing verses in the shape of a hatchet or an

egg, they have metres where the lines increase in arithmetical progression, and poems composed with such studied ambiguity that the reader may at his own option read in them either of two distinct stories totally unconnected with each other.

There is a class of writings not uncommon in Sanscrit called *champú*, consisting of a mixture of prose and verse, in the manner of the History of the Civil Wars of Grenada, in the Spanish, great part of which is related in those simple and pathetic ballads we have seen occasionally translated. And there are some exquisitely polished prose works, which from their extreme elegance are ranked among poems like *Telemaque* and *Tod Abels.*

The story of one of these so nearly resembles the Oberon of Wieland that I cannot resist giving it to you, only observing, that the Hindu hero is not required so far to transgress the bounds of decorum as to steal the teeth and mustaches of his unfortunate father-in-law.

" Candarpa-cetu, a young and valiant prince, son of Chintamani, king of Cusumapura, sees in a dream a beautiful girl of whom he becomes enamoured. Impressed with a belief of the real existence of the damsel, he resolves to travel in search of her, accompanied only by his friend Macaranda. While reposing under a tree in the forests of the Vindhya mountains, the favourite overhears two birds discoursing, and learns from them that the princess Vasavadatta had refused the hands of many suitors, having seen prince Candarpa-cetu in a dream, wherein she not only became acquainted with his person and manners, but his name. Meanwhile the young lady's confidante having been sent by her mistress in search of the hero, discovers the two friends in the forest, and delivering a letter to the young prince conducts him to the palace, whence after mutual explanations he conveys the princess. Misfortune, however, pursues them, for scarcely had they reached the forest, when in the darkness of the night the lover loses his mistress, upon which after a fruitless search, being arrived at the sea-shore, he resolves to cast himself into the sea, but is arrested by a voice from heaven promising the recovery of the princess and indicating the means. Here the resemblance to the story of Wieland stops, for Vasavadatta is discovered spell-bound, in the form of a marble statue from which Candarpa-cetu alone can release her. After her restoration, she relates her separate adventures, and they proceed together to Cusumapura, where they pass a long life in uninterrupted happiness.

Probably if we knew a little more of the native tales of India, we might trace the sources whence many of the early romances of Europe came to us through the Arabs and Moors; and possibly also, the origin of some of the Norse and Scaldic fables; but I am, unfortunately, so totally unacquainted with any oriental language, that I am obliged to stop where I find English guides fail, but it is scarcely possible not to be struck with the singular resemblances one finds in the Hindû legends and customs, to those of our ancestors.

One of the most obvious of these, is the custom of entertaining a family bard to sing the exploits of the heroes whose descendants he serves, and which has not entirely ceased in the East, any more than the family musician in the Highlands of Scotland, though in the latter the song be exchanged for the pibrach. Sometimes these bards, or bawts as they are called, are employed to tell tales of pure invention, sometimes to chant the productions of ancient poets, and oftener to recite the adventures of the ancient heroes who have become the gods of Hindostan. There is also a set of itinerant taletellers and poets, who, like the ancient minstrels and troubadours, wander from province to province secure of a hospitable reception; and by their own romantic adventures, furnishing subjects either for their own future songs, or those of other bawts.

Traces of the profession of the *bardai*, as the Hindûs call the bards, may be found in almost every nation, and perhaps it is connected with the natural progress of civilization among men. Before writing was invented, the only method of transmitting history to posterity, was by oral tradition, and as verses would be more easily remembered, and besides, their harmony gave pleasure to the auditors, they became the natural vehicle of such traditions ; and those gifted men who had the power of composing them, would infallibly acquire a sacred character among their less favoured companions.

In the early part of the sacred scriptures, we find frequent injunctions to the patriarchs to teach the laws to their sons, and their sons' sons, that they might be had in remembrance. And even after the promulgation of the written law, one of the great duties of the Levites, was yearly to read or chant the law to the people, besides the prescribed lectures from the other books of scripture, containing the actions and adventures of the forefathers of the Jews.

I do not know whether you will permit me to lay any great stress on the manners described by Ossian ; which, I must confess, appear too refined for his age, if we believe that Britain had not, in some very remote period, a nearer connection than we suppose with that people, from whom we derive all the arts and sciences with our languages, and who (to use the words of a great writer) have left us every thing but a knowledge of themselves. However, the feast of the bards in the hall of shells has its foundation in nature, and, I am persuaded, existed even before Ossian. Does not the young Greenlander invite the poet of his village to celebrate his triumph over the first seal which falls by his hand, and to recite the actions of his tribe and family while the feast that places him among the men of that tribe is held? Even Mexico and Peru had their poets, or rather minstrels, who celebrated their sun-descended monarchs. And I am disposed to regard the chorus of the ancient tragedies as only a relique of the more antique bards; for such a cumbrous machine would hardly have been invented, had there not been some prototype in nature. In the stories of the East, the great personages are always entertained with concerts at a signal, which proves that the musicians were always waiting, and, therefore, naturally ready to take part in every action that was going on, and to give that information to new comers which was necessary for carrying on the action of a piece. In my favourite Sacontala, there is a chorus of wood-nymphs in the groves, and another of minstrels in the palace; and the poets fable, that the court of the great deity on Kailassa, is the abode of the gandhavas or musicians, and the bardai or poets—an idea of mag-

E

nificence undoubtedly derived from the splendour of earthly monarchs; a small remnant of
which you will be apt to remind me is preserved
among ourselves, in the appointment of the
laureat and his yearly odes; save that, unfortunately, the praises of ancestors give place
to more direct flattery in our plain-dealing
days.

I am no musician; and, therefore, can only
tell you, that the few Indian airs I had an opportunity of hearing, were remarkable for their
extreme simplicity, and some of them pleased
my uncultivated ear, as those of Scotland and
Ireland do, because they seem expressive of the
sentiments described in the songs they accompany. The instrumental part of their music did
not please me so well; however, I believe I did
not hear any of the best. It appears to me
too noisy, from the constant use of drums of all
sizes, and of trumpets and pipes, from that so
large as to require a man to bear the mouth on
his shoulder while it is played by another, to
the smallest reed. I have, however, heard
some extremely sweet pipes; and I have seen
the double pipe, which we observe in antique
sculptures, but which is not remarkable for the
beauty of its tones. There are several instruments of the guitar and lute kind, some of
which are formed with hollow gourds, by way

of sounding-boards; and I once saw a kind of triangular harp or lyre, the tones of which were charming. There is also an instrument played with a bow, which put me a good deal in mind of a dancing-master's kit. The strings of all these being of iron or brass wire, and in general the fingers used for fretting the strings being armed with thimbles of metal, the tones produced have not that mellowness which we admire in Europe.

That the ancient music of Hindostan was infinitely superior to the modern, we may reasonably infer from the treatises concerning it in the Sanscrit language, and from the effects ascribed to it by the poets, which seem not inferior to those produced by the lyre of Orpheus. It was natural that the invention of so enchanting an art should have been ascribed to the gods; accordingly, the Bramins suppose it to have been communicated to man by Brahma himself, or his consort Seraswati, the goddess of speech; and fable, that Nareda, an ancient lawgiver, who was the inventor of the *vina* (a kind of guitar) and the *cach'hapi* or testudo, was the son of Brahma and the same goddess. Bherat, the inventor of natucs or dramas represented with songs and dances, or what we term operas, was considered as inspired; and Hanumân, the friend of Rama, who is also

Pavan or Pan, is the author of a most popular mode of music. Sir William Jones, in his Essay on the musical modes of the Hindûs, quotes several treatises, particularly the *Damodar, Narayan, Bhagavi bodha*, and *Retnacara*. These describe particularly four *matas* or systems of music, by Iswara or Siva (perhaps Osiris) Bherat, Hanumân, and Callinath, an Indian philosopher : there are, however, different systems peculiar to almost each province of Hindustan. Some of the sweetest of these seem to have prevailed in the Panjâb, and in the neighbourhood of Mat'hura, the pastoral people of which, delighted in singing the loves and adventures of their hero Crishna, who was himself the patron of music, and is often represented dancing while he plays on a reed. The scale of the Hindûs comprehends seven sounds, called sa, ri, ga, ma, pa, dha, ni, and in the octave they reckon twenty-two quarters and thirds. They also count eighty-four modes, formed by subdividing the seven natural sounds; these modes are called *ragas*, a word which properly signifies passion, each mode being intended to move one or other of our affections. Hence the fabulists have sometimes imagined them so various, as to make up the number of sixteen thousand; more temperate writers, though they admit almost as many possible modes, only reckon twenty-three as applicable to practice.

The Indian poets seem to have employed the utmost elegance and richness of their talents to adorn the fables connected with this divine art.

The six chief modes are personified as beautiful youths, the genii of music, and presiding over the six seasons. *Bhairava* is lord of the cheerful, dry, or autumnal season, and his strains invite the dancer to accompany them. *Malava* rules the cold and melancholy months, and with his attendant Ragnis, complains of slighted love, or bewails the pains of absence. *Sriraga* patronizes the dewy season, which is the time of delight, that ushers in the spring, the fragrant and the flowery time over which *Hindola* or *Vasanta* presides. When the oppressive heat comes on, the soft and languid melody of *Dipaca* sympathises with the fevered feelings, while the refreshing season of the new rains bestows a double pleasure, when accompanied by the sweet strains of *Megha**. To aid the Ragas come their faithful spouses, the thirty Raginis, five of which attend each youth, presenting to him eight little genii,

* The names of the seasons are as follows :—*Sarad,* the autumnal season; *Hemanta,* the frosty; *Sisira,* the dewy; *Vasanta,* the spring, called also *Surabhi,* fragrant, and *Prispasamaya,* flowery; *Grishma,* heat; and *Versha,* rain.

their sons, whose lovely voices aid and vary the melodies of their sires.

Such is the outline of the beautiful picture drawn by the poets, and which is also a favourite subject with the Indian painters; but their works, like the music of modern Hindostan, do not furnish materials by which to judge of the state of the art, when India was in the zenith of her glory. Of the ancient music, indeed, the history has been preserved in elaborate scientific treatises and poetical tales; but ancient pictures must long ago have perished; and it is only by a detached hint, scattered here and there, in writings on other subjects, that we can guess that painting was once highly cultivated.

The specimens of Hindû art I have seen, are minute imitations of nature, on a scale in general more diminutive than our common miniatures; but there is a delicacy of handling about them, that seems like the remains of a more perfect art, which survives only in its mechanical part, while the soul and genius that once guided it are long since fled.

Sculpture had made considerable progress in Hindostan at an early period; and however rude the first attempts at hewing a stone, and polishing it into the resemblance of the human figure, still it serves as a model which other artists may improve.

Drawn in green Steatite of the bigness of a middle sized Tortoise.

Drawn by M.G.   Etched by D.S.

Specimen of Sculpture

CARLI CAVE.

The first figures of the ancient Egyptians, and even of the Greeks, had their hands straight, and attached to the body, and the legs were not divided; the Hindûs had attained to an imitation of attitude and action; and though their forms wanted that exquisite grace which even now enraptures us, when we behold the wonders of the Grecian chissel, I have seen some which are not without elegance, particularly a dancing figure at the entrance to the cave of Carli, which possesses considerable ease and gracefulness: and there is no little skill displayed in the grouping of some of the sculptures at the Seven Pagodas, particularly one representing Crishna protecting his followers from the wrath of Indra. Perhaps one great reason of the arrestation of the farther progress of sculpture, after it had advanced so far, was the attempt to represent, by gigantic bulk, the greatness of the heroes and the gods, which necessarily, as it rendered the work less manageable, made it coarse: whereas the Greeks, though, in a few instances, they formed colossal statues, commonly confined themselves to the beautiful proportions of nature, and sought to place greatness in expression. The bending of the brow of Jupiter, conveyed at once all that is sublime and majestic in the Father of gods and men; but the giant Siva must frown, and gnash his teeth, and raise his numerous terribly armed hands, ere the Hindû sees his awful divinity, or recognises the powerful father and destroyer of all. Besides, it is probable that, as the religion of the Egyptians forbade the alteration, even for the sake of improvement, of any figure intended for the service of the temples, so the same cause might have prevented the Hindû sculptor from departing from the figure and attitude which his ancestors had bestowed on his gods.

In the lower parts of sculpture, applicable to architectural ornaments, the Hindû chissel has perhaps seldom been surpassed; its light and airy foliage, its elegant volutes, and the variety of its subjects, vie at once with Italian art and Gothic fancy, to which last style it has, indeed, occasionally a remarkable likeness.

The most ancient remains of Indian architecture are most probably those wonderful excavations and sculptured rocks, in Elephanta and Salsette, at Ellora, the Seven Pagodas, and among the Mahratta mountains. In the first of these, the effect is produced by the massiness of the pillars, as much as by the great extent of the cavern and its sculptured sides, where the gigantic deities and saints give it an air of the palace of some enchanter, so unlike are they in size and form to any thing in common nature.

The caves of Salsette are interesting, as I think they present us with the civil architecture of India at a very early period. Most of these small caves appear evidently to have been private dwellings : each of them has a little portico, and a cell within, at one end of which there is a raised part, which, on my visiting them, I imagined was designed for a bed place ; but since that time, a passage in Sacontala* has made me conjecture that it was the consecrated hearth where the sacred fire was kept, and this appears to me to be confirmed by the circumstance that there is near the largest and first cavern, one to which I was obliged to be lifted up, when I found a considerable platform, and a figure of the deity in the back ground. Now, the height to which this platform is raised, corresponds with the description of Dushmanta's hearth, and might have belonged to the superior of that society, which, from the number of caverns, their contiguity, and the conve-

---

* *Dushmanta.*—Wardour, point the way to the hearth of the consecrated fire.

Wardour.—This, oh king, is the way (*he walks before*). Here is the entrance of the hallowed enclosure ; and there stands the venerable cow to be milked for the sacrifice, looking bright from the recent sprinkling of mystic water.—Let the king ascend.

(Dushmanta *is raised to the place of sacrifice on the shoulders of his wardours.*)

Sacontala, Act 5th.

niences of baths and reservoirs with which they
are supplied, we may conclude once inhabited
the now deserted mountains of Salsette. These
scenes brought to my mind the opening of
Mason's Caractacus :—

> . . . . the place
> Where, but at times of holiest festival,
> The druid leads his train.
> . . . . up the hill
> Mine eye descries a distant range of caves
> Delv'd in the ridges of the craggy steep;
> And this way still another. ·
> > On the left
> Reside the sages skilled in nature's lore, &c.

The rocky hill in which these dwellings are
dug, contains probably some hundreds of caves,
of different sizes. I saw a great number; but,
I believe, scarcely half of those which are known.
One of them appears to have been a temple:
it is of an oblong form, terminating in a semi-
circle, in which is one of those solid masses
which the Jines and Bhaudd'has suppose to
cover part of the ashes of their respective
saints, and which are sometimes, as in Salsette, and at Carli in the Mahratta mountains,
formed of rocks, wrought in their native bed;
and sometimes, as in the temple courts of
all the sacred places I saw in Ceylon, built
of brick or other materials, plaistered over with

fine *chunam* or *stucco*, and generally of a co-
nical form. These monuments or altars, as
they have been sometimes called, are often
without ornament; frequently, however, they
are very much enriched, and have generally on
the top a member which spreads a little, so as to
form a kind of umbrella, which you know is, in
the East, the ensign of dignity.

The great caverns both at Canara, in Salsette,
and at Carli, are supported by polygonal pillars,
with peculiar bases and capitals, possessing
considerable dignity and solidity, though they
are far behind the Greek columns in elegance.
I send you some sketches of specimens of these,
and also of some which supported the entrances
to some of those smaller caves which I take to
have been dwellinghouses. At Carli, these
dwellinghouses are in different stories, in the
perpendicular face of the rock, and communi-
cating with each other by stairs within, while
the outside only presents here and there a
window, or a colonnade. At Canara, the dwellings enter from without; before each door
there is usually a reservoir, and in most of them
I found excellent water. The communication
between distant parts of the mountain is facili-
tated by winding paths, or steps hewn in the
rock; and on the summit there are larger
reservoirs and baths, which were probably in

common. The hewing of all these is extremely skilful, and marks a knowledge of the sciences and arts connected with architecture, of no ordinary degree. The construction of arches, alone, is a proof of the great progress of the Hindûs in the arts which tend so materially to the comfort and embellishment of society; and the buildings erected for astronomical purposes, of which the ruins still remain, are a farther evidence of their skill and ingenuity.

The religious *buildings* of the Hindûs probably partook originally of that grandeur and simplicity so remarkable in the cavern temples; but that they very early adopted a style of excessive ornament is evident from the *pagodas,* as the English choose erroneously to call them, hewn out of the rock at Ellora and at Mahvellepoor, or the Seven Pagodas. Every moulding, every angle, is adorned with grotesque heads or images, or pinnacles, extremely enriched with pilasters, and what we should call corbels, supporting them. The roofs of the buildings are oblong, they are generally covered with a moulding, along the to pof which is placed a row of vases, or if square, they terminate in a kind of dome, ribbed on the outside with an ornament not unlike the Gothic crockets. The interstices between the ornaments of the sides of the temples, are generally filled up with sculptures re-

6

MUNTAPUM,

Specimen of Hindu Architecture

presenting the persons of the Hindû mythology,
and the pillars which support or embellish them,
are occasionally fluted or otherwise adorned. On
the whole coast of Coromandel, the modern temples are built in the style of these very ancient
sculptures, but, in general, with considerably
more numerous embellishments, and with less
taste. I, however, send you a sketch of one
which pleased me exceedingly when I saw it,
it is a muntapom or open temple, in which, on
days of festivals, the deity is placed, having
been brought from an adjoining temple to receive the personal addresses of his votaries.
The style of building is, however, very different
in different provinces, as you may convince
yourself by looking at Daniels's beautiful prints.
Those of the north appear to be the most simple;
and one might thence, perhaps, argue, that
they were the most ancient: however, the
sculptured rocks are incomparably the most
authentic monuments of the ancient architecture; and when these shall be better known, it
may perhaps be possible to class the different
models, and to form some sort of regular system
of orders.

With the Mahommedan architecture, introduced in the 12th and 13th centuries into India
by its conquerors, and probably blended with
that of the natives, I am but little acquainted.

But you will find most magnificent specimens in the tombs of the kings at Veyjeyapoor, and in the monument built by Shah Jehan to the memory of his wife, near Agra, and called after her the Taje Mahal; it is of white marble, and beautifully inlaid. The tomb itself is inlaid with precious stones, in so beautiful a mosaic, that it has been ascribed to Italian artists in the service of the Mogul. The mosques of Dehli and Agra will also excite your admiration for their grandeur and extent, as well as for the beauty of form and workmanship you will discover in them. Like the Hindû temples, their walls usually enclose a large area, the centre of which is occupied by a consecrated tank or reservoir of masonry; and often adorned with trees, pillars, and seats, along the brink, from which, to the bottom, there is usually a flight of steps. The buildings around the court, something like the cloisters to our colleges, are, with the Hindûs, the residence of priests and other holy men; with the Mussulmans, they are consecrated to hospitality, where travellers of every nation find shelter and rest. The *choultry* of the Hindûs was naturally separated from the temple to prevent pollution by the admittance of impure tribes, but near enough to answer the humane purpose of protecting the traveller from insult or danger. Some of the most admirable works of the Hindûs are their tanks or reservoirs of water; some of which have been constructed with consummate ingenuity and incredible labour, by damming up the outlets of narrow valleys, and thus making use of the surrounding rocks as walls. Others, in the flat countries, have been dug and lined with masonry, covering frequently not less than a hundred acres; and wells of every description, for the purposes of agriculture or the relief of travellers, are met with all over the country, more or less in repair, as the towns or villages near them have flourished or been destroyed by war, oppression, or famine.

Among the great public works of Hindostan, there are none more worthy of remark than the canals of Sultaun Firoze, which were dug to supply the city of Hissar Firozeh with water. The first of these passed from the Jumna to Sufedoon, a hunting palace, and thence to Hissar, and was one hundred and fourteen geographical miles in length. This canal was repaired about A. D. 1626, by Shah Jehan, who prolonged it to Delhi, making in the whole one hundred and seventy-four geographical miles.

The other canal brought the waters of the Sutlege to Hissar: it is said to have been one hundred miles in length; and both these canals are said to have been intended by Firoze to have answered the purposes of navigation, as well as giving water to the town and adjacent country.

I copy verbatim the following note of Major Rennel from Captain Kirkpatrick's manuscripts.—" Besides the main canals that have been mentioned, it seems that several others were cut, which united them in different parts and in different directions. The banks, both of the main canals and their branches, were covered with towns—such as Juneed, Dhatara, Hansi, and Toglucpoor. Firoze, by sanction of a decree of the Cauzees assembled for the purpose, levied a tenth of the produce of the lands fertilized by these canals, which he applied, together with the revenue of the lands newly brought into cultivation, to charitable uses. The lands of Firozeh, which before had produced but one scanty harvest, now produced two abundant ones. This Sircar, ever since the conquest of Hindostan by the Moguls, has constituted the personal estate of the heir apparent of the empire."

Such works as these are really worthy of a great monarch; and the labours of Firoze, and the laws of Akbar, are among the most honourable monuments of conquest that the warriors or monarchs of any age, or any faith, have left.

The early military architecture of India must

have been of that inartificial kind which was sufficient to guard against the incursions of wild beasts or the surprise of a human enemy, whose bow and arrow were his chief weapons; these were constructed either of kneaded clay, brick, or stone, according to the nature of the country which was to be defended, and were more or less strong according to the treasure to be guarded or the importance of the situation. Many of the ancient forts were on the summits of steep rocks, and required little assistance from art to be impregnable, except by starving their garrisons; but as civilization advanced, the arts of war kept pace with those of peace, and that of fortifying towns, of course improved in proportion to the improvement in the modes of attack. The Mahomedans would naturally introduce such methods of defence as were used in their native country when they found those of the conquered people defective; but the science of fortification has always continued in the East in an extremely rude state, although many of the Mussulman monarchs, particularly Aureng Zebe in the 17th century, and Tippoo Sultaun in our own times, employed European engineers in constructing works for the defence of their principal cities.

On the coast of India you will everywhere find the forts of the Portuguese, Dutch and

F

other Europeans, who have usually been obliged
to construct such defences for their factories.
Many if not most of these are in a ruinous condition, and it is only at the three presidencies
that you will see them on a very extensive scale
and carefully kept up. The inland forts I am
less able to speak of, but I believe some of them
to possess considerable strength against any
native force, though few, excepting those whose
natural situations are strong*, could resist a regular attack from European troops. Among
these the mud forts are probably the best calculated for resistance, as the substance of which
they are built being kneaded clay, possesses a
tenuity which deadens the effect of shot and
renders it difficult to effect a breach.

But you will think I am straying out of my
proper province and trenching upon yours, and,
to say the truth, the useful and exact lines of a
fortress have in general few charms for a lady's
eyes, however she may delight in the more
showy structure of palaces and temples. There-

* Such as the fortress of Dowlat-abad, which stands on the
summit of a high insulated rock. It is surrounded by a ditch
I am told fifty feet wide, and the rock is scarped to an astonishing height. Across this ditch a narrow bridge leads to an
aperture in the rock, by which you enter a winding passage
cut in the hill, the egress of which is defended by a grating of
metal, which is let down at pleasure, and thus renders the
place completely inaccessible.

fore I will take leave in time, and beg you to
believe me as ever, &c.

LETTER V.

In mentioning the fine arts as they
once flourished in Hindostan, I ought not to have
omitted Calligraphy, which, in a country where
printing is unknown, becomes really an art, of
no trifling importance. Accordingly we find in
the East, where the means of multiplying books
by printing have not yet superseded the pen of
the scribe, the most beautiful and correct manuscripts often enriched with costly illuminations
and gilding. Though paper be now pretty
generally used to write on in India, and that of
a very smooth and even kind, yet the more ancient methods still prevail in some districts.
One of these which is most frequently practised
is writing upon the leaf of the palmyra with an
iron style; so that you see people going about
with their little bundle of leaves in appearance
like a large fan, tied up between two bits of
wood cut to fit them, either as ledgers and bill-
books, or the legendary tales of their country,
or the holy texts of their shastras, which may
possibly have been originally written with the
same materials. Another kind of writing of

which you will see a particular account in Wilks's excellent History of the South of India, is the *Cudduttum*, Curruttum, or Currut. It is a strip of cotton cloth covered on both sides with a mixture of paste and charcoal. The writing is done with a pencil of lapis ollaris, called *Balapum*, and may be rubbed out like that on a slate; the cloth is folded in leaves like a pocket-map, and tied up between thin boards painted and ornamented. This mode of writing was anciently used for records and other public papers, and in some parts of the country is still employed by merchants and shopkeepers. It is very durable, indeed probably more so, than either paper, parchment, or the palm leaf. Col. Wilks supposes it to be the linen or cotton cloth on which Arrian states that the Indians wrote.

Many grants of land and other public documents have been discovered engraved on copper-plates, a number of which are frequently fastened together with a ring and seal, and numerous inscriptions on stone are met with on the sites of most ancient towns and places of worship.

The writing on paper and parchment is performed with a reed shaped nearly like our common pens; the ink in substance and colour resembles a thick solution of the common Indian ink, but the writing is often traced in various colours, such as red and azure, or occasionally with gold.

The character in which the Sanscrit is written is called Deva Nagari, the etymology of which name does not seem determined, excepting that the first part of it proclaims its holiness*. It is written from the left to the right-hand like our own, and has a square appearance as if a line were drawn on the top of each word. You will see some beautiful manuscripts in the museum of the India-House, especially one of extraordinary length, illuminated and embellished with pictures of the gods of the Hindû Mythology, which is most delicately written upon very fine parchment.

Among other substances used for writing upon, there is a very precious, because very scarce, kind of yellow parchment, made of the skin of the hogdeer, which is used on occasions of ceremony, when the writing is commonly coloured and gilt.

Although it be generally understood that learning in all its branches is interdicted to the lower castes of the Hindûs, this ought only to be understood of such parts as are contained in the sacred books, the Vedas, Vedangas and sacred poems. But there are many treatises

* It is supposed by some to have taken its name of *Nagari*, from the city where it is said to have been invented; but this is doubtful.

written expressly for the use of the lower people, and in case they do not find occupation in
their own callings they are permitted to have recourse to any other, excepting the reading and
teaching the Vedas, among which writing is
enumerated, and in so populous a country where
literature had become a luxury, we may be sure
that very many hands must have been employed
in administering to that luxury. We may suppose without any great stretch of imagination,
that the lords and ladies of king Vicrama's court
would, after the representation of Sacontala, be
eager to read so charming a production, and
the ornamented and perfumed manuscript
would eagerly be offered to her, whose dark eyes
emulated those of the interesting princess, and
the hope of recommending himself to favour
and wealth would incite the writer to excel his
competitors, till the perfection of the art itself
became a primary object.

We have often smiled at the *naïve* account
which Froissart gives of presenting his rich
manuscript to his patron, and I cannot suppose
that the Indian poet was less eager for distinction than the western chronicler, or that the
Hindoo monarch would with less complacency receive the legends of his heaven-descended ancestors, than the Count de Foix did those of
his own contemporaries.

The warriors of Hindostan whose family Barts

led their troops on to battle, chanting the strains of victory, on returning to their halls of peace, held feasts in honour of the gods or heroes, where the minstrel after the martial exercises, made the lofty roofs resound with the songs of other times, or in his own numbers drew tears from eyes that seldom wept; sometimes the drama with all its pomp delighted the eyes and ears of the attentive audience, and at others the historic and legendary scrolls were unfolded, and the reading of past events occupied the heroes who were one day to be enrolled on the same list with their progenitors.

Far different were the scenes in which these legends were composed; retired in the deepest recesses of the sacred groves consecrated to the

> Hidden power, that reigns
> 'Mid the lone majesty of untamed nature.

Was the abode of

> Sages skilled in nature's lore:
> The changeful universe, its numbers, powers
> Studious they measure, save when meditation
> Gives place to holy rites.
> *Caractacus, Act 1st.*

These sages controuling, by their sacred character of mediators between the gods and men, the councils of monarchs and the enterprises of warriors, appeared but to command respect; and in their hours of solitude composed or compiled from ancient tradition the codes of religion, morality and law, which have acquired such unbounded influence over their countrymen, and which time seems to strengthen rather than to diminish.

Of all the writings left by these extraordinary men, the Vedas are the most interesting. Their existence was long doubted by the learned in Europe, perhaps owing in some degree to the unwillingness of the Brahmins to impart them to strangers. But early in the seventeenth century they had been partly translated for the use of the accomplished prince Dara Shekoh*, into the Persian language, and considerable portions had been rendered into the Hindûi tongue. At length several English gentlemen, among whom the most distinguished was Sir William Jones, procured copies of valuable portions of the originals; but it is to Mr. Colebrooke that we are indebted for the most complete accounts of these ancient writings.

Some persons have hastily pronounced the Vedas to be modern forgeries; but Mr. Colebrooke has brought forward the most convincing arguments corroborated by various proofs, that notwithstanding the possible inaccuracy of a few passages, the great body of the Vedas as now

* See Bernier for an account of this interesting and unfortunate brother of Aureng Zebe.

received consists of the *same compositions which under the title of Vedas have been revered by the Hindús for hundreds if not thousands of years.*

These Vedas are four in number: the Rigveda, the Yajurveda, the Samaveda, and the At'har-va Veda; and some writers reckon the books It'hasa and the Puranas as a fifth or supplemental Veda. By the age of the Vedas is not meant the period at which they were actually composed, but that in which they were collected and arranged by the sage Dwapayana surnamed Vyasa or the Compiler, or about fourteen centuries before the Christian æra, and nine hundred years before Pisistratus performed the same office for the works of Homer, in danger of being lost, owing to the practice of the public rehearsers who only declaimed detached passages and episodes.

The At'herban or more properly At'herva Veda is supposed to be more modern than the other three books, and indeed to be a compilation from them. The antiquity also of many of the puranas is questioned, but their real author and precise date is of little consequence, since the fact of their being really the sacred books of India is acknowledged.

The Vedas consist of a compilation of prayers or *Muntras* and hymns, the complete collection of which is called Sanhita, and of precepts and maxims called Brahmana. The theology of

2

Indian scripture including the argumentative part or Vedanta is contained in tracts called Upanishads, and to each Veda a treatise called Jyotish is annexed, explaining the adjustment of the calendar for religious purposes.

The Rigveda contains chiefly encomiastic muntras, and its name is derived from the verb *Rich* to laud ; these prayers are mostly in verse, and together with similar passages in any other Veda are called *Rich*. The authors of these hymns are various, some of them being ascribed to different deities male and female, others to kings and princes, or to sages and holy men. This Veda contains in its last chapter the celebrated Gayatri, or Indian priest's confession of faith, which is thus translated by Mr. Colebrooke.

" This new and excellent praise of thee, O splendid playful sun! is offered by us to thee. Be gratified by this my speech, approach this craving mind, as a fond man seeks a woman. May that sun (Pushasi) who contemplates and looks into all worlds be our protector.

" LET US MEDITATE ON THE ADORABLE LIGHT OF THE DIVINE RULER (SAVITRI). MAY IT GUIDE OUR INTELLECT. Desirous of food we solicit the gift of the splendid. sun *(Savitri)* who should be studiously worshipped. Venerable men, guided by the understanding, salute the divine sun *(Savitri)* with oblations and praise."

I do not wonder that one of the first objects
of worship should have been him who

> With surpassing glory crown'd
> Looks from his sole dominion like the
> God of this new world.

Or that the " splendid playful sun," should have
been regarded as the embodying of that divine
intellect which pervades and governs all things.
But soon the type was considered as the thing
typified, and the sun once adored as God, there
were no bounds to the wanderings of the human
imagination; and though the instructed sages ever
considered the sun, the air, the fire, as types of
their Creator, the vulgar soon adopted that mythology which personifies the elements and planets, and peoples heaven and earth with various
orders of beings. Thus though the Vedas distinctly recognize but one God, their poetic language does not sufficiently distinguish the Creator
from the creature; and though the numerous
titles of the deity be all referable to the sun, the
air and fire, and these three again but signify
the one God, these titles insensibly became
the names of separate deities, who usurped
the worship due only to the Supreme intelligence.

The name of the Yajurveda signifies that it
concerns oblations and sacrifices. Soon after it
was compiled by Vyasa it became polluted, and

a new revelation called the White Yajush was granted to Yajnyawalkya, while the remains of the former Yajush is distinguished by the title of the Black Yajurveda. Some of the prayers called Rich are included in this Veda, but its own peculiar muntras are in prose.

A peculiar degree of holiness is attributed to the Samaveda, as its name signifies that which destroys sin. Its texts are usually chanted, and I have occasionally been delighted with the solemn tones issuing from the domes of the native temples, at sunset, before the moment for the ceremonial ablutions had arrived.

The last or At'harvan Veda is chiefly used at rites for conciliating the deities, or for drawing down curses on enemies, and contains some prayers used at lustrations. As a specimen of the Hindû taste in curses, I send you the following : " Destroy, O sacred grass*, my foes; exterminate my enemies ; annihilate all those who hate me, O precious gem !"

The most remarkable part of the At'harvan Veda consists of the treatises called Upanishats. The meaning of this word is divine science, or the knowledge of God ; and the whole of the Indian theology is professedly founded on the Upanishads, which are either extracts from the

* *Darbha.* Poa Cynosuroides.

Vedas, or essays belonging to the Indian Scriptures.

To give you an idea of the doctrines contained in the Vedas, and of the style in which they are conveyed, I shall transcribe some passages from that portion of the Rigveda called Aitareya Aranyaca, the four last lectures of which, containing the most sublime account of the creation, excepting that in the book of Genesis, that I have ever met with, are translated by Mr. Colebrooke in his essay on the Vedas, published in the eighth vol. of the Asiatic Researches.

The fine passage, however, which opens this portion of the sacred writings, is followed by some of a very different cast; which make it " lose discountenanced, and like folly show;" so that one knows not whether most to admire the great man who conceived the first, or to despise the compiler who could place such ill-assorted materials together.

" Originally this universe was indeed SOUL only; nothing else whatever existed, active or inactive. HE thought, I will create worlds. Thus HE created these various worlds; water, light, mortal beings, and the waters. That water, is the region above the heaven, which heaven upholds; the atmosphere comprises light; the earth is mortal; and the regions below are the waters."

After proceeding to describe the production of all beings from the mundane egg floating on the waters, the Aitaréya asks, " What is this soul? that we may worship him. Which is the soul? Is it that, by which a man sees? By which he hears? By which he smells odours? By which he utters speech? By which he discriminates a pleasant or an unpleasant taste? Is it the heart, or understanding? Or the mind, or will? Is it sensation? or power? or discrimination? or comprehension? or perception? or retention? or attention? or application? or taste (or pain?) or memory? or assent? or determination? or animal action? or wish? or desire?

" All these are only various forms of apprehension. But this (soul consisting in the faculty of apprehension) is BRAHMA ; he is INDRA, he is (PRAJAPATI) the lord of creatures : these gods are he ; and so are the five primary elements, earth, air, the etherial fluid, water and light; these, and the same joined with minute objects and other seeds of existence, and again other beings produced from eggs, or borne in wombs, or originating in hot moisture, or springing from plants ; whether horses, or kine, or men, or elephants, whatever lives, and walks, or flies, or whatever is immoveable, as trees and herbs : all that is the eye of intelligence. On intellect every thing is founded : the world is the eye of intellect; and intellect is its foundation. Intelligence is (*Brahme*) the great one.

" By this intuitively intelligent soul, that sage ascended from the present world to the blissful region of heaven, and, obtaining all his wishes, became immortal. He became immortal.

. " May my speech be founded on understanding; and my mind be attentive to my utterance. Be thou manifested to me, O self-manifested (intellect!) For my sake, O speech and mind! approach this *Veda*. May what I have heard be unforgotten: day and night may I behold this, which I have studied. Let me think the reality: let me speak the truth. May it preserve me; may it preserve the teacher; me may it preserve; the teacher may it preserve; may it preserve the teacher."

To this long quotation I will only add the conclusion of a hymn on the same subject, which is found in a different part of the Rigveda.

" Who knows exactly, and who shall in this world declare, whence and why this creation took place? The gods are subsequent to the production of this world; then who can know whence it proceeded? or whence this varied world arose? or whether it uphold itself or not? He, who is in the highest heaven, the ruler of this universe, does indeed know; but not another can possess that knowledge."

Perhaps you will be as much struck as I was with the grandeur and simplicity of " *He* thought, I will create worlds; thus He created these worlds." But you must be aware that this is the creed of the learned, and not that of the people, who are taught the common mythological fables of the alternate destruction and renovation of the earth, with the periodical sleep of Brahma, or rather of Vishnu, the preserving power, during whose slumbers the genius of destruction prevails.

These better notions of the Vedas, and particularly those of the Aitaréya Aranyaca are professedly the fundamental doctrines of the philosophers of the Vedanta sect, whose speculations appear to coincide nearly with those of Berkeley, and perhaps, of Plato. The Sastra which contains the doctrines of the Vedantas is ascribed to Vyasa, and the commentator is Sancara, who explains and enlarges the very ancient and almost obsolete texts of this author. The opinions of this school concerning matter are, that it has no existence independent on mental perception, and consequently that existence and perceptibility are controvertible terms. That external appearances and sensations are illusory, and would vanish into nothing if the divine energy which alone sustains them were suspended but for a moment.

Their notions concerning the human soul approach nearly to the *Pantheism* of some other philosophical sects, and may be understood from the following text. " That spirit from which these created beings proceed; through which, having proceeded from it, they live; toward which they tend, *and in which they are ultimately absorbed*, that spirit study to know; that spirit is the great one*."

The oldest philosophical sect in India appears, however, to have been that of the followers of Capila, inventor of the Sanc'hya or numeral philosophy which Sir William Jones thought resembled the metaphysics of Pythagoras, who is said, indeed, to have travelled into India in search of knowledge, and who might possibly have adopted the tenets of the

---

* " Know first that heaven and earth's compacted frame
And flowing waters, and the starry flame
And both the radiant lights, one common soul
Inspires and feeds, and animates the whole.
This active mind, infused through all the space
Unites and mingles with the mighty mass.
Hence men and beasts the breath of life obtain,
And birds of air, and monsters of the main.
Th'etherial vigour is in all the same;
And ev'ry soul is filled with equal flame."
6th Æneis. Dryden's Translation.

G

Brahmins his instructors. Next to the Sanc'hya, Gotama and Canáda invented the Nyáya or logical philosophy, admitting the actual existence of material substance in the popular sense of the word matter, and comprising a body of dialectics, with an artificial method of reasoning, with distinct names for the three parts of a proposition and even for those of a regular syllogism*.

. The philosophy of the Baudd'ha and Jaina religious sects is branded with the name of atheism by the orthodox Brahmins, who assert that they deny the existence of spirit independent on matter, and consequently that of the supreme intelligence. But we may, I think, doubt how far the assertions of enemies and rivals are entitled to belief.

Thus you see the forests and groves of Hindostan produced systems of philosophy long before she

> From heav'n descended to the low-roofed house
> Of Socrates.

---

* Sir William Jones, in his eleventh Discourse, printed in the 4th vol. of the Asiatic Researches, p. 170, mentions the following curious tradition which, according to the author of the *Dabistan*, prevailed in the Panjab. " Among other Indian curiosities which Callisthenes transmitted to his uncle, was a *technical system of logic* which the Brahmins had communicated to the inquisitive Greek," and which the Mahomedan writer supposes to have been the groundwork of the famous Aristotelian method.

And conjecture, and even tradition seem to point them out as the origin of all the

> Streams that watered all the schools
> Of academies old and new, with those
> Surnamed Peripatetics, and the sect
> Epicurean, and the Stoic severe.

A thousand circumstances concur to identify the ancient religions of India and Egypt; and to render it most probable that the relation of their sciences and philosophy was not less intimate. Which was the most anciently civilized of the two countries will probably ever remain undetermined; but the Indians seem on many accounts to lay claim to a superior antiquity. Their physical situation, so well adapted to the production of all that nature requires, while it must have been long before the muddy shores of the Nile were habitable, is not the least argument in their favour; besides, their traditions and poems all seem to point to the north as the quarter whence they received their religion, their science, their language, and their conquerors, which could not have been the case if they were originally from Egypt. It is possible that the same origin may be common to them both, and that the similarity observed in the monuments of every kind in the two nations may be drawn from one common source.

Now the Greeks confessedly borrowed from

the Egyptians, but transporting their coarse and clumsy imagery into their own charming climate, genius refined and purified it with her magic touch, and formed even in the infancy of happy Greece those models, which like the ideal beauty of the painter, future times have sought unceasingly to emulate, but sought in vain; while the ancient mothers of art, continued their massy and ill-formed works, as if the palsied hand of time had brought them back to a state of infancy and fixed them in irrecoverable mediocrity. You have only to compare the rude sketch I send you of a still ruder deity*, with the beautiful head of the Apollo, and if for a moment you can forget its deformity to think of the ingenuity that made the elephant's head the symbol of the god of letters, I shall think you deserve to be born a Brahmin in your next visit to this world, and to be one of Genesa's especial favourites, with whose name I conclude this letter, the subject of which is peculiarly his own.

LETTER VI.

You flatter me extremely by desiring the continuance of so grave a correspondence as mine on the subject of India has hitherto

* See the plate of Genesa.

been, and, what is worse, I fear I cannot promise to be much more amusing in future. The
truth is, that the literature of the East has hitherto been kept so totally distinct from that
of Europe, that the moment one touches on an
oriental subject, one conjures up the figures of
grave professors with cauliflower wigs, and ex-
pects to hear beef and mutton talked of in the
original Hebrew. Now really it has often mor-
tified me, to think I was living under the same
government and protected by the same laws
with my fellow-subjects in India, and that I
knew as little about them as about the inhabitants of Mercury, who are so enveloped in sun-
beams as to be dark with excess of light; so
that you owe to my vanity all these long
stories of philosophers and poets with which I
have treated you for some time past.

I am not sure that I was not once liable to
the reproach of European prejudice so far as to
despise immeasurably the Hindu meekness, and
half polish; and perhaps I should be ashamed to
own that I had so far strayed from good-nature
and good-sense, as to forget, that whatever re-
proaches may be deserved by some of the Hindus for their moral practices, the fundamental
principles of morality itself are so firmly im-
planted in the soul of man that no vicious
practice and no mistaken code can change

their nature, and that we should look on the
historian who should tell us of laws which
enacted theft and murder, or punished honesty
and benevolence, with as little credit, as on him
who should talk of " men whose heads do grow
beneath their shoulders."

Our missionaries are very apt to split upon
this rock, and in order to place our religion in
the brightest light, as if it wanted their feeble
aid, they lay claim exclusively to all the sublime maxims of morality, and tell those they
wish to convert, that their own books contain
nothing but abominations, the belief of which
they must abandon in order to receive the purer
doctrine of Christianity. Mistaken men ! could
they desire a better opening to their hopes than
to find already established that morality which
says, it is enjoined to man even at the moment
of destruction to wish to benefit his foes, " *as
the sandal tree in the instant of its overthrow sheds
perfume on the axe that fells it.*"

How happy would it be if instead of fighting
with the air as these good men persist in doing,
they were employed in teaching the rudiments of
knowledge, in searching for, and compiling such
moral passages from the ancient Hindû books,
as, taught to the young Indians, might improve
them, and render them worthy of still further
advantages, an improvement they would be far

from refusing, as it would accord with their prejudices, and being founded on the wisdom of their forefathers would carry with it the authority of religion and the attractions of affection. Should we hear of the habitual want of truth in the Hindûs, if from their infancy they were exercised in those sacred passages where truth in all her sublime and attractive array is identified with the universal soul, and made familiar with the strains of the poet, who speaking of the inviolability of a promise, sings, " Before the appointed hour even thou thyself art not able to destroy the tyrant to whom thou hast promised life; no more than the sun is able prematurely to close the day which he himself enlightens*."

In short I consider morality like the sciences and arts, to be only slumbering not forgotten in India; and that to awaken the Hindûs to a knowledge of the treasures in their own hands is the only thing wanting to set them fairly in the course of improvement with other nations.

Everywhere in the ancient Hindû books we find the maxims of that pure and sound morality which is founded on the nature of man as a rational and social being. Their laws themselves

* From Magha's poem on the death of Sisupila.

pronounce future punishments against the hypo-
crite and fraudulent; while the violation of the
social relations by the commission of adultery is
punished with a severity beyond that exercised
by almost any other people. Even the minor
moral or rule of courtesy has not been neglected by the lawgivers, for Menu says, " Let one
not insult those who want a limb, who are un-
learned, who are advanced in age, who have no
beauty, no wealth, or who are of ignoble birth."
Maxims which might have become the noble
courtesy of the Spartans, while Athenian po-
liteness scarcely exceeds that other saying of
the sage, "Let a man say what is true, but let
him say what is pleasing."

The Hindûs claim the honour of having invented the method of teaching by apologues,
and whatever we may think of the justice with
which the claim is made, when we remember the fables used by Samson, it is beyond a
doubt that one of the oldest collections of fables
in existence is that long known in Europe by
the title of Pilpay's Fables, but which Mr.
Wilkins has restored to its original name of
Heetopadesa, where rules and maxims for the
government of a state, a household, and one's
own conduct, are aptly illustrated in a series of
apologues related by a Brahmin tutor, to his

pupils, two young princes whom he prepares for the exercise of regal power at the request of their father.

I am not sure that I need defend the laws of the Hindûs as I have done their morality, because I do not recollect ever having been unjust towards them myself; but I think that they bear the impression of a certain state of civilization, which does not appear to have been far enough advanced, to have restored to men that portion of liberty which in times of high cultivation is naturally recovered from the laws instituted in the early stages of society, when lawgivers, delighted with their first triumphs over savage man, attempt to render their regulations perfect, by making them reach to every offence and degree of offence whether public or private. Accordingly we find among the Hindû laws, a number of frivolous and vexatious details interfering with almost every employment and every action of human life; for instance, the laws of Menu contain prohibitions against biting the nails, or washing the feet in a pan of yellow mixed metal, with cautions not to walk in the shadow of a copper-coloured or red-haired man, besides tedious sumptuary laws, especially regarding the dress of women.

However, there are among these laws many that shew the legislator to have been wise and

humane, and give us a high idea of the governments of ancient India. The laws of Menu
which you may read in Sir William Jones's
Translation, are said to have been compiled
about nine centuries before Christ; but as the
age of the Vedas is fixed considerably earlier,
we may conclude that the laws themselves are
much more ancient, whether handed down by
tradition or preserved in writing *.

From this code it appears that the ancient
Hindû courts were held openly by the king or
by his judges, who might be chosen from either
of the three first or *twice-born* castes, although
a Brahmin was preferred. The judges are enjoined to understand the expedient, but to pronounce according to the strict interpretation of
the law. Three witnesses were required to prove
an accusation, which witnesses might be of any
class, and where women were concerned, women
were also to be witnesses. I am sure you will
admire the address which the judge is directed
to make to the witnesses. " The soul itself is
its own witness, the soul itself is its own refuge:

---

* There are eighteen principal titles of law according to
Menu, the ten first of which concern debts, deposits, part-
nerships, boundaries, sale and purchase, and masters and
servants; 11th and 12th, assault and slander; 13th, larceny;
14th, robbery; 15th, adultery; 16th, matrimonial disputes;
17th, inheritance; 18th, gaming.

Offend not thy conscious soul the supreme internal witness of men! The sinful have said in their hearts, None sees us; yes, the gods distinctly see them; and so does the spirit within their breasts*." I think you must recollect my telling you that the Parsees in Bombay regulated their own affairs by their Panchaït or village council. This Panchaït is borrowed by them from the Hindus, and consisted of a little jury which received and decided on evidence under the head man of the village or Patel, who was again subject to the governor of a larger district, and so on through several gradations to the sovereign himself. Every village or rather township was surrounded with its fields, which were sometimes cultivated in common, but more frequently each man tilled his own ground, and there was besides a village waste, which served for the common pasturage of the inhabitants. In each township there were twelve principal persons, 1st, the patel or magistrate; 2d, the registrar; 3d, and 4th, the watchmen of the village and of the crops; 5th, the distributer of the waters; 6th, the astrologer, who an-

---

* It is true that a species of pious fraud is not only allowed but honoured, by being called the speech of the gods, when by bearing false witness one may save an innocent person. This vicious principle of course leads to perjury on other occasions.

nounced the seasons for sowing and reaping;
7th, the smith; 8th, the carpenter; 9th, the
potter; 10th, the washerman; 11th, the barber,
and 12th, the silversmith, who is sometimes ex-
cluded from the number, and his place filled by
the village poet or schoolmaster. These twelve
received a compensation for their labour in land
or in fees from the crops of their neighbours;
and such was the constitution of each township,
whose internal regulations suffered no change,
whatever political revolutions might happen in
the state. The laws or customs concerning the
property of land have unfortunately either been
lost or are so vaguely expressed as to have led
to considerable controversy in our times; and
to a more serious disadvantage in the difficulty
of settling a fixed revenue without committing
injustice to the landholder. Very many authorities have been adduced to prove that the
sovereign was the possessor of the soil, and that
the usufruct only belonged to the landholder. But
I own that to me the arguments for the contrary
opinion appear the strongest, inasmuch as the
right of sale and inheritance are unquestioned *.
The king's revenue arose from a sixth of the
produce of the land, which might be legally,

* See Wilks's History of Mysoor, who quotes Menu, ch. 9th,
v. 44, thus: "Cultivated land is the property of him who cut
away the wood, or first cleared and tilled it."

and indeed often was, redeemed for a price in money.

The Hindû law of inheritance divides the property into equal shares, two of which go to the eldest son, one and a half to the next, and one to each of the others; or the eldest son takes one share, and the best article out of the chattels of his father; besides which, a single sheep or other animal may not be divided, but is given to the eldest. To the unmarried daughters the brothers give each a fourth of his share as portions. The sons inherit first, then the daughters and wife, after whom all descendants, male or female, real or adopted, before collateral relations.

Should a whole family choose to remain together, the eldest son takes his father's place, and enjoys the property undivided, providing for all the rest as his father did in his lifetime; a custom which reminds one of the patriarchal times when Lot sojourned with Abraham till they increased so greatly, when Abraham divided the property and they parted, Lot journeying towards the East, and Abraham dwelling in the land of Canaan.

I feel a little angry however with one part of the code of Menu, where he says that a woman may never be independent, but that in her youth she belongs to her father, on her marriage

2

to her husband, and on his death to her sons or other male relations; and again, that a wife, a son, and a slave can have no property independent on the husband, father or master; thus classing them together.

However we must not look upon the state of slaves in the East in the same light in which we have been accustomed to consider the negroes in the West Indies. A man purchased by a Hindû or Mahomedan becomes one of his family, and is liable to no greater hardships than the son of his purchaser, and is frequently treated with as much consideration. The eldest servant of Abraham's house ruled over all that he had, and was charged by his master with the care of providing a wife for his only son; and the manners in the East have been so stationary that no material change has taken place in the situation of slaves. All the laborious occupations of husbandry which European merchants forced their slaves in foreign climates to perform, have always been carried on in the East by free husbandmen, and all the mechanical arts by free persons of particular classes, so that the slaves could only be household servants, and by living constantly in the families to which they belonged, they acquired claims to tenderness and consideration which were seldom if ever resisted.

In perusing the laws of Menu you will no

doubt be struck as I was with the number of laws favourable to the Brahminical order. For instance, in the 8th chapter, " Never shall the king slay a Brahmin though convicted of all possible crimes : let him banish the offender from his realm; but with all his property secure and his body unhurt. No greater crime is known on earth than slaying a Brahmin, and the king therefore must not even form in his mind an idea of killing a priest." And again, in the 1st chapter, " Whatever exists in the universe is all in effect, though not in form, the wealth of the Brahmins, since the Brahmin is intitled to it all by his primogeniture and eminence of birth."

Would one not imagine that the spirit, if not the letter, of these laws had transmigrated into the popes and their myrmidons during the middle ages? If the unfortunate brother of Chandragupta, whom the Greeks call Sandracottus, fell a victim to his expressions of contempt for a filthy and deformed Brahmin, we have seen an emperor (Henry IV.) distinguished for many virtues and possessed of considerable talents, standing for three days barefooted in the depth of winter, at the gate of the haughty bishops of Rome ; and another Henry, among the most virtuous of the English monarchs, receiving stripes at the tomb of him who had made his life a constant martyrdom. If the Brahmins, protected in their persons and property, yet presided in courts where they condemned others to the severest penalties of the laws, the priesthood of Europe, no less privileged, while they claimed exemption from all secular jurisdiction, exercised the power of life and death in their own courts, to which every man was amenable, whose strength in arms was not sufficient to protect him. Happily for Europe the priesthood was not hereditary or confined to one class. The constant influx of new members who brought something of the common world into the cloister, preserving their family relations and the connections of country, prevented their becoming a distinct caste, an evil which would inevitably have prolonged the darkness which so long overwhelmed the western world, if it had not confirmed it for ever. It is scarcely possible to imagine any two systems more nearly allied than those of the Brahmins and of the priests of the middle ages. The monasteries in the West, endowed by royal patrons, and enriched by the pious contributions of all ranks, were only rivalled by the magnificence of the Hindû temples, supported by royal and private grants of land, and other valuables, and adorned with the jewels of the pious, or the expiatory offerings of the offender. The priests of both classes esteemed it more honourable to subsist by alms than to labour, and both arrogated to themselves the right of instructing and guiding the people, and of directing the secret councils of their monarchs.

The trials by ordeal so common in Europe in the middle ages, have subsisted from time immemorial in India, and, though generally disused, they are still of authority, and have been appealed to at Benares so late as A. D. 1783. Robertson, in his History of Charles the Fifth, supposes that these trials were invented in Europe to remedy the defects of the judicial proceedings of those times, and to guard against the numerous frauds, and the injustice which could not but arise from the practice of allowing a man to clear himself from any accusation by compurgation, or the oaths of himself and his neighbours or relations. But the extreme similarity between the trial by ordeal as practised in India, and the appeal to the justice of God common in Europe, would lead us to believe that they had a common and more ancient origin. The principles on which such appeals rest, are indeed founded in human nature, and have given rise not only to these absurdities, but to the belief in magic, and the train of follies attendant on it. It is natural for the savage, in such cases as his own sagacity is incompetent to investigate and to decide, to look to some superior power for aid, and in many cases the workings of conscience itself, on being brought to a test, which it was firmly believed was directed by a Supreme omniscient Being, would produce effects consonant to the justice of the cause, and every such event would give strength to the popular faith in the efficacy of the trials. The rocking-stones which are found on the coast of Cornwall, and other parts of England, were used as an ordeal by the Druids ; and well might fear palsy the hand ere it touched the rock of trial, while innocence boldly approached and moved the mighty mass *. Notwithstanding these considerations which account for a similarity of principle, the exact coincidence of many of the forms used, persuades me, that they are so many traces of the ancient and intimate connexion which Sir William Jones pronounces, it would be possible to prove, between the first race of Persians and the Indians, to whom we may add the Greeks and Romans, the Goths and the old Egyptians or Ethiops, who according to him originally spoke the same language, and professed the same popular faith : And probably the more familiar we become with the antique customs, laws and manners of Hindos-

---

* See Mason's Caractacus, for a beautiful exemplification of this superstition of our forefathers.

tan, the stronger will the resemblances be found, and the clearer the traces of the ancient connexion and subsequent separation of these various tribes.

But I will not detain you with my own opinions on the subject, but state the facts on which they are grounded. The trial by ordeal is of nine kinds, 1st, by the balance, 2d, by fire, 3d, by water, 4th, by poison, 5th, by the cosha, 6th, by rice, 7th, by boiling oil, 8th, by red-hot iron, and 9th, by images.

The first, a trial by the balance, is made by the accused person performing worship to the fire, and afterwards fasting a whole day, when he is weighed twice or thrice, and if at the second or third weighing he is found heavier than at first he is guilty. The writing on the wall over against Belshazzar king of Babylon, " thou art weighed in the balance, and found wanting," (Daniel, chap. v. ver. 27) of which text Milton has made so noble a use in the end of the 4th book of the Paradise Lost.

> The fiend looked up and knew
> His mounted scale aloft, nor more but fled -
> Murmuring, and with him fled the shades of night.

Probably refers to a similar trial used by the Babylonians; and Homer also makes Jove hang out the scales of life to weigh the fate of his son Sarpedon.

The second and third ordeals, those by fire and water, were administered pretty much in the same manner as in the western courts. In the former, the culprit after his accusation had been publicly declared, walked through fire or over hot embers. The antiquity of this trial needs no farther proof than the passage of the Ramayuna, where Sita to dispel the suspicions of Rama passed through the fire. Its existence in ancient Persia is proved by Ferdousi, one of whose heroes, Syawousch, the eastern Hippolytus, passes through the fiery ordeal to clear himself from the guilt imputed to him by his mother-in-law. But the most extraordinary use of the fire ordeal that I recollect, belongs to Europe: I mean the famous trial of the Musarabic and Romish liturgies in Spain, during the eleventh century, which was had recourse to after the trial by judicial combat; when, contrary to the wishes of the court, and the interest of the superior clergy, the champion of the Musarabic book, had triumphed over the knight of the Roman faith*. The last legal trials by fire or by water in England were in King John's

* A story similar to this is related of a kazee and a missionary at Delhi, under Jahanghire, who not being troubled with much faith, proposed the trial. The kazee shrunk from it. The Jesuit, knowing the emperor's disposition, accepted the proposal, but the good-natured Shah interposed and saved him.

reign; but I suspect that since that time many an old woman has been drowned in endeavouring to prove her innocence of witchcraft, by the trial whether she sank or swam in water. This mode of trial differs but little from that of the Hindûs, among whom the accused is compelled to put his head under water, and if he raises it before a person appointed for the purpose has walked a certain distance, he is guilty.

The trials by poison are of two kinds. One is by swallowing poison from the hand of a Brahmin after worshipping the fire, when the culprit is absolved if he survives, and the other method is to take a ring out of a vase in which a venemous snake has been confined, who at once convicts and punishes the unfortunate wretch if he bites him.

The trial by the Cosha resembles that mentioned in the fifth Chapter of Numbers, which treats of the law of jealousy. Among the Hindûs it is conducted by making the accused person drink of the water in which idols have been washed, while the Jews put the dust that covered the floor of the tabernacle into the water. In both cases indisposition within a prescribed time after the draught was the sign of guilt.

The trial by rice was performed by chewing consecrated rice, and if it came out of the mouth bloody or dry the accused person was

condemned.   The trial by images, called Dherma and Adherma, or justice and injustice, consisted in taking out of a covered vase a figure of
lead or other base metal, or one of silver.   The
silver image absolved, and the base metal condemned.   Sometimes pieces of black and white
cloth with the images painted on them were used.

The trial by red-hot iron has been used in
Europe in various forms.   In the early history
both of France and England, there are instances
of accused persons of high rank, particularly
women, walking over red-hot ploughshares; and
you doubtless remember the anecdote of one of
the Paleologi, who, when required by the patriarch of Constantinople to take a red-hot ball
off the altar, begged the holy man to set him the
example, as certainly his innocence must be
sufficient to guard him from harm, if it were
possible that a soldier might remain unhurt.
In this latter form of handling a hot ball, a man
was tried at Benares, in the year 1783, on the
following occasion.   A man accused one Sancar
of larceny, who pleaded not guilty, and as the
theft could not be proved by legal evidence, the
trial by ordeal was offered to the appellee, and
accepted by him; and after obtaining permission
from the Honourable Company's government, it
was conducted as follows, in the presence of
Ali Ibrahim Khan, chief magistrate of Benares,
from whose account of it, in the first volume of

the Asiatic Researches, I take the story, and indeed the rest of the history of Indian ordeals.

" The Pandits of the court and city having worshipped the god of knowledge*, and presented their oblation of clarified butter to the fire, formed nine circles of cow-dung on the ground; and, having bathed the appellee in the Ganges, brought him with his clothes wet, when, to remove all suspicion of deceit, they washed his hands with pure water; then having written a state of the case, and the words of the Muntra, on a palmyra-leaf, they tied it on his head; and put into his hands, which they opened and joined together, seven leaves of pippal, seven of jend, seven blades of darbha grass, a few flowers, and some barley moistened with curds, which they fastened with seven threads of raw white cotton. After this, they made the ball red-hot, and taking it up with tongs, placed it in his hands: he walked with it, step by step, the space of three *gaz* and a half, through each of the seven intermediate rings, and threw the ball in the ninth, where it burnt the grass that had been left in it. He next, to prove his veracity, rubbed some rice in the husk between his hands, which were afterwards examined, and were so far from being burned, that not even a blister was raised on either of them. Since it is the nature of fire to burn, the officers

* Ganesa.

of the court, and people of Benares, near five
hundred of whom attended the ceremony, were
astonished at the event; and this well-wisher to
mankind was perfectly amazed. It occurred to
his weak apprehension, that probably the fresh
leaves and other things which, as it has been
mentioned, were placed in the hands of the accused, had prevented their being burned; besides, the time was short between his taking the
ball and throwing it down: yet it is positively
declared in the Dherma Sastra, and in the
written opinions of the most respectable Pundits,
that the hand of a man who speaks truth cannot be burned; and Ali Ibrahīm Khan certainly
saw with his own eyes, as many others also saw
with theirs, that the hands of the appellee in
this cause were unhurt by the fire: he was,
consequently, discharged; but, that men might
in future be deterred from demanding the
trial by ordeal, the appellor was committed for
a week.

Nearly about the same time, another man
submitted to the trial of hot oil, plunging his
hand into a vessel full of it, to take out a ring;
but the result was different, for his hand was
burnt, and he was obliged to pay the value of
the property he was accused of stealing.

Such are the Indian ordeals, for the practice
of which I know no absurdity more like than the
practice of sitting in *dherna*—a method of ob-

taining justice, or of enforcing a petition, founded, I suspect, on the fear of drawing down punishment by injuring a Brahmin, by whom this species of importunity is chiefly practised. When a person wishes to gain a point that he has no other means of carrying, and therefore resolves to sit in dherna, he places himself at the door of the person of whom it is to be obtained with a dagger or poison in his hand, which he threatens to use if the master of the house goes out, or attempts to molest him; and as no sin is comparable to that of causing the death of a Brahmin, the unfortunate person is thereby completely arrested. The Brahmin continues to sit fasting; and it is customary for the person arrested to fast also; so that it generally happens that the prosecutor obtains his wish, partly by the dread of his death, and partly by his importunity. I believe this custom properly belongs to the Brahmins; but I recollect a curious instance of it among a lower tribe in Bombay. Shortly after I went there, my tailor brought me a letter, intreating me to beg the magistrates to take away a man who sate in dherna at his door. On inquiring into the case, I found that it was to recover a wife. It seems the prosecutor having a wife whom he was unable to support, during a time of scarcity, had made her over to the tailor, who having a good business, was not only able to maintain her, but to dress her so well, that in time of plenty she never thought of returning to her former husband; who nevertheless, as she was able to do a good deal of work, wished to have her back again. Not being able to obtain her by intreaty, he had recourse to the method by dherna, which I believe did not succeed, the tailor rather choosing to give him a sum of money than to part with the lady.

Many Brahmins obtain a subsistence from other Hindoos by sitting in dherna before their houses; but their demands in this case are so moderate, as to be readily complied with. Some of the Pundits admit the validity of an obligation extorted by dherna, while others reject it.

There is another kind of extrajudicial method of extorting justice, called the koor. A circular pile of wood is erected, and on it is placed a cow, or an old woman, when the whole is set fire to at once. The object of this is to intimidate the officers of government or others from importunate demands, the whole guilt of the sacrifice being supposed to fall on those who force the constructor of the koor to adopt the cruel expedient.

These two barbarous methods of obtaining justice, mark a greater degree of insecurity than the general tenor of the Indian laws and police would induce us to attribute to the state of society in ancient India. It is probable, therefore, that they had their origin during the civil wars, which desolated that country for some time previous to the Mussulman invasion, or were borrowed from some of the savage tribes who occasionally made their inroads from the North. Some other circumstances seem to give colour to such a supposition—such as the murder of innocent persons, in order that their ghosts may haunt an enemy. Of this crime, you will find several instances detailed in the twenty-second article of the ninth volume of the Asiatic Researches, but which are too shocking to dwell upon: however, I cannot help noticing the custom which prevailed in some of the Rajpoot tribes, of putting to death their female infants.

It was only in the year 1789 that this custom was known to prevail; and shortly afterwards, measures were taken to induce them by arguments sanctioned not only by natural feeling and humanity, but also by the religion they profess, to enter into an agreement to bring up their female children. Happily, this measure was productive of the best effects, and it is probable, that at present the custom scarcely exists.

Here is a very long letter; I only hope it may entertain, or rather interest you, and that my endeavours to shew the Hindûs, upon the whole, in a more favourable light than you allow them to deserve, or that I confess I once thought them worthy of, will not have entirely failed: at the same time we see them men, and men fallen from a high state of civilization to one the most humiliating, with all the train of vices which that humiliation is calculated to produce.

But we must not forget what they were once. Athens herself, alas! groans under the sway of a Turkish Janissary; and the " mother of arts and eloquence"—she who was " native to famous wits, or hospitable"—now languishes in her ruins; and instead of the voice of commerce in her streets, and of the Muses in her groves, echoes only the pitying sigh of the traveller. If indeed her genius still survives, and watches over her august ruins, she has been soothed by one bright gleam, which has shone upon her from our North, though it has been but to gild her tomb.—

'Tis Greece—but living Greece no more!
So coldly sweet, so deadly fair,
We start;—for soul is wanting there.
Hers is the loveliness in death
That parts not quite with parting breath:
But beauty with that fearful bloom,
That hue which haunts it to the tomb—
Expression's last receding ray,
A gilded halo hovering round decay,
The farewell beam of feeling past away!
Spark of that flame—perchance of heav'nly birth—
Which gleams, but warms no more its cherish'd earth!

GIAOUR.

LETTER VII.

You will think me very presumptuous when I tell you I am going to mention the Indian astronomy in this Letter : but I measure my endeavours to give you the little information I have myself, by the curiosity I know you to possess, rather than by my abilities.

Of all the sciences cultivated by man, astronomy is that which seems to raise him highest in the scale of beings. Sublime as the heavens in which it is conversant, it seems to detach him from earth, and to place him in the midst of beauty, order, and harmony. The magnificent vault of heaven, studded with its brilliant gems, revolving in ceaseless and silent course, must naturally have attracted the earliest regards of man ; and to trace the progress of astronomy from its first rude observations, would be to follow the history of human progress from the beginning of the world.

It was natural that the remains of a profound knowledge of the laws of the heavenly bodies, with exact and perspicuous rules for calculating their phænomena, when first discovered in India, should have attracted no common share of attention from the European philosophers. But on examination, the state of astronomy in modern India exhibits the same melancholy traces of decline and ruin which are discernible in every other science which once flourished in that venerable country.

The antiquity which may be assigned to the Indian astronomy has been disputed; but the general conclusion, drawn from the most respectable authorities, gives its earliest recorded observations in from three to four thousand years before the Christian æra. The arguments of those who contend that the Indians received their astronomy from the Greeks or Arabs, are refuted by the fact, that though the astronomers of Greece had every advantage over those of Hindostan, excepting what they derived from the antiquity of their science, they fell into errors which the Hindûs entirely avoided; to which may be added, that the calculus of the Hindûs, more correct than that of Greece, agrees in its delineation of the heavens at a remote period with the improved state of astronomy in modern Europe. Of the many proofs, however, of the originality of the science in Hindostan, the most remarkable is the rectification of the circle, the rule for computing the length of its circumference, being used in India before it was known in Europe*.

The existence of the Indian astronomy was not known in Europe till M. de la Loubere, ambassador of Louis XIV. at the court of Siam, brought with him to France some tables and rules for calculating the places of the sun and moon, which were examined by Cassini, who bore testimony to their accuracy. Other tables were sent to Paris by the French missionaries; and M. le Gentil, on his return from India, where he had been to observe the transit of Venus, A. D. 1769, brought with him another set of tables, and the Indian methods of calculating; and in 1787, M. Bailly published his *Astronomie Indienne*, while in 1789 Mr. Playfair's paper on the same subject appeared in the Edinburgh Transactions. Such was the state of knowledge on this highly interesting subject when the Asiatic Society was established. Since that time, the volumes of their Researches have been enriched with a variety of papers on the Indian astronomy, from which I take the facts I write to you, in hopes that though I understand nothing whatever of the science myself, you may be induced, in the East, to go

* See Mr. Davis's paper, in the second volume of the Asiatic Researches.

8

on with studies in which I know you have already made some progress.

The Hindû books on astronomy have the general name of the Jyotish Sastras, in which are to be discovered traits of a bright light, which must have illumined mankind at so very early a period, that M. Bailly seems to doubt whether we should not regard them as remains of antediluvian science, fragments of a system that is lost, and whose ruins only serve to excite our admiration.

The Surya Sidd'hanta* seems to be the Jyotish Sastra of highest authority, if it be not the oldest. It is said to have been revealed by Surya, or the sun, to the sage Meya, according to some about the year of the world 1956. The obliquity of the ecliptic is stated in it to be 24°, which, if founded on actual observation at the time of compiling that Sastra, would confirm its supposed antiquity.

The Hindû division of the zodiac into signs

---

* Abul Fazzle, in the Ayeen Akberi, enumerates nine sidd'hantas or treatises on astronomy: 1st, the Brahma Sidd'-hanta; 2d, Surya Sidd'hanta; 3d, Soma Sidd'hanta; 4th, Vrihaspati Sidd'hanta; 5th, Goorg Sidd'hanta; 6th, Nareda Sidd'hanta; 7th, Parasara Sidd'hanta; 8th, Poolustya Sidd'-hanta; 9th, Vashishtha Sidd'hanta. But there are many other treatises on the subject, either original works or commentaries on the ancient books.

and degrees, is the same as ours. Their year is
sidereal, and commences at the instant of the
sun's entering the sign Aries, each astronomical
month containing as many days and fractions of
days as he stays in each sign. The civil time
differs from the astronomical year, in rejecting
the fractional parts, and the civil year and
month are begun at sunrise instead of mid-
night.

The epocha from which the Hindûs compute
the motions of the planets, is that point of time
counted back, when, according to their motions,
they must have been in conjunction at the first
point of Aries, or above a thousand millions of
years ago, it will take nearly double that period
before they are again in the same situation; and
the enormous interval between these conjunc-
tions is called a calpa, and mythologically a day
of Brahma. The calpa is divided into manuan-
taras, and great and little yugs, the use of some
of which divisions is not now apparent; but the
greater yug is an anomalistic period of the sun
and moon, at the end of which they are found
together in the first of Aries. The division of
the great yug into the Satya, Treta, Dwapar,
and Cali yugs, are by some supposed to have
originated in the precession of the equinoxes
(*Cranti*), but by others they are considered
as purely mythological, like the golden,

I

silver, brazen, and iron ages, among the western poets.

The really learned Jyotish Pandits have just notions of the figure of the earth, and of the œconomy of the universe; but they, in appearance, agree with the popular notions on these subjects—such as, that eclipses are caused by a monster who occasionally interposes his head or his tail (*Cetu* and *Rahu*, or the ascending and descending nodes) between the earth and the sun and moon; and that the earth is a plain, supported on the backs of elephants, resting on a tortoise, and other equally puerile superstitions.

But to return to the Jyotish Brahmins: one of their methods for finding the latitude is by an observation of the *Palabha*, or shadow projected from a perpendicular gnomon, when the sun is in the equator; and the longitude is directed to be found by observation of lunar eclipses, calculated for the first meridian, which the Surya Sidd'hanta makes pass over Lanca Rohitaca, Avanti (now Ougein) and Sannihitasaras. In the Surya Sidd'hanta, the method of observing the places of the stars is briefly hinted, " *The astronomer should frame a sphere, and examine the apparent latitude and longitude.*" Commentators on this passage describe the method of making the observation. They direct a spherical instrument (*golayantra**) to be constructed. On the pins of the axis of the sphere must be suspended an intersecting graduated circle, which appears to be a circle of declination. The golayantra is then rectified, so that the axis points to the pole, and the horizon is true by a water level. " The instrument being thus

---

* This is an armillary sphere. Various directions for constructing it occur in different astronomical books of the Hindûs, among others in the Sidd'hanta Siromani, by Bhascara an astronomer, who flourished in the twelfth century of the Christian æra. But there is one contained in the Surya Sidd'-hanta as follows, in a literal translation.

" Let the astronomer frame the surprising structure of the terrestrial and celestial spheres.

" Having caused a wooden globe to be made (of such size) as he pleases, to represent the earth; with a staff for the axis, passing through the centre, and exceeding the globe at both ends; let him place the supporting hoops [1] as also the equinoctial circle.

" Three circles must be prepared (divided for signs and degrees) the radius of which must agree with the respective diurnal circles, in proportion to the equinoctial: the three circles should be placed for the ram and following signs, respectively, at the proper declination in degrees north or south; the same answer contrariwise for the Crab and other signs. In like manner three circles are placed in the southern hemisphere for the Balance and the rest, and contrariwise for Capricorn and the remaining signs. Circles are similarly placed on both hoops, for the asterisms in both hemispheres, as also for *Abhijit,* and for the seven *Rishis, Agastya, Brahme,* and other stars.

[1] They are the colures.

" In

placed, the observer is instructed to look at the star Revati through a sight fitted to an orifice at the centre of the sphere; and having found the star, to adjust by it the end of the sign Pisces on the ecliptic. The observer is then to look, through the sight at the chief (*yóga*) star of Aswini, or any other proposed object, and to

" In the middle of all these circles is placed the equinoctial. At the intersection of that and the supporting hoops, and distant from each other half the signs, the two equinoxes should be determined, and the two solstices, at the degree of obliquity from the equinoctial; and the places of the Ram and the rest, in the order of the signs, should be adjusted by the strings of the curve. Another circle, thus passing from equinox to equinox, is named the ecliptic: and by this path, the sun illuminating worlds, for ever travels. The moon and other planets are seen deviating from their nodes in the ecliptic, to the extent of their respective greatest latitudes (within the Zodiac.)"

The author proceeds to notice the relation of the great circles beforementioned to the horizon; and observes, that, whatever place be assumed for the apex of the sphere, the middle of the heavens for that place is its horizon. He concludes by shewing that the instrument may be made to revolve with regularity by means of a current of water; and hints that the appearance of spontaneous motion may be given by a concealed mechanism, for which quicksilver is to be employed.

Mr. Colebrooke's Essay on the Indian and Arabian divisions of the Zodiac, Asiatic Researches, vol. IX. From that gentleman's and Mr. Davis's papers I take with very little exception all that I have presumed to say on the subject of Indian astronomy.

bring the moveable circle of declination over it. The distance in degrees, from the intersection of this circle and the ecliptic to the end of Pisces (*Mina*), is its longitude in degrees; and the number of degrees on the moveable circle of declination from the point of intersection to the place of the star, is its latitude. These latitudes and longitudes of course require correction, for which some rules are given; but, I imagine, the manner of observing will be sufficient for you at present. Another mode is taught in the Sidd'hanta Sundara*, and expound-

* " A tube adapted to the summit of a gnomon, is directed towards the star on the meridian; and the line of the tube, pointed to the star, is prolonged by a thread to the ground. The line from the summit of the gnomon to the base is the hypothenuse, the height of the gnomon is the perpendicular, and its distance from the extremity of the thread is the base of the triangle. Therefore, as the hypothenuse is to its base, so is the radius to a base, from which the sine of the angle and the angle itself are known. If it exceed the latitude the declination is south; or, if the contrary, it is north. The right ascension of the star is ascertained by calculation from the hour of the night, and from the right ascension of the sun for that time. The declination of the corresponding point of the ecliptic being found, the sum or difference of the declinations, according as they are of the same or different denominations, is the distance of the star from the ecliptic. The longitude of the same point is computed; and from these elements, with the actual precession of the equinox, may be calculated the true longitude of the star; as also its latitude on a circle passing through the poles of the ecliptic."—Mr. COLEBROOKE.

ed in the Sidd'hanta Sarvabhanma, the only work in which the true latitudes and longitudes of the stars are attempted to be given.

The notion of a polar star common to the Indian and Greek astronomers could not be taken from the present polar star in the Little Bear; Bailly conjectures that one of the stars in the Dragon* was the polar star mentioned by Eudoxus, which was nearest to the pole 1326 years before Christ; and it is possible, that either that, or the great star in the same constellation† which was within one degree of the pole 2836 years before Christ, may be the polar star of the ancient Hindû astronomers.

The Hindûs have a division of the ecliptic and zodiac into twelve signs or constellations, agreeing in figure and designation with those of the Greeks, and differing merely in the place of the constellations which are carried by them a little further to the westward than by the Greeks. But their most ancient distribution of the ecliptic was into twenty-seven parts, nearly agreeing with the Manzil or mansions of the moon used by the Arabs, who might either have borrowed it from the Hindûs, or derived it from the same common source of some more ancient astronomy‡.

---

* η Draconis.   † α Draconis.

‡ Names of the twelve signs from Sir William Jones's paper on the antiquity of the Indian zodiac. Asiatic Researches, Vol. II.   *Mesha*

The principal star of each Nacshatra is called Yogatara, but they are not the same with the Yogas which regard astrology, and are also employed in regulating moveable feasts. The yoga is a mode of indicating the sum of the longitudes of the sun and moon; the rules given for its computation make it obvious that the yogas are twenty-seven divisions of 360° of a great circle measured on the ecliptic. The twenty-eight yogas of the astrologers correspond with the nacshatras, but vary according to the day of

Mesha.........the Ram.	*Tula*............the Balance.
Vrisha.........the Bull.	*Vrishchica*.....the Scorpion.
Mithuna......the Pair.	*Dhanus*........the Bow.
Carcata........the Crab.	*Macara*......the Sea Monster,
Sinha..........the Lion.	*Cumbha*........the Ewer.
Canya.........the Virgin.	*Mina*...........the Fish.

The figures of these twelve asterisms are thus described in a translation by Sir William, from the *Retnamala* of *Sripeti*:

The *Ram, Bull, Crab, Lion,* and *Scorpion* have the figures of those five animals respectively: the *Pair* are a damsel playing on a vina, and a youth wielding a mace: the *Virgin* stands on a boat in water, holding in one hand a lamp, and in the other an ear of rice-corn: the *Balance* is held by a weigher with a weight in one hand: the *Bow* by an archer whose hinder parts were like those of a horse: the *Sea Monster* has the face of an antelope: the *Ewer* is a water-pot borne on the shoulders of a man who empties it: the *Fish* are two with their heads turned to each other's tails; and all these are supposed to be in such places as suit their several natures.

The lunar mansions, Nacshatras, from Mr. Colebrooke's most interesting paper, are

Names

the week; they have also a division of the zodiac, called dreshcana, answering to the Decani of European astrologers. Each of the twelve signs is divided into three dreshcanas, and over these divisions thirty-six guardians are appointed whose figure and habit are described minutely: these dreshcanas are used in casting nativities and de-

Names of Nacshatras.	Figure.	No. of Stars.	Star supposed to be meant.
1 Aswini	a horse's head	3	α Arietis.
2 Bharani		3	Musca.
3 Kritica	a knife	6	η Tauri, Pleiades.
4 Rohini	a wheel-carriage	5	α Tauri, Aldebaran.
5 Mrigasiras	an antelope's head	3	λ Orionis.
6 Atdra	a gem	1	α Orionis.
7 Punarvasu	a house	4	β Geminorum.
8 Pushya	an arrow	3	δ Cancri.
9 Aslesha	a potter's wheel	5	α 1 & 2 Cancri.
10 Mag'ha	a house	5	α Leonis, Regulus.
11 Phalguni	a couch	2	δ Leonis.
12 Phalguni	a bed	2	β Leonis.
13 Hasta	a hand	5	γ or δ Corvi.
14 Chitra	a pearl	1	α Virginis, Spica.
15 Swati	a coral bead	1	α Bootis, Arcturus.
16 Vaisac'ha	a festoon	4	α or η Libræ.
17 Anurad'ha	a row of oblations	4	δ Scorpionis.
18 Jyist'ha	a ring	3	α Scorpionis, Antares.
19 Mula	a lion's tail	11	ι or υ Scorpionis.
20 Ashad'ha	a couch	2	δ Sagittarii.
21 Ashad'ha	an elephant's tooth	2	τ Sagittarii.
22 Abhijit	a triangular nut	3	α Lyræ.
23 Sravana	three footsteps	3	α Aquilæ.
24 Danisht'ha	a drum	4	α Delphini.
25 Satabhisha	a circle	100	λ Aquarii.
26 Bhadrapada	a figure with two faces	2	α Pegasi.
27 Bhadrapada	a couch, a bed	2	α Andromedæ.
28 Revati	a tabor	32	ζ Piscium.

termining fortunate and unfortunate days or
hours, and the figures of their guardians are in-
scribed on amulets or other charms. They correspond not only with the Decani of the Greeks,
but with the Rab ul Wajeh of the Arabs who
were not less addicted to judicial astrology than
the Hindûs.

A modern Hindû will upon no account under-
take a journey or an enterprise of any kind
without consulting the astrologer, and you may
remember that I mentioned him as one of the
twelve chief persons in a village, where his office
is to declare the proper times for the different
operations of agriculture, to adjust the calendar
for religious festivals, besides the proclamation
of lucky and unlucky days. All of which, after
all, only proves that men are the same in every
climate and under every circumstance : the au-
gurs of Greece and Rome, the soothsayers of
Israel, and the conjurors of modern Europe, like
the astrologers of Hindostan, had equally the
credulity of their fellow-mortals to work upon,
and as a knave sometimes ends in being as great
a dupe as those he deceives, the deception that
was begun from interested motives may be carried on with the good faith of superstition.

Thus the most sublime science that the mind
of man ever aspired to grasp, has been made
subservient to purposes the most ridiculous, as if

3

poor human nature was destined to be humbled even where she might justly have exalted herself. Thank Heaven the days of the triumph of astrology in the West are over, and there is little danger of our seeing an army run away in consequence of a bad omen, or a general keep his tent because of an unlucky conjunction of the stars! The lights of heaven now shine with beneficent lustre to guide the mariner over the trackless deep, and the " bands of Orion and the sweet influences of the Pleïades*" cheer the traveller as he wanders on through distant nations, imparting and receiving knowledge.

The industry and ability of Mr. Strachey has lately furnished us with a translation of a Sanscrit work on algebra, called Bija Gannita, written by Bhascara Acharya about the year 1188 of our æra. The work appears to have been written with a view to astronomy, and seems to have been compiled from more ancient materials : I would fain refer you entirely for an account of it to the Edinburgh Review for July 1813, where, among other curious remarks, you will find a very ingenious explanation of the use of the word *colours* for unknown quantities. As the operations of arithmetic received the name of

* If the translation be true, the stars were named and classed in Egypt and Chaldea before the time of Moses, since the book of Job is as old as that lawgiver.

calculus from the pebbles with which they were carried on before the invention of numerical signs, so the unknown quantities of the Indian algebra must have received those of the colours from the use of different coloured shells, flowers, or pieces of cloth, when the first rude essays towards inventing the science were made. This may rationally be considered as a collateral proof of the originality of the Hindû algebra; but there appear to be others much more direct in the solutions of various difficult problems given in the Bija Gannita, some of which continued to be unknown in Europe until the time of Euler, which could scarcely have been the case if they had been derived from the Greek and Arabian writers, whose works are the foundation of modern science. But I am so ignorant on this subject, that I have written even the name of algebra in fear and trembling, and only ventured to do so as an excuse to tell you where you might look for the best account of it in its Indian guise that we yet possess in this country.

The mode of dividing time in India is very unequal, as it depends on the seasons and consequent length of day and night : the great divisions are four day watches and four night watches, each of which must of course vary with the season; but the watches are subdivided into ghurrees which are fixed, and contain twenty-

four English minutes, so that there are sixty
ghurrees in the twenty-four hours, although the
number of ghurrees in each watch or *puhur* is
perpetually changing. The *ghurree* is divided
into sixty *puls*, the *pul* into sixty *bipuls*, and the
bipul into sixty *till* or *anoopul*. The way in
which these periods are measured for the common purposes of life is with a *kutoree*, or thin
brass cup perforated at the bottom and placed
on the surface of water in a large vessel where
nothing can disturb it, when the water has filled
it to a certain line, which has been previously
adjusted astronomically by an astrolabe, the
ghurree allee or watchman strikes the ghurree
with a wooden mallet on a shallow bell-metal
pan, like those we bring from China under the
name of gongs, and besides the number of the
ghurree, that of the *puhur* is rung at the end of
each watch. The same kind of water measure,
but very delicately arranged, is used for astronomical purposes. None but great men can afford the luxury of a *ghurree al*, or clock, as it
requires the attendance of numerous servants,
and the only public clocks in India are those
attached to the armies.

LETTER VIII.

MY DEAR SIR,

A THOUSAND thanks for the patience you have had with my last letter, which has really encouraged me to begin this, and to go on with the plan I had proposed. Since, then, we have done with the heavens, it will not be amiss to inquire what the ancient Hindûs thought of the earth.

Their systems of geography are extremely curious, though involved in considerable obscurity, owing to the exuberance, or poverty, shall I say, of the Hindû imagination, which delights in describing mountains of precious stones, seas of milk, and rivers of honey or butter; and has pleased itself with rendering the world so equal, that for every mountain in the south there is its equivalent in the north, and that no river can flow without a sister stream in an opposite direction. Notwithstanding these disguises, however, it is plain that the Hindûs had a very general and tolerably correct notion of the old continent; and though at first sight they appear completely separated from the rest of the world, the means by which they acquired their true notions of it, become, on a little attention, abundantly apparent.

In the first place, the rich productions of their country, and the excellence of their manufactures, would naturally draw a number of traders to their cities, and as naturally lead them to travel with their merchandise. Besides, they believe that their ancestors came from the north, and it is certain that to this day several places in Tartary are visited by pilgrims as places of worship; and Mr. Duncan, the late governor of Bombay, told me he had seen one who had even been to Moscow on a similar errand*. A pretty regular intercourse has been at all times kept up between India and Samarkand, Balkh, and other northern cities where there are colonies of Hindûs, established from time immemorial; and one of the great pilgrimages from Hindostan is to the place called the Fiery Mouth, on the borders of the Caspian Sea.

We must not wonder that, in the early stages of society, the recitals of pilgrims and merchants concerning remote countries, should have been embellished not only by themselves, but by those who took upon them to record and preserve them; and hence, in all probability, arose part, at least, of the absurdity we remark in the Hindû systems of geography.

---

* An account of that man is published in the Asiatic Researches.

7

These systems differ considerably among themselves, even as related in the Puranas; but, for the most part, they divide the earth into seven *Dwipa*, or islands, the first of which, Jambhu Dwipa, is evidently India itself, with the countries surrounding it, bounded on the east by the Yellow Sea, on the west by the Caspian, extending north as far as the Frozen Ocean, and washed on the south by the Indian Sea*.

The Mount Meru occupies the centre of Jambhu Dwipa, and is described by the poets as composed of gold and precious gems, three-peaked, the habitation of the immortals, and from it flow four rivers to the four quarters of the earth, among which the Ganges rolls through the southern quarter, and its source leads us to the true position of Meru, the base of which is the land of Illavrati, surrounded on all sides by lofty mountains. Now this inclosed land is found in Western Tartary, having on the south Thibet, on the east the sandy desert of Cobi, on the west the Imaus, and on the north the Altai mountains; and from the four extremities of this raised plain four of the largest rivers of the old continent take their rise.

North and south of Meru three parallel ranges

* See Edinburgh Review, April, 1808.

of mountains are described. The first range, on the north, is the Nila, or blue mountains, which appears to be part of the Altai, and is said to inclose Ramanaca, or Dauria. Second, the Sweeta, or white mountain, divides Ramanaca from Heranya, or the gold country, whose inhabitants are tall, robust, and rich in gold[*]. Thirdly, the Sringavan mountains separate Heranya from Ottara Curu, the northern Curu, or Siberia, which Pliny calls Ottorocoro. Here the river Bhadra, probably the Irtush, flows into the Northern ocean at the extremity of Jambhu Dwipa. South of Meru are the Nishada mountains, corresponding with the northern range of Thibet hills, which country is named Herivarsha, and is separated by the Himacuta mountains from the land of Kinnara, comprising Srinagur, Nepal, and Butan, and divided from Bharata, or India, by the snowy chain of Hymaleya or Imaus.

To the east of Meru, the mountains of Málayaván divide Illavritta from the land of Badraswa, which is bounded by the Golden Sea (called by our geographers the Yellow Sea), into which a river, called the Eastern Sita, empties

---

[*] They are denominated *Yara*, or workers in mines. The metallurgic labours of the ancient inhabitants of the Altaï mountains are still traced by the traveller. Ed. Rev. for April, 1808.

itself, after passing through the lake Arunda, *(Orinnor)* and is probably the Whang-ho, Hara-moren, or Yellow river. To the west of Meru lies mount Vipula, an extension of Imaus; and between it and the western sea, or Caspian, lies the country of Cetumálá, comprising Sogdiana, Bactriana, and Margiana, with part of the country of the Sacæ. A river, called in some Puranas, the Chaxu, in others the Javanxu, (Oxus, or Jaxartes) after flowing through the lake Si-toda, falls into the Caspian.

Major Wilford supposes the other six Dwipas to comprehend all the rest of Asia and Europe, even as far as Iceland, dividing those countries as follows:—*Cusa dwipa* contains the countries from the Indus to the Caspian and the Persian Gulph. *Placsha dwipa* occupied the space between those seas and the Mediterranean and Euxine, or Lesser Asia, Armenia, Syria, &c. *Salmali dwipa* from the Tanais to Germany. *Crauncha dwipa* contained Germany, France, and the adjacent countries. *Sacam* the British islands, and *Pushcara dwipa* Iceland.

This gentleman, whose learned and ingenious works adorn the Asiatic Researches, has an idea that the British Isles are the sacred isles of the West, mentioned in the Sastras of the Hindûs. Should this opinion prove to have been unfounded, no one will regret, however, that Major

K

Wilford has been induced to entertain it; for the researches in which he engaged, in order to support it, have made us acquainted with the geographical systems of the Hindûs, and with the true situations of almost all the kingdoms and cities mentioned by ancient writers, both native Hindûs, and Greeks and Romans, whose descriptions are thus verified, and new confirmations added to history.

Of the books from which the Hindû systems of geography are to be learned, the Puranas are the chief. To each of these there is a book annexed, called Bhuvana Cosha, or dictionary of countries. Besides these, Major Wilford mentions several geographical treatises* of the orthodox Hindûs, and others of the Jines and Baudd'has. The Hindûs, as I before mentioned, consider Mount Meru as the center of the world; and some of their books describe the seven dwipas as disposed in concentric circles around it, descending gradually from its summit, and separated from each other by seas, some of which they imagine to be salt, others milky, or of the juice of the sugar cane,

* One of these, *Vicrama-pratidesa-vyavast'ha,* was written in the fifth century; and another, *Munja pratidesa vyavast'ha,* in the tenth. The *Trilocya despana,* or description of the three worlds is said to be like St. Patrick's book on the same subject.

with other similar absurdities. The Baudd'-
has of Thibet suppose Meru to be a square
pillar, and the dwipas, of course, square also;
while others among the Baudd'has imagine
the dwipas to be disposed in circles between
Jambhu dwipa and Mount Meru, which they thus
place at the north pole. This notion of the
circular divisions of the earth with interposing
seas, is not peculiar to the ancient Indians. The
Hindûs make the sacred Ganges wind seven
times round the base of Meru, thus forming the
seven dwipas; the Baudd'ha's sea of milk en-
compasses the same mountain eight times, while
the Styx* of the western mythologists wound
nine times round the earth.

And with nine circling streams the captive souls inclosed.

6th Æneis.—Dryden.

The fables of the Ædda agree also remarkably with these notions; and perhaps their common origin may be traced in Genesis, chap. II.
v. 10.

" And a river went out of Eden to water the
garden; and from thence it was parted, and became into four heads."

* Hesiod, speaking of the Styx, says,

> *In nine streams,*
> Round and around earth and the ocean broad,
> With silver whirlpools mazy-rolled, at length
> It falls into the main.
> *Theogony.—Elton's Translation.*

The four rivers of the Hindûs, into which the Ganges separates, after circumambulating Meru, are discharged from rocks having the faces of different animals. Ganges descends from the cow's mouth, and is collected in the lake Mana-Sarovara, to rest itself, after its fall from Meru, before it descends to earth. Pliny and Q. Curtius both mention this resting of the river in this lake, the usual name of which is Mapanh. It lies between thirty-three and thirty-four degrees of north latitude, and between eighty-one and eighty-two of east longitude. The Chaxu, the Sita, and the Bhadra, which I have already mentioned, flow in like manner through the heads of animals: the last through that of a lion, the second through that of an elephant, and the first through that of a horse; which different animals are supposed to impart their characters to the nations watered by their streams, after their sacred repose in their appropriate lakes.

This, I fancy, will be a sufficient specimen of the geography of the Hindû books: I shall therefore detain you no longer with it, but, with the help of Major Wilford, endeavour to reconcile the accounts of India, left us by the ancients of the West, with the actual positions of the places now existing, or whose remains can yet be traced; and afterwards the ancient divisions of the peninsula of India, according to their own historians, with those to which we are now familiarized.

I cannot do better, I believe, than begin by Major Wilford's account of the famous royal, or Nyssæan road, as described by Pliny and the Peutingerian tables. Some of the measures and distances given by the ancients, as they received their accounts only by hearsay, are naturally enough wrong, though, upon the whole, they agree wonderfully well with the distances calculated by Major Rennell.

This road, according to Dionysius Periegetes, was made out with great care, and at the end of every Indian itinerary measure a small column was erected. To accompany this description, I send you a little map which I made for my own use ; and, if not very exact, it will at least serve to show the general line of the road. The first part of this road, from the Indus to the Hyphasis, is that pursued by Alexander in his expedition into India, and the rest is that leading to Palibothra, at that time the capital of the Hindû empire.

Alexander crossed the Indus at the ferry of Tor-Beilam, or the black shore, to the westward of Peucolais, now Pirhola or Pucauli, and advanced to Taxila, the true name of which was Tacsha Syala, or Tacshila. It is now completely in ruins, as well as a city which was built on its

site by the Mussulmans, and called Turruck
Pehri. Thence he proceeded to Rotas, whose
Hindû name was Hridu, and on to the Hydaspes, whose native names are Jailam and Behat.
Near the ferry there, was Alexandria Bucepha-
los, remarkable for the neighbouring mountain,
called by Plutarch the mountain of the elephant,
by which title it is still known, and is remarkable as a holy place, whence it is commonly
called Bal-Nath-Thileh, or the mountain of the
lord elephant. He then crossed the Acesines,
Chandra Bhaga, or Chinab river, near the town
called Spatura or Simtura by the Europeans,
and probably the modern Sadhorah. The city
of Lobaca, on the Hydraotes, or Ravi (the Ira-
vati of the Puranas) was the next station. It is
the modern Lahore, whose real name is Lavaca
or Labaca, from Lava or Laba, a son of Rama,
and Lahore is corrupted from Lava-wara, the
place of Lava.

From Lahore the road crossed the Hyphasis or
Beya, and the Zadadrus or Satadru rivers, to the
town called Tahora in the Peutingerian tables,
and now Tehoura or Tihotra; thence to *Ketrora*, really C'hettri-wara, the capital of a
powerful tribe of C'hettris or Xetries, who lived
in a beautiful and woody country, whom Pliny
calls Cetriboni, from Xetri-ban, the forest of
Xetries. Ketrora is now Tanehsar. From Ke-

trora the road led to the Jumna, which it crossed at Cunjpoora, and to the Ganges at Hustinapour, the true situation of which was first discovered by Major Wilford. This magnificent capital, the seat of the monarchs descended from Puru, had been supposed, by Abu Fazzle and his followers, to have stood near Tanehsar, to the west of the Jumna; but its true situation is a few miles south-west of Darinagar, on a branch of the Ganges, formerly the bed of that river. It is the Bacinora of the Peutingerian tables, and the Storna of Ptolemy. Bacinora is a corruption of Hastinora or Wastinora, synonymous with Hastinagara or Hastinapoor. Of so large a city, there now remains only a small place of worship, and the site of the city is covered with large ant-hills. The next stage from Hastinapoor was the Rodapha of Pliny and the Rapphe of Ptolemy, now called Hurdowah, from which Calinipaxa, properly Calinibasa, of which there is no remains but the river that gave it name, led to Allahabad, called Gangapoor, or the town of the Ganges by Artemidorus. From Allahabad to Palibothra the road lay along the southern bank of the Ganges; and Ptolemy gives the following stations: First, the river Tuso, now the Touse; thence to Cindia, now Cauntee, on the banks of the Ganges, almost opposite to Goopy Gunge, which, though now not in the road, might have been so formerly, as the course of the river is considerably changed.

After Cauntee, two cities, called Sagala, are mentioned, one of which is Mirzapoor, and the other Monghir. These places are said to have a subterraneous communication, opened by lightning, which may account for their having the same name, while both the ancient Sanscrit and modern names are different. The true name for the first, Sagala, is Vindhya Vasini, and of the second Mudgala. The first is a name of the goddess Cali, and the second descriptive of the charms of the situation. From Sagala the distance is short to Palibothra or Baliputra, called also Raja Griha. There is every reason to believe that the Baliputras, or sons of Bali, whose capital Palibothra was, abandoned it as soon as the kings of Gaur or Bengal became powerful, as it was too near their frontier; and they afterwards fixed their residence at Padmavati or Patna, which had also the names of Magad'ha, Elimaied, and Almaied.

You have here the great Indian road, which extends over a space of 1,476 British miles at least, as mentioned by the western ancients; but the regular road, instead of beginning with the Tor Beilam, probably crossed the Indus at Attock Benares, a few miles farther to the north.

Ptolemy mentions some other roads used by the traders to China; one of which departed from Cabolitæ, or Cabul, and went through the mountains north of the Panjab, where it was joined by one from Tahora, at a point called Aris, in the mountains of Haridwar. These two roads are frequented to this day, and the place of meeting called Khama lang. The road then goes to Aspacora, in Thibet, mentioned by Ptolemy, where it met with another from the Gangetic provinces, and passed through Parthona, now Kelten, with the epithet of Panjuling, whence, perhaps, the Paliana of Ptolemy. This road ends, in the tables at Magaris, corruptly for the Thogaris of Ptolemy, now Tonkar, near Lassa.

The road from the Gangetic provinces came from a place called Carsina or Cartasina, now Carjuna, near Burdwar, thence through Scobaru, now Cucshubaru, to Aspacora, which it is probable was the rendezvous also of the caravans which, according to Pliny, went by land from Ceylon, or Taprobane, to China.

I have marked these routes on my little map, in which I have abstained from putting any names but those absolutely necessary.

The first division of India, which I noticed while speaking of the languages of Hindostan, is into the five Gaurs and the five Draviras, and concerning these authorities nearly agree. That they really formed separate states, I should think admitted of no doubt, as they each had a separate language, which had been cultivated by poets, if not by prose writers; and a nation must have been long consolidated and independent before it could form its language and polish its style; and, on this account, I chuse to begin with this division rather than with those which have obtained in later times, but which I shall notice.

The first of these nations was named from the principal river which flowed through their country, namely, the Sareswata. They probably occupied all the Panjab as far west as the Indus, and bounded to the south by Guzerat. In this tract we find Lahore, Multan and part of Ajmere, and that portion of Dehli, which contains Hissar Firoze, which I mentioned to you before, on account of its canals. This country is particularly interesting, as it contains the whole space marched over by Alexander, and the course of his fleet down the Hydaspes and Indus to the ocean.

The Canyacubjas, whose capital was Canoge*, appear to have been a warlike nation, and oc-

* 27° 10' N. Lat. and 79° 50' E. Long.

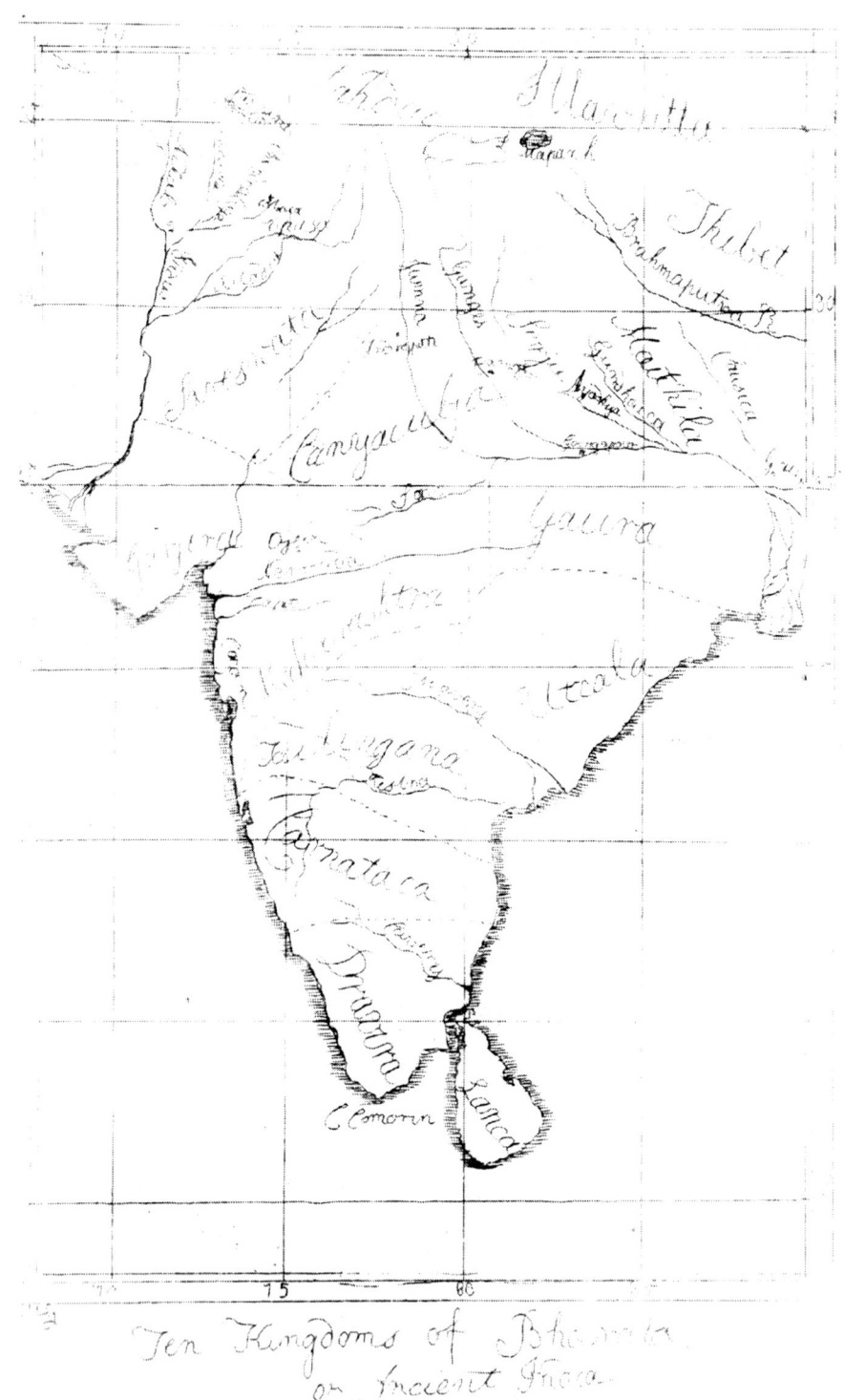

Ten Kingdoms of Bharata
or Ancient India

casionally to have carried their arms, and extended their dominion, over great part of India, so that it would be difficult to fix their boundary, especially as the language formed upon theirs is understood over almost the whole of Hindostan and the Deccan. Their dominion, however, may be considered as extending over part of the province of Dehli, with Oude, Agra, Serinagur, and, probably, Allahabad and Kashmeer. It was bounded on the north by the Himaleyah, or snowy mountains, whence flow the Jumna, Ganges, Serju, and other rivers; and it was also watered by the Sinde, Chumbul, Tonsa, and Sona, from the Ricksha hills. I should be inclined to think this kingdom the paradise of Brahminism. Canoge itself is situated on the Holy Ganga. Delhi, anciently Indrapati, or the city of Indra, occupies a station, little inferior in sanctity, on the Jumna. Hastinapoor, the residence of the kings of Puru's race, surrounded by its sacred groves, and washed by the daughter of Jahnu (Ganges) divided with Canoge the honours of the capital; and the two holy cities, Gungapoor (Allahabad) and Casi (Benares) still pride themselves on their antiquity and sanctity.

Mait'hila, or Tirhut, extended from the Cusi *(Causica)* to the Gundhuc (Gandhaca) and from the Ganges to the mountains of Nepaul,

7

and contained the modern Sircars of Tirhut, and the adjoining districts of Hajipoor, Betnah, and perhaps Teriani. Its ancient capital was Tirhut, or Tirhucti, celebrated for its race of Brahmins, its schools, and its learning.

Gaura, or Bengala, extended over the province of Bengal, and probably part of Bahar, the ancient Maghada, whose monarchs succeeded to those of Canoge, if they were not the same race, in the extensive dominion they possessed in India. This province formed part of the kingdom of the Prasii, or Prachii (people of the East,) whose capital, the famous Palibothra *(Baliputra)* occupied the place of the modern Rajemahl, and was only abandoned for Patali Putra, or Patna, when the kings of Gaur Proper began to emerge from obscurity, and fixed their residence at the city of Gaur, on the opposite side of the Ganges.

Utcala, or Odradesa, now the Subah of Orissa, extended along the shores of the bay of Bengal from Balasore to Point Godavery, and inland, as far as Sammalpoor; it comprehended the Company's provinces of Mednapoor, Cuttack, and the Circars, and the Nizam's countries of Singboom, Mohurgunge, Gangpoor, and Sumbulpoor. It is watered by several fine rivers, the chief of which is the Mahanuddy. On the low sandy shore stands the celebrated Jaggernaut Pagoda, where Crishna is worshipped under the figure and attributes of Jagnaut'h. The province of Cuttach is low and swampy, and I assure you, from experience, that the coast is not the most agreeable in the world for navigators. Point Palmyras is only discovered, when within dangerous distance, by the tops of the Palmyra trees, whence it takes its name; and from thence begin the sand-heads, as they are called, an assemblage of shoals continually shifting, as the matter brought down from the interior by the rivers that fall into the head of the bay increases. A number of pilot-vessels continually cruize in the neighbourhood, to conduct ships bound for Calcutta up the Hoogley, which, without them, would be inaccessible, as nothing but experience can enable men to perform the navigation with safety. The inhabitants of Orissa, and their language, were anciently called Urrigas.

Dravira extends from Cape Comorin to between twelve and thirteen degrees of north latitude, and comprehends Madura, Travancore, and the intermediate provinces up to Mysore and the Carnatic part of each of which are within its boundary. It is watered by the Cavery, which rises in the Sahya hills, or that part of the Ghauts near Poona, and by several tributary streams which flow from the mountains of Malaya and Mahendra. This country has been

famous from the spirit and enterprise of its mountain tribes, the extreme beauty of its landscape,
and above all, for the great place of Hindu pilgrimage, which rivals if it does not exceed even
Jaggernaut,—I mean Ramisseram, situated on
a point at the head of the Gulf of Manar, and
appearing to communicate with Ceylon by the
little chain of islands which the Hindûs call
Rama's Bridge, but which the Mussulmans,
and after them the Christians, have transformed
into the Bridge of Adam.   Here it was that the
indefatigable Hanumân made a road for the
armies of Rama Chandra, when he invaded
Ceylon, whence the sacredness of the place and
the yearly offerings to Rama.   The western part
of Dravira is remarkable, as the country of the
Christians of India, and on its coast is Calicut,
where the first Europeans, under Vasco de
Gama, visited India by way of the Cape of Good
Hope.

North of Dravira was the kingdom of Carnataca, which has given name both to the Carnatic
on the east, and Canara on the west coast; it
occupied the rest of the Mysore and the Carnatic, and the shores of Choromandel or Shola
Mandel (*the country of Shola,*) on which stood
the famous city of Maha Bali Pooram, now better known as a sea-mark by the name of the
Seven Pagodas, and presenting, even in its ruins,

marks of early grandeur. Its sculptured rocks and antique buildings are among the most curious monuments in India.

> On the sandy shore, beside the verge
> Of ocean here and there, a rock-hewn fane
> Resisted in its strength the surf and surge
> That on their deep foundations beat in vain.
> In solitude the ancient temples stood,
> Once resonant with instrument and song,
> And solemn dance of festive multitude:
> Now, as the weary ages pass along,
> No voice they hear, save of the ocean flood
> Which roars for ever on the restless shores;
> Or, visiting their solitary caves,
> The lonely sound of winds, that moan around
> Accordant to the melancholy waves.
>
> *Southey's Curse of Kehama.*

Tailingana extended over the country between the Kistna and Godavery, and even beyond them on either side, and lay between Odradesa, Muru, and Carnataca, and probably contained part of the provinces of Bejapoor and Aurungabad, with Beder and Hydrabad. Its three rivers, the Godavery, Kistna, and Beema, are sacred. It is part of the Deccan, properly so called, and was the seat of the great Mahomedan kingdom of Bejapoor, under the Bhamani dynasty. Its mountains and forests furnish the scenery of some of the great poems of the Hindûs; and within its limits is the celebrated fortress of Dowlatabad, formerly Deogir, which Major Wilford has identified with the Tagara of the ancients.

The country of Muru, or the Maharashtras, now called Marhattas, occupied the mountainous district south of the Nermada (*Nerbudda*) and the maritime country of the Kócán, or Candeish, part of Berar, Aurungabad, and Bejapoor, and the Cocan, still retaining its ancient name. The Brahmins of this country are supposed to have been raised from the people of low caste, after an extirpation of the priesthood, who had made themselves obnoxious to their monarchs. The people are warlike, and have distinguished themselves particularly in the last century. The inhabitants of the coast have, from the earliest times, carried on both trade and piracy, for which their numerous small ports are admirably adapted. The Marhattas have also cultivated literature and philosophy in a remarkable degree, and are said to possess even books of history.

In the country of Muru we find most of those wonderful excavations which the ancient Hindûs have left as monuments of their power and ingenuity. Elephanta and Salsette, Carli and Poonah, with the caverned mountains near Fort Vittoria or Bancoot, where my friend Shahabo'-

dien, a native of the place, assured me there were thirty-two caves, are all in Muru; and I believe that the mountains of Ellora may also have been within its limits. Gurjera, the modern Guzerat, seems not to have changed its ancient limits. Being well situated for commerce, it has at all times been the resort of strangers. The ancient Barygaza, now Baroach, was frequented by the Roman merchants from Alexandria, and by the Arabs and maritime Persians; and it was the Rajah of Guzerat who hospitably received the expatriated Persees, after the famous battle that ended the dynasty of the ancient Persian monarchs in the person of Jesdegird.

These are the ten great divisions of Bharata, or India, which were of sufficient consequence and stability to have formed distinct languages, and to have cultivated science and literature. At what period they were formed, or when they were mingled and redivided, is hitherto unknown; but centuries before the Mahomedan conquest they had already changed their names and relative importance.

The Great Akbar divided Hindostan Proper into twelve soubahs, or viceroyalties, which were again subdivided into sircars or provinces, and kusbahs or townships*. The soubahs were

* See Letter 6th, for the œconomy of the village or township.

L

Allahabad, Oude, Agmere, Ahmedabad, Bahar, Bengal, Delhi, Cabul, Lahore, Multan, and Malwa; and upon the conquest of Candeish, Berar, and Ahmednuggur, they were formed into three other soubahs, though their limits were not precisely defined.

Abu Fazel begins his account of the Soubahs with that of Bengal, in which he includes Orissa and Cuttack, with the country to the south-east, as far as Chitagong. He describes the country as rich in the extreme, and particularly mentions that the revenue was paid in gold and silver, and not in produce; and that Akbar, in the assessment, conformed to the established custom. The periodical rains begin in April, and continue about six months, with intervals, however, of charming weather.

Bahar, lying west of Bengal, and watered by the Ganges and Soane, was also very fertile, and paid its proportion of produce in money, and the rainy season is the same as in Bengal. The natives of this province, to the north of the Ganges, on the banks of the Gunduck, are afflicted with a kind of *goître*, and the historian of Akbar observes, that young people are most frequently affected.

The capital of the soubah of Allahabad is a town of the same name, but anciently called Piyang or Gangapuri: it is called the king of worshipped places, because the Ganges and Jumna meet there; and it is said that the Sareswata joins them at that place by a subterraneous channel. Like the other Gangetic provinces, it appears in the time of Akbar to have been not only fertile but highly cultivated, abounding in towns and villages, and flourishing manufactures.

Oude, watered by the Goggra or Sarjew, and the Goomty, is remarked by Abu Fazel for the perfection of its agriculture, its manufacture of earthen ware, and the flourishing state of its commerce, as well as the antiquity and sanctity of its capital. In the soubah of Agra were mines of copper, and hot and cold springs. It produces excellent sugar and indigo, and was celebrated for its agriculture and its manufactures of blankets and fine stuffs.

The climate of Malwah is described as charming—in summer cool, and in winter temperate; abounding with wheat and fruits; the country naturally beautiful, and ornamented with buildings, and the people warlike. One province, Gurreh, is noticed as paying its share of the revenue in money.

Candeish, called in the Ayeen Akbery Dandees *, is a rich province, abounding in rivers,

* A compliment to the prince Daniel, son of Akbar, who was its governor when Abu Fazel wrote; but on the death of Daniel, the new name was dropped, and the old one resumed.

and enjoying an agreeable climate. In the time
of Akbar it was highly cultivated, had some
manufactures, and its cities were famous for
their handicraftsmen. The banks of the Tap-
tee, its principal river, are consecrated by the
site of many holy places, particularly on the
spots where it is joined by its various tributary
streams.

Berar is also distinguished by its sacred stream
the Godavery, to the source of which annual
pilgrimages are made. This extensive province
contained cultivated lands, and also wilds, so
extensive as to harbour wild elephants and monkeys. It contains mines of the most useful and
the most useless of minerals—namely, iron and
diamond: it also furnishes other precious stones,
and there are in it several petrifying springs.

The soubah of Guzerat is a maritime country,
and when Abu Fazel wrote, produced chiefly
jewary and bajeree, two coarse grains, which
were the principal food of the inhabitants, but
rice was imported from the Deccan, and wheat
and barley from Candeish. At present, the po-
tatoe is cultivated to a considerable extent. The
whole country produces abundance of fruit and
vegetables, and was famous for painters, carvers,
and other workmen, and its manufactories of
swords, dirks, and bows and arrows, besides
silks, velvets, and gold and silver stuffs.

The magnificent city of Ahmedabad was

its capital; it contained one thousand stone mosques, with many tombs, some erected to royal personages, and two considerable forts. West from Ahmedabad is a natural salt pan, of considerable extent; beyond that the territory of Cutch; and still farther west, the country of Sinde, full of woods and uncultivated sands.

South of Cutch, the territory of Surat extends from the port of Gogeh, or Gogo, to that of Aramray: it is divided into nine parts, each inhabited by a different tribe; the fifth being Juzzet or Daurka, famous in Hindû fable, as the favourite abode of Crishna; and the ninth is distinguished as the residence of the bawts and charums, whose profession is, like that of a minstrel or troubadour, to sing hymns, recite genealogies, and in battle to animate the troops by eloquence and song. Abu Fazel says, Gurgera contains nine circars, divided into one hundred and ninety-eight pergunnas, of which thirteen are sea-ports.

Agmere contains seven pergunnas; it is situated to the west of Agra. The soil is sandy, and water scarce, and the summer heat is intense. The southern part is mountainous, and contains mines of iron and copper. The following romantic story of some of the ancient landholders, called Rawel or Ramsa, is told by Abu Fazel. Ancient historians relate, that Alla o' dien Khuljee, king of Dehli, hearing that Rawel

Rutten Sein, of Meywar, had a wife of uncommon beauty, sent to demand her of him. The Rawel refused to part with her, upon which the army of the sultan besieged him in Chitore, where he held out so long, that Alla o' dien had at length recourse to artifice, and offered peace, inviting Rutten Sein to be his guest. The Ranna was at first received with great respect, but on a signal given he was seized, and carried to the sultan's camp, where he was respectfully treated. Meantime, seven hundred soldiers equipped themselves as women, and placing themselves in palankeens, sent word that the Rannee was coming in state with her women, to present herself to the sultan, but first requested an interview with the Ranna, which request being complied with, the soldiers had no sooner been admitted to their prince, than they threw off their disguises, and rescued him: his return to Chitore being covered by posts stationed previously, and who stood against the pursuing enemy till their sovereign was placed in safety, when the sultan returned disappointed to Dehli. A second expedition was equally unavailing; but, at length, the Rawel being decoyed to his presence, was treacherously murdered.

The soubah of Dehli, divided into eight sircars, was rich in natural productions and manufactures. Its mountains were filled with mines, and its plains with corn and cattle. It is wa-

tered by the Ganges and Jumna, with many of
their tributary streams, and is studded thick
with towns and villages. Here the monuments
of Hindú piety raise their venerable forms amid
the shades of Thanessar; and there the magnificence of the Moslemin displays itself in the
canals of Firoze, and the tombs of the Alla o'
diens and the Toglucks. Throughout the East,
a tomb is not, as with us, left neglected amid a
crowd of others, where the bat " folds his dank
wing " on the over-spreading yew, but placed
in gardens of public resort, where the placid joy
diffused by the charms of nature combine with
the remembrance of the departed friend, and
mellow our grief for his loss, into that softer
feeling, which, as the twilight reminds us of the
departed sun but to give us hope of his again
rising, persuades us that our separation is not
eternal.

The soubah of Lahore contains five divisions.
Great part of it is now called the Panjáb, or five
waters, from the five rivers flowing through it,
and falling into the Indus, which is its western
boundary. In the time of Akbar, its inhabitants
were famed for their handicraft and manufactures, as well as their agriculture; and the
country produced abundance of fruit and grain,
besides metals and minerals, found in the sandy
beds of the rivers, and mines of rock salt. La-

7

hore, the ancient Labaca, is the capital of the soubah, and was for some time the seat of the Mogul government, when it was the resort of merchants, who admired its magnificence and its riches, the elegance of its buildings, and the beauty and variety of its gardens.

Multan lies along the banks of the Indus, and is intersected by some of the rivers of the Panjáb, but it nevertheless contains much desert, and is plagued with the *Semoom*, a wind, hot and dry, like the siroc, and equally pernicious. Tattah, one of the three sircars of Multan, is famous for its breed of horses, which, if not so handsome as the Arabs or Persians, are strong, and capable of bearing greater fatigue. The camels of Tattah are also esteemed; and its inhabitants were a warlike race; they were also navigators, and when the Ayeen Akbery was written, possessed forty thousand boats. Rice, in this sircar, was good and abundant, and the fruits and flowers, fish, which was a chief article of food among the inhabitants, and salt and iron, were produced in great plenty. Tattah was divided into five sircars, though itself a sircar of Multan. Abu Fazel mentions among its curiosities, an extraordinary and disgusting set of witches, called Jiggerkhars or liver-eaters, who were supposed to have the power of fascinating people by their evil eyes, and thus stealing their livers, on which they made their detestable meal. It seems that they possessed the European witches' faculty of not sinking in water, and, like them, were ill-treated and destroyed wherever they were found.

The soubah of Cashmere comprehended Cashmere, Pehkeli, Bhember Sewad, Bijore, Kandahar, and Kabulistan. Of Cashmere, Abu Fazel says, " the whole of this soubah represents a garden in perpetual spring, and the fortifications with which nature has furnished it, are of astonishing height, so that the grand and romantic appearance cannot fail of delighting those who are fond of variety, as well as those who take pleasure in retirement. The water is remarkably good, and the cataracts are enchantingly magnificent. It rains and snows here at the same seasons as in Tartary and Persia; and during the periodical rains of Hindostan, there also fall light showers. The soil is partly marshy, and the rest well watered by rivers and lakes. Violets, roses, and narcissuses, with innumerable other flowers, grow wild here. The spring and autumn display scenes delightfully astonishing. The houses, which are built of wood, are of four stories, and some higher, and they are entirely open, without any courtyard. The roofs of the houses are planted with tulips, which produce a wonderful effect in the spring." Such is the description of the appearance of Cashmere by a Mussulman; and if you will read Bernier, who accompanied Aureng Zebe in a journey to that delightful country, you will find the French physician as enthusiastic an admirer of it as the Mogul historian.

All Cashmere is holy ground to the Hindús, a peculiar sect of whom, calling themselves Rishis, professed celibacy and abstinence. They reviled no other sect, and asked nothing from any one; but made it a duty to plant fruit trees by the road side to refresh the traveller, and to perform similar acts of benevolence.

Cashmere produces in abundance all the fruits of Europe and of Asia: it furnishes a great deal of silk, and all those beautiful shawls called Indian shawls, which are worn wherever Commerce has extended her sails or rested her caravans. The country is exceedingly populous, and the inhabitants addicted to *simple* pleasures I believe I should call them, to distinguish them from vicious indulgencies. A weaver of Cashmere has no sooner earned a little money, than he proceeds to the banks of a lake or river, and there with his family hires a boat, in which they pass the day, rowing or sailing amidst the most beautiful scenery in the world, and only landing to take refreshment, or walk in the meadows and gardens which are fertilized by the streams and lakes formed by the heads of the Indus, ere he leaves their happy valley. The country is free from poisonous snakes and scorpions, but produces excellent sheep, elks, and partridges ; hawking and hunting are favourite amusements, and the principal food of the inhabitants is rice and fish.

I once saw a picture or map of Cashmere, which was brought to Calcutta by some shawl-merchants. It was painted upon a square of cotton cloth, and professed not only to trace the situations of the towns, lakes, and rivers, but even the houses, bridges, and public pleasure gardens. The encircling mountains were coloured with all the gradations from the deepest verdure at the foot, to the snowy hue of the summits ; and among the valleys, on the side towards Cashmere, there was scarcely one which had not a Hindû temple or a Mussulman mosque. In the public pleasure ground, called Almeidân, parties were represented sitting under the shade of spreading groves ; and at the different bridges over the canals, or on the banks of the reservoirs which water the gardens, were multitudes of boats for hire, and the lakes and rivers were crowded with parties in barks of various sizes and degrees of beauty. I immediately thought of the demesnes of the Castle of

Indolence, and half expected to hear the syrens' witching flute, and feel the softened air : but the knight of arts and industry had already been there, and the leisure which the Cashmerians seem so passionately fond of, is the fair reward of toil and ingenuity.

The inhabitants of this terrestrial paradise are partly Hindû and partly Mussulman, with a mixture, however, of Jews, who are supposed to be part of the ten tribes carried into captivity by Nebuchadnezzar; and Bernier, who took some pains to ascertain the fact, seems to believe it.

The other sircars which in the time of Akbar formed part of the soubah of Cashmere—namely, Pekhely, Bhember, Sewad, Bijore, Kandahar, and Kabul, partake more or less of its physical advantages, being all diversified with woods and mountains, and watered with abundant streams. They occasionally procure gold in some of their rivers, by laying a fleece in the water, and the next day they usually find the grains of the metal entangled in it, so that they have only the trouble of watching it. The whole soubah abounds in springs, many of which are intermittent, others are hot, some petrify, and others produce salt. The hills and mountains, besides the mines of various metals, contain many singular caverns, to which the superstition of the people has, as usual, ascribed a miraculous origin.

Such is the picture of Hindostan left us by Abu Fazel, who wrote in the sixteenth century: a picture probably flattering, and certainly very different from that presented on our acquiring possession of the territory; but the long and happy reign of Akbar, which lasted half a century, and was distinguished by the most regular and wise government that ever blessed Hindostan, since the first Mussulman invasion, had restored to the cultivator confidence, and to the manufacturer security. Although the taxes were in some districts extremely high, in Cashmere for instance, equal to one half the produce of the land, the mildness and equity of the government, and the greater commerce carried on by the *highest taxed soubahs*, in proportion to their cultivated lands, made the taxes on real property as light as in those actually rated at less.

In my next letter I shall endeavour to give you an account of the Deccan or South. This name has sometimes been applied to the whole peninsula south of the Nermada; but, since the Mahomedan conquest, seems not to have extended further than to the banks of the Kistna.

The twelve soubahs of Akbar comprehended some parts of the Deccan; but they may be

easily distinguished from the true provinces of
the empire of Dehli by their situation, and perhaps I ought to have reserved them for their
proper place, but I thought it better to present
you with the statement of the Ayeen Akbery,
without changing any thing, as it is unquestion-
ably the most authentic document we possess of
the former state of India.

LETTER IX.

AFTER my last long letter on the geography of India, you will, I fancy, think me
unreasonable to begin another with the same
subject. But I had only laid before you the
ancient divisions of India, more properly called
Bharata, when we are speaking of it before the
Mahomedan conquest, and the provinces of
Hindostan Proper, or the country north of the
Nermada or Nerbudda, with the very small portion of the Deccan, annexed by Akbar to the
Mogul empire. I must now mention the kingdoms of the South, or Deccan, in its widest extent, that is, from the Nermada to Cape Comorin, about fifteen degrees of latitude.

The greater part of this tract consists of high
table-land, elevated from three to five thousand

feet above the sea, called the Balaghaut or land above the mountains; the rest is a belt of unequal breadth surrounding this land, and called Payeen Ghaut, or below the mountains. In the Deccan you may place the ancient kingdoms, distinguished and circumscribed by their languages, called the five Dravirs, but omitting Guzerat and substituting Orissa. The ancient divisions were however lost, among new and more numerous partitions, long before any intimate intercourse between Europeans and India.

Telingana, divided into Andra and Kalinga, seems to have retained its distinctive name longer than most of the Dravirs, for it was known to the Mahomedans by it; and, at the period of their invasion, its capital was Warankal.

Carnataca was early divided into a number of separate states, the south-western portion of which was Mysoor. Of the modern Carnatic a small portion only formed part of the ancient province, and Bejapoor occupied the northern part, and perhaps a small part of Telingana. The ancient capital of Carnataca was Dhoor Summudra, about a hundred miles north-west of Seringapatam; but the seat of government was removed to Tonoor, only twelve miles from that city, upon the Mussulman invasion in 1326, when the ancient city was destroyed by the army of Mahommed III.

About the same time a new kingdom was
founded upon the banks of the Toombudra by
some officers of the dethroned king of Warankal,
and its capital was named Videanaggur, sometimes called Bisnuggur. This kingdom was sub-
sequently enlarged by the acquisition of the
greatest part of Dravira or Draveda. From
Niliseram, near which there is a considerable
wall in ruins, the country of Toolava extended
to the neighbourhood of Goa; and bordering on
it to the East is the small country of Coorg,
whose present Rajah and his father have distinguished themselves by the desire of improving
their country and people. The three principal
parts into which Dravira was divided, were named
from three rival dynasties, the Chola or Chora*,
the Cheran and the Pandian. Combaconum and
Tanjore, upon the Cavery, appear to have been
the capitals of the former, which comprehended
the provinces of Tanjore, Trichinapoli, part of
the modern Carnatic, including probably Gingee
and Wandiwahi. The kingdom of Pandian included Madura, Tinivelly, Marawas, and probably part of Dindigul, and the country of the
Polygars; and the country of Chera compre-

* From Chola, or Chora, con. our name of Coromandel.
Mandala signifies a circle or country, thus, Chora Mandala the
country of Chora.

8

hended Kerala or Malabar, Cochin, Travancore,
Shallam, and Coimbatoor. In this division is
Calicut, where the first European ships, under
Vasco de Gama, touched, after doubling the
Cape of Good Hope. The coast is bold, and
the most picturesque I ever saw; and the country abounds in the finest timber in the world.
There are no harbours for any thing larger than
a boat; and it is only during the rains that the
small rapid rivers, that fall directly from the
mountains, are deep enough to float the timber
to the coasts.

At the time when the Mahrattas or Maha-
rastras emerged from obscurity under Sevajee
and his successors, the country anciently known
by their name was divided into a number of distinct provinces, which were successively seized
by the Mahomedans, with the exception perhaps
of the mountainous districts near Poonah and
the Cokun. Candeish and Berar were added to
the Mogul empire; Aurungabad, Beder, Beja-
pore, and Gundwana, with their subdivisions,
formed the greatest part of the Mahomedan dominions in the Deccan, to which must be added
Hydrabad, Golconda, and other provinces of
Telingana north of the Godavery.

Such is the general view of the division of
India at two very different periods. The first,
when its ancient kingdoms were so settled and

M

polished as to have formed and cultivated each
its own language; the last, as it was found
at the time of the first permanent European
establishments in the country. Had it been
possible to have been more minute in stating
the precise ancient boundaries of the different provinces, I am not sure that I should
have attempted it, for the task of tracing their
perpetual variations would have been endless,
and perhaps useless.

The British dominions extend over by far the
greater part of the above provinces, and accident, rather than convenience, seems to have
fixed the situations of the three presidencies
from which they are governed. Calcutta, the
seat of the supreme government in India, stands
on that branch of the Ganges called the
Hoogly, about eighty miles from Saugor island,
where that river falls into the sea. The approach to it is defended by a most dangerous
coast, owing to the shoals called the sand-heads,
which are deposited by the thousand mouths of
Ganges as it rolls into the ocean, and which,
during the floods occasioned by the rains, are
continually changing their places. The bed of
the Hoogly is also encumbered by similar sands,
and the bays formed in its low woody shores are
in general extremely unhealthy. The aspect
improves as you approach the capital, and the

clearing of the grounds has also materially improved its salubrity. Calcutta itself is now far from an unhealthy place, which is in great measure owing to draining the streets of the Black town, and constructing good roads in all directions from the presidency, a work, which does the Marquis Wellesley even more honour than his magnificent palace at the presidency, or his charming gardens at Barrackpoor.

In the rainy season the Hoogly is navigable quite to the Ganges; but in the dry weather boats of all descriptions are obliged to pass through the sunderbunds, or channels, that intersect the Delta formed by the Ganges, into the main stream. The country round Calcutta is perfectly flat and very woody. In the immediate neighbourhood are some extensive salt-lakes, and the country in general, like the rest of Bengal, is extremely fertile. Fort William, which defends this presidency, is strong, but perhaps larger than is necessary under the present circumstances, as the army that would be required to garrison it might certainly keep the field, but it was built before the English possessed either the territory or the resources they are now masters of in India, and while the French, Danes, and Germans possessed settlements on the river above Calcutta.

Madras, the second in rank of our presidencies, is perhaps more central to our dominions than any of the others, but it has not a single natural advantage. Built upon a low sandy shore, against which a tremendous surf continually beats, in the best seasons hardly to be crossed without risk, it has no port, or even headland, to protect the ships that resort to it. The soil around is so arid that it scarcely produces rice, and the most assiduous cultivation is necessary to raise the commonest vegetables. Nevertheless, being the seat of government for the south of India, it is amazingly populous; and it is the depôt for all the manufactures carried on in the northern circars, and the countries south of those provinces. The stuffs made there, though imported to Madras, take its name, instead of those of the countries where they are fabricated, and are known in Europe as Madras muslins, long cloths, and chintzes.

The fort of Saint George defends this settlement. It is situated so near the sea that a hurricane, which happened in 1805, so completely changed the face of the shore, that the watergate, which had before been at some distance from the beach, was washed by the surf. A canal has been cut from Fort George to Pulicat, about sixteen miles to the northward, whence the inhabitants of Madras are supplied with charcoal and other necessaries.

Bombay possesses more natural advantages than any other European settlement in India, but it is, unaccountably, that which has been most neglected; however, it is only a few years since the Mahrattas have been so far subdued as to render the surrounding districts safe. The island of Bombay lies in 18° of north latitude; it is nine miles in length and three in breadth; full of towns and villages, and every foot of the land in cultivation. It is connected by a causeway, with the large and fruitful, though neglected, island of Salsette, and forms with it, Caranja, and Elephanta, a most commodious harbour. It has the advantage over every port in India in the rise of the tides, which is seventeen feet, whereas the highest springs in Prince of Wales's Island, and the wonderful harbour of Trincomale only rise to ten feet. It is consequently well adapted for building and docking large ships, the timber for which is furnished by the Malabar coast; and its situation opposite to the Persian and Arabian shores makes it peculiarly fit for commerce. I know no place so well situated. Its excellent well-defended harbour, the fertility of the adjoining districts, the agreeableness of the climate, and the extreme beauty of the scenery, all contribute to make it one of the most charming spots in the world, as far as the gifts of nature are concerned, and with the

state of its society I have at present nothing to
to do, although I feel it difficult to restrain myself from talking of a place which is rendered
interesting to me by a thousand agreeable recol-
lections.

I shall not attempt to delineate the present
political divisions of India, but confine myself to
the external features of the country, some of
which I have already described. The northern
part of Hindostan Proper is bounded by the
stupendous range of mountains which separates
it from Tartary and Thibet, running in a direction north-west and south-east, called the Hima-
layah mountains, or Himavat. These mountains furnish the sources of the Indus and its
tributary streams, which water the country of
the Panjab, the Ganges, with the Jumna, and
other rivers which unite with that majestic flood,
and the Brahmaputra.

The mountains of Paryatra lie in the neighbourhood of Ogein, to the north of the Nermada, and from them flow the Mahie, the Sipra,
and Betwa, with some other rivers. The Recsha
mountains give rise to the Nermada, the Soane,
and many streams of less note, which, with the
exception of the Nermada, fall into other rivers.

The Vindhya mountains, among which lies
the Arcadia of India, lie to the south of
the Nermada, and contain the sources of the

Tapi, Tapti, and several smaller rivers, while those of the Godavery, Kistna, Bhima, Tungabadra, and Cavery are in a less elevated range south of the Vindhya chain, called the Tahya hills. Four inconsiderable streams rise in the Malaya mountains, and some others from the high Mahendra. In general there is a deficiency of water in the Deccan, none of the rivers south of the Nermada being navigable for any distance from their mouths; those on the eastern side of the peninsula being choaked with sand-banks, thrown by a violent surf against their openings; and those on the western coast descend so abruptly from the mountains of the shore, that they have not time to collect into streams of any magnitude before they join the king of rivers. There are no lakes but those formed artificially, for the purposes of sustenance and agriculture, but some of these are of such vast extent, as to appear more like the work of nature than of man; and though in some places the mountain torrents form cascades of exquisite beauty, there are none of sufficient magnitude to bear a comparison with the stupendous features of the New World.

Although travellers report that many districts of India bear the marks of extinguished volcanos, and many specimens of minerals, apparently formed in these tremendous laboratories of nature, have been brought from different parts of the country, there is not at present any burning mountain in action, nor are there, I believe, records of any such, although the *mouths of fire*, as several streams are called which emit flame, are frequently mentioned : such, for instance, are those in the neighbourhood of the Caspian, and that at Chitagong, where a temple is built over the spring, and due oblations performed to the sacred fire. Warm springs are not uncommon on the western coast, nor, I believe, in other parts of the country. Coal is found in the north-eastern provinces; mines of copper, gold, silver, and iron abound in those of the north; diamond has long rendered the name of Golconda famous; Cambay furnishes cornelian and other opake stones; the neighbourhood of Hydrabad produces garnets; while Ceylon seems the great magazine of the beautiful coloured and transparent gems.

Of that island little is known beyond the Belt occupied by the English, which encircles the whole island, and is from ten to thirty miles in width; a district woody, fertile, and in general healthy. On the western side is one of the finest harbours in the world at Trincomale; and on the northern coast is the pearl fishery, in the Straits of Manar, the product of which, however, is by no means equal to that in the Arabian seas. The interior of Ceylon is mountainous and woody, but it is so dangerous to the health, to pass any time in the Jungle, and so difficult for an European who has once entered the country to leave it, that I can only refer you to the old traveller, Knox, for an account of it, whose picture is of that kind, that though one does not know the original, one feels sure of the resemblance.

One great natural feature of India is the singular diversity of its coasts. That of the western side is high and bold, with some small harbours formed by insulated rocks and promontories; such as that of the river at Goa, and the bay at Bombay, than which there are few finer. The eastern, or Choromandel coast, on the contrary, is low and sandy, full of banks, against which a tremendous surf at all times beats, and not offering a port of any kind. The seasons also differ on the opposite shores, the rains setting in at Bombay in May or June, as they do in Bengal and the other northern provinces, while at Madras they begin nearly as the dry weather sets in on the western coast. During the rainy seasons the climate is subject to violent storms and hurricanes, particularly at the setting in and breaking up of the Monsoons; but for eight months in the year the weather is clear; the land and sea breezes constantly blow; and one may, if any where, forget the proverbial inconstancy of the winds and waves.

But it is time to take leave of you for the present. I have done with local descriptions for some time, as I wish, if possible, to present you with a sketch of such a part of the history of ancient India, as has come to our knowledge with any degree of certainty. Adieu.

LETTER X.

THE prodigious antiquity claimed by the Brahmins for their country and their history, extending to millions of years, is evidently fabulous. It is however reconcileable with truth by the consideration that the assumed periods of the Hindû astronomical cycles, have been mistaken by the poets for actual revolutions of years on earth, and M. Bailly has shewn that in ancient times the word signifying a year was employed for any revolution whatever, and that among some nations the times of the equinoxes and solstices were the periods of three months each, by which time was computed, while others who enjoyed a shorter summer, had one warm and two cold seasons, each of four months, and equally called years. The revolutions of the moon, and even that of day and night have also passed for years, and hence the confusion of early chronology when the true length of

the solar year being undetermined or disregard-
ed, the revolutions by which time was counted
were perpetually changing, and consequently
present those anomalies which have appeared
irreconcileable with reason and truth.

Major Wilford places the beginning of the
astronomical and unchangeable Cali Yug * at
3100 years before Christ †, but its commence-
ment as a civil or historical period is by no
means agreed upon; though there are reasons
for placing it about 1370 before Christ, when
Yud'hishthira, Minos, and Crishna lived ‡.

The æras used in more modern times are
those of Vicramaditya, beginning 56 years
before Christ, and of Salivahana whose period
commences seventy-eight years after the Christian æra. The history of the two extraordinary
personages who gave names to these periods is
enveloped in fables and contradictions which
can only be plausibly explained by the supposition of several persons of the same name whose
history has been confused.

* The four Yougs, i. e. the Kruty Youg, the Treta Youg, the
Dwapar Youg, and the Kali Youg are poetical periods like the
four ages of the western poets ; but they are besides probably
all astronomical periods. Their extravagant length shews them
to have been in every case supposititious, and it is very possible that they were chiefly adapted for the purposes of judicial astrology.

† Or before Vicramaditya 3044.

‡ The Jines place it 1078 B. C. others 1835 B. C.

Major Wilford mentions four Vicramadityas whose histories appear to be a mass of heterogeneous legends taken from the apocryphal gospel of the infancy of Christ, the tales of the Talmud concerning Solomon, and some of the Persian history of the Sassanian kings.

Vicramaditya was a king of Ogein, who made a desperate tapassya* in order to obtain long life from the goddess Kali; but as she seemed deaf to him he prepared to cut off his own head, when she interposed and granted him the empire of the world, till the appearance of a divine child, who was to be born of a virgin, and whose father was to be a carpenter, when he was to be deprived of his crown and life, in the year of the Cali yug 3101, answering to the beginning of the Christian æra. Vicramaditya after this promise lived surrounded by pleasures for a thousand years, when, remembering the prophecy, he sent messengers to seek the wonder-

* After the publication of the Curse of Kehama, it is probably unnecessary to explain the nature of a Tapassya, or those sacred austerities which have power to force boons of monstrous import from the gods, to overturn the laws of nature, and to subject immortals themselves to human controul. The opinion of the efficacy of severe self-mortification, if it has produced the Tapass of Vicrama, Bali, and Arjoon, has also, combined with a purer faith, produced the pillared saints of Egypt, the Anchorets of Palestine, and peopled the convents and monasteries of Europe. Man is always and everywhere the same.

VICRAMADITIA or KALI

ful child, and followed with an army to destroy him ; but the young Salivahana then five years old defeated and slew the longlived votary of Cali, and established his own æra instead of that of his rival.

Another account of Vicrama makes him live only one hundred and forty-five years, during all which time he waged war with the Romacas or Romans, and took one of their emperors prisoner, whom he dragged in triumph through the streets of Ogein, which tale is probably founded on the imprisonment of the emperor Valerian by the Persian prince Shapour. The Vicrama cotemporary with Solomon is like him said to have discovered the great muntra or spell by which he ruled the elements and subjected the spirits and genii.

But the great features in which all the histories of these Vicramas agree is the war with the divine child king Salivahana, and the tapass to Cali, at whose feet on the least fit of ill-humour they cast their heads, which are then picked up and replaced on the trunk by an attendant spirit, who however, *as every body knows*, is only empowered to perform this service ten times. The last Vicrama however appears really to be a distinct person, whose true name was Bhoja. It is doubted whether this is not the king whose court Calidasa and his learned cotemporaries adorned, but most Orientalists seem of opinion that it was the king of Ogein of that name who reigned fifty-six years before our æra, and who is the true Vicrama of the chronologists. Bhoja waged war with the Mahomedans, and must have lived about the year 1000 of the Christian æra.

The ancient history of India like its chronology, is lost in remote antiquity, and the traces of it are so faint and imperfect that we might be tempted to imagine that for some political purpose all regular documents had been systematically destroyed. Of the different races now inhabiting Hindostan, it is conjectured that the scattered tribes of the hilly countries, whose language, customs and religion differ entirely from those of the Brahmins, are the aboriginal inhabitants, and it is certain that the Brahmins and their brethren have traditions stating themselves to have come from the North, to have conquered the fertile country of Hindostan, and to have established their customs, their religion, and their languages. At whatever time this conquest took place, the Brahmins were considered as the masters of India from the remotest antiquity, long before the days of Alexander, and the descriptions left of them by the Greek writers proves that no material change has taken place in their manners and customs notwithstanding the Mahomedan conquest and the subsequent intrusion of European settlers.

The ancient Hindú historians begin their accounts of the world with seven dynasties or races of men, six of which have entirely passed away, and the seventh race, of whom Satyavrata the seventh Menu is the patriarch, now inhabit the globe, and it is predicted that on the extinction of this dynasty, seven others will succeed. This Satyavrata appears to be the same person with Noah, like him he was preserved in a boat during an universal deluge, and with him his sons, Charma, Shama and Jyapeti. After the deluge Atri, a son or grandson of Menu, had three sons who became monarchs and legislators. The eldest was an incarnation of the moon or Soma, called also a portion of Brahma, and founded the Chandra varsha or lunar race of kings, who sate for many centuries on the throne of Magad'ha, a country properly comprehending South Bahar only, but which under that powerful race of monarchs occasionally spread over the greatest part of India.

From Ikshwacu, another son of Satyavrata, descended the monarchs of the Surya Varshas or solar line, whose capital at one time appears to have been Hastinapoor, a city built however by a monarch of the lunar race of kings.

The lunar race of kings of Magad'ha have particularly engaged the notice of Sir William Jones and Major Wilford, partly on account of their more authentic history, and partly because the Greek and Chinese writers throw some additional light on their chronicles.

There are two periods of which the chronology may be fixed with tolerable accuracy, before the birth of Christ, namely, the great war of the Mahabharat, and the reign of Chandra Gupta, the cotemporary of Alexander. All the space before and between these dates is lost in uncertainty, excepting when occasionally a votive inscription serves to fix the date of a particular reign.

The fifth monarch in descent from Atri was Puru, the ancestor of the family of Pandu, whose adventures are the subjects of the epic poet, the dramatist and the musician throughout India. Dushmanta, the hero of Sacontala, was also of the royal and fortunate house of Puru, and his son Bharata gave his name to the whole of India. Hasti bequeathed his name to his descendants in the magnificent city of Hastinapoor which he built, and the sons of Curu, Jahnu and Sudana, began that rivalship between their families which caused the longest and bloodiest war in the annals of India.

While these great men adorned the race of Soma, that of Surya produced her Raghu, her Dusarathra, and other heroes, forerunners and worthy relations of the hero Ramachandra, the

incarnate Vishnu, whose exploits are celebrated by Valmeeki, and whose praises are still chaunted by the Hindû warrior as he marches to battle.

The same family also boasts of Parasa Rama, son of the Brahmin Jemadagmi, who destroyed the tyrants of the earth, and gave freedom to thousands of the oppressed.

These are the great names which we meet with prior to the wars of the Mahabharat; and the histories we have of them are chiefly derived from poems so very inexact in their chronology, that little dependance can be placed on them. The heroes of that war however, are expressly declared to have been cotemporaries with Parasará, in whose time an observation of the place of the solstices was made, which fixes his date 1391 years before Christ, so that these wars must have taken place about 1350 years before our æra.

At that time Jara Sand'ha reigned in Magadha, and it appears lived peaceably in his capital Rajagriha, or Palibothra, when Crishna, whom his followers have called an incarnation of Vishnu, invaded his kingdom. Like Jara Sand'ha he was of the lunar race, his forefather being Jadhu, and his father Vasudeva nearly related to Pandu, whose sons, with Crishna, and his brother Bali Rama, made war upon their kinsman Jara Sand'ha, and having surprised him in his capital, they caused him to be split asunder. Crishna and

N

the Pandus* appear to have been great warriors, and to have carried havoc and devastation where-ever they turned their arms, nor were the re-ligious changes which they effected less remark-able than their political conquests. The ancient worship of Siva or Maha Deo, whom it would not be difficult to identify with the ancient Bac-chus and with Osiris, was almost displaced to make way for that of Vishnu or Hercules (*Crishna*), and the votaries of the former were obliged to take refuge in the mountainous districts, while those of Vishnu, under the various names of Rama and Crishna, occupy all the plain. 'Another violent revolution was also brought about in this war of the Mahabharat. The Xetries or warlike tribes were found too turbulent for the tranquil-lity of the new conquerors, and they were accord-ingly exterminated in many provinces, and Sudras and other low persons elevated in their stead. Of the extent of the conquest of these invaders, we may form some idea from the manner of dividing the spoil. After the murder of Jara Sand'ha, Bala Rama the brother of Crishna, placed Sa-hadevati the son of Jara on the throne of his father, retaining for himself, however, the great-

---

* The five sons of Pandu, the eldest of whom was Yud-hishthira, but the most famous was the hero Arjoon. To these five brothers the Hindùs are fond of ascribing every great monument, of whose real author they are ignorant.

est part of the territory, as is inferred by his
being the builder or restorer of Palipotra or
Raja Griha on the Ganges, Mahaballipooram to
the south of Madras, and Pali Pura in the Deccan. To Gada another brother of Crishna, was
assigned the country named after him Gadipoor
or Gazipoor, and many other provinces were
given by Crishna to his various followers.

From the age of Crishna to that of Alexander
the history of India continues checquered with
spots of light on a ground of impenetrable darkness, just sufficing to shew it to be made up of
the same materials with that of other nations,
with perhaps even more of vicissitude. During
the reign of a weak prince every noble seems to
have considered himself independent, hence a
multitude of petty monarchies and dynasties,
which the first movement of a superior genius
on the superior throne swept away. Great
monarchies shine with a dazzling lustre for a
while, but in a few years are divided into as
many states as there were princes to grace the
ancient court. In short, every evil attendant
on the state of society where the welfare of the
state depends solely on the individual energies
or virtues of the ruling monarch by turns prevailed. A hero was employed in conquest, a
pusillanimous prince could neither protect his
subjects from foreign invasion, nor repress the

petty tyranny of the nobles, who appear more than once to have carried their turbulence so far as to have drawn upon their whole class death or banishment.

The next period, after the great wars, upon which we can fix with certainty is the reign of Chandra Gupta, by the Greeks called Sandracottus. This prince was descended from the ancient lunar kings of Magadha, but he was illegitimate, his mother being the daughter of a barber, and he only succeeded to the throne by intrigue and crimes. Sacatara, prime minister of Nanda, the father of Chandra Gupta, murdered his master, but was in turn with the whole of his family, except one son named Vicatara, put to death by Upadhanwa, the son and successor of Nanda. The young man however whom Upadhanwa had spared, watched for an opportunity of revenge, and having provoked the young monarch to offer an affront to a Brahmin, he took advantage of the confusion occasioned by the excommunication of the king, and with Chandra Gupta entreated the assistance of the neighbouring monarchs to overturn the kingdom of Prachi*, half of which he promised to Par-

* Prachi, or the East, comprehending all the country eastward from Allahabad. The Greeks called the inhabitants of this district Prasii, and its capital was Raja Griha or Palibothra. Prachi included, 1st, the country from Allahabad to Raja Griha, and 2d, Bengal, or Gaucavadesa, whose inhabitants were called by the Greeks Gangarides.

vateswara, *lord of the mountains,* king of Nepaul, in case of success. That monarch not only assisted Chandra Gupta with his own troops, but also procured the help of the Yavans or Greeks, when after a disgusting scene of alternate cruelty and treachery, Chandra Gupta was seated on the throne of Prachi, where he soon forgot his promise to Parvateswara.

The new monarch put to death all the noble and legitimate children of his father, after which his reign appears to have been peaceful and prosperous, respected abroad and beloved by his subjects. The accounts of the Greek cotemporary historians agree remarkably well with this Indian account of Sandracottus, only that they hint that the minister Sacatara was his real father. The most remarkable event in the latter part of his reign was the invasion of his kingdom by Seleucus, about A. C. 300; but the inroad ended in a treaty, by which the Greek gave his daughter in marriage to Chandra Gupta, who agreed to furnish him annually with fifty elephants.

The same good intelligence is recorded to have subsisted between the descendants of the two kings, for Antiochus the Great went to India to renew the ancient alliance with Sophagasemus (*Shivaca Sena*) the grandson of Chandra.

From this period the race of Bala Rama, called the Bali Putras, gradually declined on the throne of Maghada till A. D. 191, when Sipaca or Sri Carna Devi established the dynasty of the And'hra monarchs, which in its three branches made a conspicuous figure on the banks of the Ganges for nearly eight hundred years. The interval between Chandra Gupta and Sipaca was filled up by twenty-four kings, the ten first of which were of the family of Soma, who were succeeded by ten of the Surya Varshas, the most remarkable of whom was Vicramaditya, whose reign furnishes the date of the common æra of India, beginning fifty-six years before that of Christ. During the reign of four insignificant monarchs of the Canwa race, the Andharas gradually rose to power and virtually governed the kingdom, when in A. D. 151 the murder of the last Canwa prince placed Sipaca on the throne.

The first race of Andharas was of the genuine family, the second was a spurious branch, and the third consisted of the servants of the latter, who at first governed and afterwards dethroned their masters.

The native country of this family was Gaur, but they took their name from the province of Andhara, between Nellore and the Godavery, of which they were at one time the sovereigns, but in what manner or at what period they obtained possession of it we are ignorant.

Sri Carna Devi or Sipaca, styles himself in some grants of land Lord of Tri Calinga or the three shores, so that his dominion must have extended over the whole of India, if not the peninsula of Malacca, at least its western shore, if the expression be not merely intended to mark his superiority over the inferior monarchs his neighbours. His descendant Puloman, the last of the second family of Andharas, was a most pious and warlike prince, and after a life of heroic exploits he put an end to his life in the holy stream of the Ganges, a kind of death which seems to have been fashionable in his family, as his grandfather closed a brilliant career of conquest, by the voluntary deed of death near the uprising ocean. The death of Puloman happened A. D. 648, a date corroborated by the Chinese annals, and after that event the empire of India was divided into a number of small monarchies, and *Maharajahs* or great chiefs, established themselves at Canoge, in Guzerat, at Mait'hila*, Sacita†, Varanesa‡, and Tamralipta§. Magad'ha was reduced to its original limits or South Bahar, and the kings of Gaur or Bengal quickly became so powerful,

* Tirhut.   † Oude.   ‡ Benares.   § Tamlook.

that the seat of the government of Magad'ha was removed from Palibothra to Patna, as being farther from the enemy's frontier.

While these changes were going on in the kingdom of Magad'ha, the countries to the westward, or that part of Hindostan called the Panjáb, was ravaged by a horde of Huns, who seem to have met with little resistance from the native monarchs.

The situations of the different kingdoms of the south of India I described in a former letter, their history is buried in obscurity till about the time of the Mahomedan conquest, but they appear to have been occasionally under the dominion of the powerful monarchies of the North, though the distinct characters of their languages and alphabetical writing prove that they must have been for the most part either totally independent or only nominally in subjection. When the Mussulmans first appeared in the south of India, Bulal Raï was the sovereign of Carnata, Dravida, and Tulava, and his capital was Dwara Summudra, 155 miles north-west from Seringapatam; but the city being shortly ruined by the invaders, the seat of government was removed to Tonara near Seringapatam, and Bulal Raï built the city of Vejeyanuggur as a defence against the Moslems. This new city soon became famous all over the East for its riches and splendor under a new dynasty, who ruled the whole of India south of the Kistna, till the year 1564, when the Rajah, Ram Rajah fell in the battle of Telicotta, and his descendants fled before the Mahomedans, first to Pennaconda and thence to Chandragheri, whence the last branch of this ancient family was expelled in 1646.

After the battle of Telicotta the remaining Hindû nobles, and landholders or Udiars, endeavoured to render themselves independent, and those of Mysore succeeded in establishing a kingdom, the capital of which was first Mysore but afterwards Seringapatam, where nine kings of one family reigned successively till A. D. 1761, when Hyder Ally deprived the last of his throne. These Mysore Rajahs appear to have been men of abilities, and probably in more favourable times might have established a permanent monarchy; but the miserable political and military state of all India at that time, distracted no less by the wars which strangers waged with each other within her territories, than by the ravages of her own various nations, prevented the possibility of securing a small kingdom both from foreign conquest and domestic treachery.

As I am purposely refraining from all mention of the Mahomedan history of India in this letter, the Mahratta State is the only one which remains to be mentioned. Could its history be accurately given, it would furnish a perfect example of all that must take place where a nation hardy and warlike, with just civilization enough to make it follow its leader in the field, and obey its monarch at home, rises suddenly by conquest to vast importance, and when the spirit of conquest is over, sinks again to its native insignificance. But I only mean to give you such a sketch of this extraordinary nation as may excite your curiosity and make you seek information where alone it can be found, in the country you are going to. I regret that my stay in India was too short to learn half of what I wished, and still more that I lost a great deal of time; because, having no guide to my curiosity, my attention was distracted by the multitude of new objects that presented themselves.

But to return to our Mahrattas. The ancient Maharashtra nation appears for some centuries to have been subject to some of its powerful neighbours, occasionally rebelling, and carrying on trade or piracy as the opportunity offered, from the ports in the Cokun, when in the middle of the seventeenth century one of those extraordinary men arose, who want neither fortune nor power, but create the one, and command the other. Sevajee suddenly appeared. The son of an adventurer, he began his life by strokes of policy and firmness that might have become a veteran statesman. Having possessed himself of the treasures of his father Shahjee, at that time minister to one of the Mussulman kings in the Deccan, he speedily collected around him a band of adventurers, with whom having made himself master of the hill-forts and strong places along the Ghauts, he plundered and harassed the neighbouring states, carrying terror even into the armies of Aurung Zebe, in whose power the chance of war once placed him and his son, but from whom he found means to deliver himself, to gain new victories, and at length to organize his kingdom.

It was in 1674 that he caused himself to be crowned at Poonah, and had money coined in his name, and from that time the authority of a monarch being added to the spirit of an adventurer and the boldness of a warrior, his arms were irresistible, and though he died in 1680, the impulse he had given to his people continued, and under his successors, whether of his own family or of the usurping Peishwas, carried terror and devastation over the whole of Hindostan and the Deccan for seventy years.

The causes of the fall of the Mahratta power are even more obvious than those of its rise. When Sevajee, in organizing his kingdom, supposed it to be always at war, and its king at the head of his troops, he gave the death-blow to the power of his descendants, by leaving the whole civil authority and administration in the hands of the viceroy and Peishwa. Accordingly his grandson Shahoo, the third of his family who succeeded him, was soon confined in the fortress of Sittara, and the ambitious Peishwa Balajee governed, in his master's name it is true, but entirely by his own authority. The other nobles of the council, of course jealous of the Peishwa, formed their separate parties, and pursued their separate interests, and while they pillaged Dehli and Agra, overrun Guzerat, ravaged Bengal and Orissa, and even carried their incursions to the gates of Madras, those internal quarrels were fermenting, which after the battle of Pamput, A. D. 1761, disunited the Mahratta chiefs for ever, and have thus secured the peace of India.

When I visited Poonah in 1810 the melancholy spectacle of ruined towns and villages but too plainly marked the camps of the rival chiefs, who alternately pretended to defend, or openly attacked the capital, and it would not be easy for Sevajee to recognize, in the British cantonments which surround the capital and imprison its chief, the scene of that greatness which he raised, and of that power which rendered him the dread of the greatest monarch of Hindostan.

In the slight sketch I have given you of the different Hindû kingdoms of India, I have not attempted to give all the details which I might have collected, but only to awaken your curiosity. Before I quit the subject I must mention the kingdom of Nepaul, which, although without the limits of India proper, must be considered as a Hindû kingdom, as its inhabitants are believers in the Brahminical religion, and their customs and manners prove them to be of the same families. Like that of the other Hindû kingdoms, the early history of Nepaul is obscured by superstitious fables, and its beautiful valley is reputed to have been a favoured dwelling-place of the gods, after the lake which once filled it had been dried up.

The historians of Nepaul preserve the memory of several dynasties who have reigned over the country, the greater number of which have proceeded from foreign conquerors, who appear always to have found that beautiful country an easy prey. If the first dynasty was of native princes, the second was of invading Rajepoots, deposed by the Kerats, a mountain tribe from the East, and these were displaced by a tribe of Xetries, who reigned in different branches, nearly three thousand years. The kingdom was then divided into three separate sovereignties, in which state it continued for two centuries, when

one of the rival monarchs calling in Prithi Nar-
rayn, a powerful prince of the Rajepoot tribe,
and surnamed Goorkhali, from his dominion of
Goorkha, that artful stranger contrived to re-
unite the divided branches of the kingdom under
his own dominion, and in A. D. 1768, became
sole master of Nepaul. His son succeeded him
in 1771, and dying two years after, left his
kingdom to his infant son, who still occupies
the throne, and whose minority was passed under
the alternate guidance of his uncle and his
mother, both of whom appear to have possessed
uncommon abilities, and it is only to be regretted that their want of cordiality produced
much evil, when a better understanding between
them might have been of service to the state.
Our chief knowledge of Nepaul we owe to Col.
Kirkpatrick, who visited that country in the
capacity of an ambassador when the English
were applied to by the Nepaul government, for
their good offices in the war between Nepaul
and Thibet, when a Chinese army marching to
the defence of the Lama, brought the Nepau-
lese to humiliating terms, before the arrival of
the British embassy.

LETTER XI.

THE first attempt of the Mahomedans towards the conquest of India was made during the reign of the Kalif Omar*, who sent Maganeh Abul Aas, from Bahrein to the mouth of the Indus; but the expedition failed of success, and it was not till the reign of the Kalif Walid † that Sind was occupied by the Mussulmans, from which period their incursions into the fertile countries of Hindostan became more frequent and successful, till they at length obtained complete possession.

The first Mussulman prince however who made a serious impression on India, was the Sultan Mahmud Sebectaghin, who reigned at Ghazna. His father Sebectaghin appears to have been a soldier of fortune, and being too far from the seat of the Kalifat to fear its power, he erected an independent sovereignty at Ghazna, nominally however subject to the Kalif; for on the accession of Mahmud to his father's power, after a successful expedition to Balk, we find him receiving the robe of honour and the investiture as Sultan, from Kalif Cader, in the year of the Hegira 389 ‡.

---

* A. D. 636. A. H. 15.   † A. D. 717. A. H. 99.
‡ i. e. A. D. 998—9.

Three years after this event he made his first expedition into India with considerable success*, but remained but a short time in that country, as he made a conquering excursion into Segestan the following year, whence he returned to India in 1005 of our æra †, and seized Habeth and Multan. No sooner had he completed this expedition, than he was obliged to turn his arms against Ilek Khan, who had profited of his absence in India to invade Khorassan, and besiege Balk; but the victorious Mahmoud overcame and slew the invader and drove his army beyond the Oxus ‡, when he returned to India to spread his conquests and his faith, it being no less his object to make converts to Islam than to extend his dominions. A. D. 1014 and 1018 § he again visited or rather overrun the north of India, taking among other cities, Benares and Patna; but in the latter year allured by the reputed treasures of the South, he left the northern provinces to a tranquillity they enjoyed for near a century, while his successors on the throne of Ghazna were continually employed in protecting Khorassan, or in incursions towards Syria and the frontiers of Arabia. In 1025|| Mahmoud invaded Guzerat, which appears to have fallen an easy prey.

* A. D. 1001. A. H. 392.　　† A. H. 396.
‡ A. D. 1006. A. H. 397.　　§ A. H. 405 and 409.
|| A. H. 416.

The most remarkable events of that expedition were the destruction of the famous Hindû temple of Soumenat, and the choice made by Mahmoud of a descendant of the ancient rulers of the country of the race of Debschelim, to be its governor and king.

After an active and successful reign of thirty-one years, this great prince died in the year of the Prophet 421. Amid the constant activity as a warrior which distinguished Mahmoud, we feel almost surprised to contemplate the elegance of his court, which was not only the theatre of magnificence, but the temple of the muses. It was by his order that the materials of the Shahnameh were collected, and under his eye that Ferdousi composed that immortal poem, where the wisdom of the sage and the genius of the poet combine 'to preserve and adorn the early history of his native country. I once before referred you to the Chevalier D'Ohsson's interesting account of the life and character of Ferdousi prefixed to his *Tableau Historique de l'Orient*, a work confessedly taken from the Shahnameh.

The Negharistan from which D'Herbelot chiefly takes his account of Mahmoud, which you will perceive I scrupulously follow, relates many interesting anecdotes of this prince, but none which pleases me so much as the following, which, while it shews the virtues of the

o

Sultan most conspicuously, displays the vices of the oriental government and administration of justice, holdiug out little safety to the wretched except from the private virtues of the judge!

A poor man complained to Mahmoud that a Turk had broken into his house in the night, and after robbing him, had beaten and abused him cruelly.. After every inquiry that might lead to the detection of the culprit, without effect, Mahmoud desired the poor man not to oppose the thief the next time he came, but to come instantly to him. It was not long before the Turk repeated his attack. The sufferer immediately gave information to the Sultan, and led him to his house. Mahmoud having surrounded it with his guards, caused all the lights to be extinguished and the robber slain, which being done, he called eagerly for a lamp, examined the person of the wretch, and exclaiming, God be praised, he fell upon his knees, returned a thanksgiving, and called for food. The poor man had nothing but the coarsest bread and water to offer, but Mahmoud ate and drank eagerly, and prepared to depart, when the man to whom he had done justice, entreated to be informed why he had caused the lights to be put out, why he had thanked God, and called for food. " I caused your lamp to be extinguished," said the Sultan, "because I thought that none could dare to commit so flagrant a piece of injustice but one of my own sons, and I was not willing that the sight of my child should prevent me from inflicting the punishment such a crime deserved; when I thanked God, it was because I discovered the body to be that of a stranger, and I called for food, because, since the day you preferred your complaint, fearing that it might be my son, I have fasted while I doubted of his virtue!"

Of the successors of Mahmoud on the throne of Ghazna little need be said. They were constantly occupied either in petty warfare at home, or in the defence of their distant provinces with various success; and the usual intrigues of the Harems and the viziers, rebellion and slavery are not likely to furnish pictures of a pleasurable nature.

Thirteen monarchs of the dynasty of Sebectaghin reigned at Ghazna*, but with very various

	Yrs.	Mths.		Yrs.	Mths.
* Mahmoud Sebectaghin reigned	31	0	Massoud III	18	0
Massoud I.	13	0	Schirzad	1	0
Maudoud	7	0	Arslam Shah	3	0
Massoud II.	0	1	Bahrâm Shah	32	0
Ali	2	0	Khosru Shah was imprisoned		
Abdul Raschid	1	0	A. H. 551, and died A. H.		
Ibrahim	42	0	561 or A. D. 1156 and 1165.		

The

influence or interest in Hindostan. It was reserved for the princes of the next family, who, by deposing Khosru, obtained possession of his empire, to fix their capital in India, and to establish permanently the Mussulman belief on the throne of Dehli. The father of Hassan ben Hossain owed his fortunes and advancement to the government of Gaur to the seventh Ghaznavide Sultan Ibrahim, but Hassan taking advantage of the weak and disordered state of the empire of Ghazna under Bharâm Shah, invaded it, and after various success, both in his reign and that of his successor Khosru Shah, he took the latter prisoner, and he died in confinement ten years after the loss of his kingdom.

Previous to the final conquest of Ghazna, Hassan met with one of those singular reverses of fortune which are only to be met with in oriental story : having invaded the dominions of the Seleucidæ, he was taken prisoner, and appears to have been made the personal attendant of Sangiar the then reigning monarch, in which situation he so much ingratiated himself by his talents for poetry and for flattery, that the conqueror sent him back laden with gifts to his own ca-

The succession of these princes is a little different in Dow's Ferishta, where we find two Khosrus after Bahrâm, the first of whom reigned seven years; and it was his son who was imprisoned by the Gauride Mahommed.

pital, where he died either in the same year in which he took Khosru Shah prisoner, or that immediately following it.

Mahommed Seifeddien succeeded his father Hassan, and reigned seven years, which were of little importance to India; but the joint reigns of Giath'o'dien Abulfutteh and Shahabo'dien Abul Muzzuffur which lasted forty years, and the short period of four years during which the latter survived his beloved brother and friend, fixed the first Mussulman empire within India Proper on the throne of Dehli.

The history of the immediate cause of the revolution which subverted the ancient Hindû monarchy of Indra-Patti or Dehli, is among the most romantic that even the annals of the East present.

Jya Chandra, Emperor of India, whose capital was Canoge, was not in truth the legitimate sovereign of the country; that title belonged to the young hero Pithaura king of Dehli, whose noble character and unhappy fate are the theme of both Mussulman and Hindû writers: the two monarchs appear, however, to have lived for some years in good intelligence, till upon occasion of a solemn sacrifice at the capital of Jya Chandra, where the functions of officiating priests were to be performed by sovereign princes; Pithaura, not choosing to perform an inferior part while his rank as superior lord should have made him the high priest, absented himself from the ceremony, and thus incurred the enmity and persecution of the monarch of Canoge. Shortly afterwards, a more romantic adventure terminated not only in the destruction of Pithaura but in his own ruin. Jya Chandra had adopted as his daughter a beautiful and accomplished damsel with whom the king of Sinhala-Dwipa or Ceylon had presented him, during an excursion he had made to that island under pretence of a pilgrimage, but in reality to exact tribute from the kings of the southern provinces. This damsel he had promised in marriage to a neighbouring monarch, but she, being enamoured of the valorous and noble Pithaura, refused her consent. Pithaura being at that time at Dehli and hearing of her affection, disguised himself, his brothers and attendants as the servants of a bard whom he sent to the court of Jya Chandra; and having by his means obtained an interview with the fair prisoner, for such she had been since her avowal of her affection for Pithaura, he carried her off in safety to Dehli during a species of tournament held by Jya Chandra, though not without a combat which deprived him of some of his bravest warriors.

The king of Canoge, in order to revenge himself the more completely for this insult, implored the assistance of Shahab'o'dien, who ac-

cordingly marched with a powerful army against
Pithaura, who roused himself from the delights
of his capital and the indulgence of his love to
meet the Mussulmans in the plains of Thanessar,
where he was defeated and slain A. D. 1194*.
His capital immediately fell, and Shahab'o'dien
fixed in it the first and greatest of the Mahomedan monarchies of India; and very shortly afterwards overthrew Jya Chandra himself, and thus
obtained the most extensive and richest provinces of Hindostan.

When Shahab'o'dien found himself sole master of the extensive dominions of the Ghaznavide sultan, increased by his recent conquests,
his regret at having no male children induced
him to adopt several of his slaves, among whom
he divided his empire. Of these, Tegh Ildiz in
Ghazna, Nassuro'dien in Multan, and Cuttubo'-
dien Ibec in Dehli, founded powerful dynasties
after the death of Mahmoud the immediate successor of Shahabo'dien, of the Gauride family,
and who reigned seven years. Mahmoud fell a
victim to the indignation excited by his treachery in betraying the young prince Ali Shah
into the hands of his rival on the throne of
Khouaresm, Mohammed Shah, and was consequently murdered in his bed A. D. 1212†;

* A. H. 591.   † A. H. 609.

when the crown of Ghazna was seized by the same Mohammed Shah the Khouaresmian*.

But his dominion in India was rather nominal than real, as he was employed during the whole of it in war with Gengis Khan, whom he had imprudently provoked. In 596 of the Hegira†, sultan Mohammed invaded Khorassan, and in one of those battles which in the East have usually decided the fate of nations, obtained entire possession of that country. The following year he made an incursion into Tartary, during which he took Samarkand and Bochara, and defeated the eastern Tartars and Turks in a pitched battle, on which occasion he received the name of Iskender Thani. Meanwhile his lieutenant in Transoxania, who was governor of Otrar the

---

* The Khouaresmian dynasty takes its name from the country of Khouaresm on the Oxus. The first of these sovereigns Cottub'o'dien Mohammed ben Bousteghin Gurckeh, who reigned thirty years, established himself under the Seleucidæ in the year of the Hegira 491, A. D. 1097; his successors were: Atsiz who reigned twenty years; I lArslan seven years; Sultan Shah twenty-one years; Takash eight years; Cuttub o'dien Mahommed ben Takash twenty-one years: this king was succeeded by Rocneddin Gorsang, Gaiath o'dien Mirsha, and Gelal'o dien Maubek Berni, who at different times reigned eleven years to the extinction of the dynasty in A. H. 628, or A. D. 1231. It was the sixth of these, Cuttub o'dien Mahommed ben Takash, who obtained the dominions of the Ghaznavide sovereigns.

† A. D. 1199.

capital of that province, had seized and put to death some Tartar merchants, travelling with a caravan from the camp of Genghis Khan, who sent to demand an apology which was inconsiderately refused. That conqueror immediately invaded Khorassan*, and in spite of the incomparable valour of Jellaleddin or Gelal o'dien, eldest son of Mohammed, defeated the Khouaresmians and forced the sultan to retire; which he at first wished to have done, towards his Indian dominions, but being intercepted, he fled to Mazenderan and for greater security went to Abgoum an island of the Caspian, whence he was driven by the Tartars to another island in the same sea, where he died A. H. 617†.

His brave successor Gelal o'dien fought long and valiantly against Genghis, but in vain: one of his most desperate actions was, swimming across the Indus in sight of Genghis and his victorious army, after having drowned his women to save them from the conqueror; who, at the sight of this honourable though perhaps cruel exploit, turned to his children and exclaimed, " Behold my sons, a hero worthy of his father‡!" Five years afterwards he returned into Persia, where the celebrity of his name soon raised him an army with which he gained some battles, and

* A. H. 615, A. D. 1218. † A. D. 1220.
‡ This exploit was performed A. H. 618, A. D. 1221.

conquered some small states towards the frontiers of Arabia; but his native dominions were hourly falling a prey to the arms of Octai the grandson of Genghis and his generals, who had already possessed themselves of Cabul, Candahar and Multan; and

> He left the name at which the world grew pale
> To point a moral or adorn a tale.

For A. H. 628*, being surprised by a party of Moguls, he disappeared, and nothing is known certainly of his fate.

Genghis Khan, whose family in its various branches has reigned with such various fortune in India, and whose name and exploits spread terror even in Europe, was born at Diloun Joloun in the year of the Hegira 549†. His father dying when he was at the age of thirteen, the Mogul chiefs his subjects rebelled against the government of a child, and obliged him to take refuge with Avenk Khan a Tartar prince, at whose court he soon distinguished himself by his great qualities; and having upon one occasion preserved the crown of his benefactor when attacked by a revolted brother, he was rewarded with the hand of the daughter of Avenk, who thus added the ties of relationship to those of gratitude.

But this harmony did not last, for the Tartar

* A. D. 1230.   † A. D. 1154.

nobles, jealous of the young foreigner, formed
cabals against him, and excited the suspicions
of his father-in-law ; so that that to save himself,
Genghis, or as he was then called Timegin, had
recourse to arms, and having obtained a complete victory over the Tartars, took possession
of the dominions of Avenk, and regained the
kingdom of his father. Upon this signal success he assembled the *Kuriltai* or national military meeting of the Tartars*, at which he was by
acclamation named their sovereign, and the title
of Genghis Khan conferred upon him by the noble
Tubi Tangri†. The eleven years immediately suc-
ceeding were employed in conquests towards China, Korea, and Cathay; and the twelfth year was
that of his invasion of the states of Mohammed,
but it is unnecessary to enter into a detail of his
rapid conquests; the towns destroyed, and the millions of human victims which were sacrificed, have
sufficiently often blanched the cheek of the reader
of the history of that scourge of mankind; and yet,
there are generous actions recorded of him, and
generous sentiments expressed, which show that
the heart though wild was not without those feelings of humanity, which by no means belong

* Something resembling the Wittenagemotes and Weapon-
schaws of our forefathers.

† From the war with Avenk to the meeting of the Kuriltai occupied from A. H. 600 to 602, or from A. D. 1203 to
1205.

peculiarly to the more polished societies of the West. Perhaps, judging by modern examples, we might be tempted to believe that where the passions for conquest and for fame are strong enough to overleap the bounds of modern education, which naturally tends to equalize the genius by assimilating the habits of men, there must be a natural ferocity of character insensible to the charities of human life, though capable of the exertions which may exalt it to fame.

Genghis Khan became the nominal sovereign of the empire of Dehli in the year of the Hegira 619*, but never actually took possession of the throne, as his life was a continued scene of moving conquest. Five years after this new acquisition, being completely worn out by his constant exertions, he solemnly assembled his family and divided his dominions among them†. These dominions extended from east to west over a space of eighteen hundred miles, and although the Tartar laws of Genghis are celebrated for their wisdom, still the miserable civil state of that extensive country, and the extreme turbulence of the military chiefs, rendered the division of so immense a territory absolutely necessary. Accordingly to Octai his grandson, whose father had fallen in battle, he gave the Mogul and Cathaïan territories. Jagathay, gave his

---

* A. D. 1222.   † A. H. 624, or A. D. 1227.

name to Transoxania or Turkestan Proper. Khorassan, Persia and India became the patrimony
of Tulikhan : and Batou the son of Giougi, another grandson, was put in possession of Arban,
Rous and Bulgaria : this is the same Batou, who,
forty years afterwards, crossed the Tanais, entered
Europe and overran Hungary and Moravia*.
Having thus divided his conquests, Genghis Khan
died in the sixty-sixth year of his age, having
first put into the hands of his sons a solemn com-
pact concluded between his great-great-grand-
father Kil Khan and his brother Fangiouli the
seventh ancestor of Timur Leng, in virtue of
which his family held the sovereignty of Tartary;
and which Timur himself so much respected,
that he chose rather to claim honour as descended from a female of the family of Genghis,
than as being himself of an older branch of the
house of Kil Khan.

That you may form some idea of the terrors
of a Tartar army, I repeat the following account
from D'Herbelot, of the destruction of the city
of Herat : It had been taken and kindly treated
by one of the generals of Genghis Khan ; but a
report of some reverses of fortune having reached
it during his absence, the city rebelled, and on
his return held out against him till most of the

---

* A. H. 656, or A. D. 1258.

inhabitants capable of bearing arms were either killed or wounded. When it was retaken, every man, woman and child was put to the sword excepting a Moola, Scheffer u'dien Khatib, and fifteen other men who hid themselves in a cave, where they were joined three days afterwards by twenty-four more, and these forty persons lived in the ruins of Herat fifteen years without seeing one other human being!

While the Tartars were thus hovering round the frontiers of India and daily threatening its cities with the fate of those of Cabul and Khorassan, the adopted slaves of Shahab o'dien were enjoying its riches and ruling its finest provinces. Kuttubo'dien* reigned at Dehli till A. D. 1219†, when he was succeeded by Aram Shah who was as soon deposed by Iletmish Shums'o'dien, who died in 1235‡, and was succeeded by Firoze Shah Rocneddin.

Firoze did not, however, long enjoy his dignity, for his sister Radiath'o'dien or Rizia, a lady of incomparable beauty and unbounded ambition, having brought over the chief nobles to her party, exiled her brother and seated herself

---

* A. D. 1207; Mahommed Bakthyr one of Kuttub o'dien's generals overcame Lakshmanyah the last king of Bengal, and that province continued subject to the crown of Delhi 140 years; its subsequent revolutions will be mentioned hereafter.

† A. H. 616.　　　　　‡ A. H. 633.

on his throne. But under a female reign jealousy was easily excited, and this enterprising princess was obliged to fly from her capital, and after a series of the most romantic adventures, she was killed in attempting to escape from her other brother Baharam, who was then raised to the throne, which he enjoyed for little more than two years, when his army rebelled and placed Massoud Shah alla o'dien, the son of Firoze, on the throne. But he, being a weak prince, was immediately deposed in favour of his uncle Nassur o'dien Mahmoud a man of extraordinary qualifications. During the time of his imprisonment, which lasted from the death of his father Iletmish, he had supported himself by writing, as he despised the imperial allowance to prisoners, saying, that those who would not labour for bread, did not deserve to eat. After he ascended the throne, he considered himself only as trustee for the state, and continued to supply his private wants by his own industry. Ferishta relates, that one day as an Omrah was inspecting a Koran of the king's writing, he pointed out a word which he said was wrong; Mahmoud smiled, and drew a circle round the word; but as soon as the Omrah was gone, he erased the circle and restored the word; remarking that it was better to erase from a paper what he knew was right, than to wound the old man by shewing him that he had found fault without reason. Mahmoud had but one wife who performed all the homely offices of housewifery without even a maid servant to assist her, and their table, as the emperors of India never ate in public, was served with the frugality of an anchoret. To these private virtues, Mahmoud added a thorough knowledge of arms, and was eminently successful in all his wars. His clemency towards those who at different periods of his reign rebelled against him, was so extraordinary that it draws forth a kind of reproving wonder from his historian; and the only shade in his government was thrown over it by a temporary favourite who abused his power; but it passed quickly away, and Mahmoud, who had the singular fortune to find a friend in his vizier Ghiaso'dien Balin, died after a reign happy both for himself and his subjects of twenty-one years; and leaving no children, was succeeded by Balin, who was of the same family with his master and predecessor.

Balin was originally a Turkish prisoner, who was sold as a slave, but making known his connexion with the reigning family at Dehli, he was advanced by the princes, his predecessors, to the highest rank, and his reign proved him worthy of his fortunes. He expelled all flatterers, usurers, and disorderly persons, from his court, and was severe in dispensing justice, but liberal in rewarding merit. His generosity was proverbial, for he had at one time not less than twenty of the unfortunate sovereigns whom Genghis Khan had driven from their kingdom, in his capital, to each of whom he assigned princely revenues. In their trains were all the men of letters and celebrated artists of Asia, so that the court of Balin was one of the most polite and magnificent in the world. Every night a society of poets, philosophers, and divines, met at the house of Shehid, the emperor's eldest son, where the noble Khosru, the poet, presided; and the fine arts were equally cultivated by Kera, the younger brother. Balin himself encouraged magnificence in architecture, equipage, and dress, although he discountenanced drinking and debauchery of every kind.

A. D. 1268, or A. H. 667, prince Mahommed Shehid was sent by his father as viceroy to Lahore, where his court became famous for its elegance and its learning; and Shehid wishing to obtain the friendship of Sadi, the poet of Shiraz, twice invited him to his court; the old man excused himself on account of his years, but sent to Shehid a copy of his works.

This great and accomplished prince met his death in endeavouring to repel an incursion of the Moguls into Multan, when his father Balin was eighty years of age. The old man died soon

P

after, and his second son, Kera, being absent in
his viceroyalty of Bengal, Key Kobad, son of
Kera, was placed on the throne of Dehli. But
this prince proved unworthy of the family whence
he sprung; and as the weak are usually the
prey of the wicked, an ambitious and profligate
minister took advantage of the young monarch's
propensity to pleasure, and brought such odium
upon him, that he was murdered A. D. 1289,
after a reign of three years, and Jellal o' dien
Firoze, an Afghan chief, was raised to the
throne, at the age of seventy. He endeavoured
to repair the evils of the last reign, but it was
too hard a task for a man of such an advanced
age; and all the virtues of Firoze could not
preserve him from treachery and violence combined : he was put to death A. H. 695*, and
Alla o' dien, his nephew and son-in-law, succeeded him.

Alla o'dien was a man of prodigious ambition
and strong passions and talents, a great warrior
and financier, and exact in maintaining justice :
but his reign, from the beginning till his death,
was marked with cruelty and hardness of heart.
We may form an idea of his ambition by the two
projects which he formed in the early part of his
life. The first was to found a new religion to
immortalize his name, like Mahommed; and

* A. D. 1295.

the second to leave a viceroy in India, and to tread in the steps of Alexander the Great, after whom he called himself Secunder Sani*. But neither the people he governed, nor the state of his empire, permitted him actually to engage in either of these attempts. That he possessed no common energy of character is proved by the following anecdote. —Being totally illiterate when he ascended the throne, he observed that his courtiers, before him, abstained from literary conversation ; he therefore privately applied himself to learn, and in a few months wrote and read the Persian character with ease, when he called learned men to his court, and neglected nothing to encourage literature.

But his tyranny met with its reward in a general insurrection, headed by his unworthy favourite Cafoor, which increased the violence of an illness under which he then laboured, and he died A. H. 716†. During a few months, Cafoor, under the name of the late king's son Omar, governed ; but he was so universally detested, that the people saw with pleasure the throne occupied by Cottub o'dien Mobarric Shah, the eldest son of Alla.

---

* Alexander Second: this is the same name elsewhere written Iskander Thani, the difference being in the pronunciation of the various dialects in which the histories are written.

† A. D. 1316.

That infamous prince, and his still more infamous favourite and murderer, darkened the throne of India for five years, when Ghiaus o' dien Tugluck, a Patan, whose father had been brought up by Balin, was crowned by the acclamation of the people, and fully justified their choice. In matters of justice and police, and the encouragement of science, art, industry, and commerce, he revived the memory of the reign of Balin.

His son Jonah, afterwards sultan Mahommed III. was everywhere victorious in the Deccan, and carried his arms to Warankul and Telingana, which had, during the late disturbances, shaken off the Mussulman yoke; Bengal, which had continued an independent Mussulman government from the death of Balin, under the posterity of his son Kera, acknowledged anew the superiority of Togluck, by appealing to him from the abuses of its sovereigns, and he seemed to enjoy every prosperity, when, in A. H. 725* he was killed by the accidental falling in of the roof of a temporary house at Afghanpoor.

Mahommed III. was a brave prince, and generous beyond example, but his character was harsh and cruel. His conquests were generally followed by massacres, and frequently of Mus-

* A, D. 1324.

sulmans as well as Hindûs, although he kept up
the outward forms of religion with extreme
strictness. In his reign, the Moguls penetrated
nearly to Dehli; and to pay the royal coffers
for the sums which bought off the invaders, the
farmers were so severely taxed, that some burnt
their houses and crops in despair, many fled
to the forests, where they subsisted by robbery;
and these evils were further increased by issuing
base money of imaginary value. In these dis-
tressing circumstances, Mahommed hearing that
there were immense riches in China, formed
the mad project of invading that country; but
the army he raised for that purpose perished by
the way, and he was soon called to quell rebellions in the southern part of his dominion,
which continued to rage with little interruption
during the rest of the reign. To increase the
miseries of his subjects, the infatuated Mahommed took it into his head to transplant the whole
of the inhabitants of Dehli to Deoghir, which he
new named Dowlatabad, and thus desolated his
capital for the sake of forming a colony which
never succeeded, and which soon remained his
only possession in the Deccan; for some of the
Hindû princes, particularly Bullal Deo, the
builder of Bejanuggur, taking advantage of the
distraction of his empire, opposed his armies,
and drove them from some of his finest pro-

vinces. At length, A. H. 752*, this tyrannical reign of twenty-seven years closed, and Firoze, the nephew of Mahommed, succeeded him.

Muezzin Mohizeb Firoze Shah, is a name which might be canonized in India. He was not a great warrior by inclination; but there is not a single instance in which he did not put down rebellion and repel invasion, although he made no conquests. His pleasure was to educate his sons properly, and to improve his country. The following list of his public works is a sufficient panegyric.—" He built fifty great sluices, forty mosques, thirty schools, twenty caravansaras, a hundred palaces, five hospitals, a hundred tombs, ten baths, ten spires, one hundred and fifty wells, one hundred bridges, and gardens without number. His name is preserved in that of his city Firozeabad, and the remains of his canals are still to be traced. The only great severity of which he was guilty, was the punishing too signally a treacherous assassination. It is to be regretted that his old age was embittered by the loss of the worthiest of his children, and a rebellion against his son Mahommed, to whom he had resigned his empire. He died A. H. 791†.

Ghiaus o'dien Togluck, the grandson of

* A. D. 1351. † A. D. 1388.

Firoze, reigned after him but five months; his vices and cruelty having incensed the nobles, who put him to death, and raised Abu Becre, his cousin, to the throne. He remained on it but a year and six months, when his uncle Mahommed returning from the exile into which the party of Togluck had driven him, recovered the crown of his father; but during his reign, and that of his son Nussur o' dien Mahmoud, the miseries of the empire increased: civil war raged in all parts till A. H. 799*, when news reached the capital that Timur Beg, or Tamerlane, had crossed the Indus with an intention to conquer Hindostan†, when a temporary union of parties took place.

Meantime, in the reign of the tyrant Mahomet the Third, an independent kingdom had been founded in the Deccan. Houssun, an inhabitant of Dehli, was dependent on one Kangoh, a Brahmin and astrologer, a favourite of Mahmoud. This Brahmin gave Houssun a plough and a pair of oxen, with two labourers, to cultivate a waste piece of ground near Dehli, on his own account. While employed on his new farm, he found a pot of gold, which he carried to the Brahmin, who commending his honesty, took the gold, and flattered the youth, by pre-

* A. D. 1397.　† See Dow's History of Hindostan.

tending to predict that he should one day rule
over the Deccan, and begging him, in that
case, to add the name of Kangoh to his own;
and with this empty prophecy, he paid him for
his gold. The prediction, however, was one
which in such turbulent times are calculated to
work their own accomplishment. Accordingly,
Houssun having been appointed to the command of a hundred horse as a reward for his honesty in delivering the gold to his master, employed every resource of his powerful mind in
advancing toward his object; and at length,
having risen by his talents to a high command
in the army, he took advantage of the distractions of the empire under Mahommed, and
seized on the provinces of the Deccan.

On the first success of his rebellion, he had
the art to make it appear that he was made
king of Deccan, by the choice of the rebel
chiefs whom he had engaged to assist his views;
and being in a manner pressed to assume the
sovereignty, he changed his title of Ziffir Khan
for that of Alla o'dien Houssun Kangoh Bah-
manee, thus remembering his promise to his old
master who became his prime minister, being
the first Hindû who had served in a Mussulman
court. Deoghir, the modern Dowlatabad, the
Tagara of Ptolemy, had been the Hindû capital
of that part of India; but Alla o'dien fixed his

residence at the ancient Koolburga, which he new-named Ahssunabad.

The dynasty of Bhamanee kings founded by him in A. H. 748, or A. D. 1347, lasted two hundred years, when the natural weakness of the Mussulman monarchies was productive of its usual consequences in the division of the kingdom into five inferior monarchies, which were finally absorbed in the Mogul empire in the reign of Aurengzebe, about the year 1650*.

---

* Table of the Bhamanee kings of Deckan from Scot's Ferishta:

	A. H.	A. D.
Sultan Alla o'dien Kangoh Bhamanee	748	1347
Mahommed Shah Bhamanee	759	1357
Mujahid Shah Bhamanee	776	1374
Daoud Shah Bhamanee, (son of Alla o'dien)	779	1377
Mahmoud, (another son of Alla o'dien¹)	779	1377
Ghiause o'dien Bhamanee	799	1396
Shumse o'dien, (brother of Ghiause)	799	1396
Abu'l Muzzuffir ul Ghazi Sultaun Firoze Roze'af'zoon	800	1397
Ahmed Shah Wallee (brother of Abu'l Muzuffir)	825	1422
Alla o'dien II	838	1434
Houmaioun Shah Zelim, surnamed the Cruel	862	1457
Nizam Shah	865	1460

¹ It was to visit this prince who was a patron of learned men, if not himself among their number, that Hafiz left Schiraze to go to India; but after embarking, a tempest forced him back to port, which, with the other disagreeable circumstances incident to being at sea when not accustomed to it, determined him never to quit his native country again.

Shumse'o'dien

Timur Leng, or, as he is called by Europeans, Tamerlane, is said by some authors to have been

	A.H.	A.D.
Shumse'o'dien wa o'Doonia Abul Nussur ul Ghazee Mahummed Shah	867	1462
Mhamoud Shah	887	1482
Ahmud Shah	923	1518
Alla o'dien III	927	1520

Kulaeen oolla the last of the Bhamanee kings of Deckan.

Of the five distinct kingdoms into which the Deckany empire was afterwards divided, the Adhel Shahee or kingdom of Beejapoor is the most interesting to Europeans, as the first transactions of Europeans in the East took place in that province; of which the famous city of Bejapoor or Visiapoor now in ruins was the capital. It was separated from the Bhamanee empire during the reign of Mhamoud Shah at the same time with the kingdom of Ahmednuggur, whose rulers are known by the title of the Nizam Shahee dynasty. The Adil Shahs were:

	A.H.	A.D.
Yusuf Adil Shah	895	1489
Ismael Adil Shah	915	1509
Mulloo Adil Shah	941	1534
Abu'l Nussur Ibrahim Adil Shah	941	1534
Abu'l Muzzuffir Ali Adil Shah	965	1557
Abu'l Muzzuffir Ibrahim Adil Shah	988	1579

Here Ferishta who was the cotemporary of Abu'l Muzzuffir ends his history of the Deckan, but according to the Leb al Tarikh, his successors were:

	A.H.	A.D.
Mhamoud Adil Shah	1036	1626
Ali Adil Shah II	1071	1660
Secunder Adil Shah	1083	1672

In whose reign Aurengzebe or Alumgeer took possession of the kingdom of Bejapoor, excepting the mountains and maritime

parts

the son of a Tartar shepherd, and by others his descent is traced from the same noble family as that of Genghis Khan : when the manners of the nation are considered, it will not appear impossible that both accounts may be true; the Tartars live as the ancient patriarchs and the modern Arabs, without fixed habitations, but remove their villages or camps as the season, caprice, or

parts which had been seized by the Mahratta Sevagee, and annexed it to the Great Mogul empire A. H. 1097, A. D. 1685.

The succession of the Nizam Shahee kings of Ahmednuggur began with Beheree, whose son, however, first actually assumed the crown; this son was

	A.H.	A.D.
Ahmed Nizam Shah	895	1489
Boorehan Nizam Shah	914	1508
Houssein Nizam Shah	961	1553
Moortiza Nizam Shah	970	1562
Meeraun Houssein Nizam Shah, (a suicide)	996	1587
Ismael Nizam Shah	997	1588
Boorahan Shah	1004	1595

This prince was the father of Ismael whom he succeeded, and the son of Moortiza Nizam Shah; he was taken prisoner by the Moguls in his capital Ahmednuggur, and sent to the fortress of Gualior, the Spandau of Asia. After this disaster a slave, Unber, under the name and by the authority of Moortiza the Second, governed with great ability, and preserved the kingdom in peace during his administration, which he employed in public works of utility and magnificence. Among these he built the town of Aurungabad or Gurkeh, and greatly improved and beautified Dowlatabad where he was buried, A. H. 1035. His son Futteh succeeded to his dignities under Moortiza and his son Houssein; but the Moguls having at length taken

Dowlatabad,

the convenience of feeding their flocks and herds may dictate. The constant disputes that, in such a state of society, must arise on account of the best pasture, or the most plentiful springs, the necessity of vigilance to guard the camps from the attacks of neighbouring hordes, or of wild beasts, maintain a warlike spirit and martial habits among the people; and, as the prince is dis-

Dowlatabad,-Houssein was sent to Gualior, and Futteh being insane was allowed to retire to Lahore.

The kingdom of Golcondah was not torn from the Bhamanee sovereigns till nearly eighty years after those of Bejapoor and Ahmednuggur. Its monarchs are known by the name of the Koottub Shahs. The first of whom was

	A. H.	A. D.
Koolli Koottub Shah	918	1512
Jumsheed Koottub Shah	955	
Ibrahim Koottub Shah	962	
Mahommed Koolli Koottub Shah..................	989	1581
Mahmoud Koottub Shah		
Abdalla Koottub Shah		
Abu Houssein Koottub Shah		

This last prince was taken prisoner by Aurungzebe, who confined him in the fortress of Dowlatabad, and annexed his kingdom to the Mogul empire.

The other two kingdoms which were founded on the ruins of the Bhamanee monarchy of Deckan, were those of the Bereed and Ummaid Shahees, the first of whom reigned over a small district of which Beder was the capital; but the dynasty produced only three sovereigns. And the latter ruled a small part of Berar, but during the reign of the fourth Ummaid Shah, these two petty kingdoms were swallowed up in the Mogul empire.

tinguished from his followers by no external mark of dignity, the appellation of a Tartar shepherd might well apply to the noble relation of the great Khan.

At the age of twenty-six, Timur married the daughter of a powerful emir, who was tributary to Togatimur, a descendant of Zagathai, the son of Genghis.   His first conquest was that of the city of Balkh, in the year of the Hegira 771*, from which time he reigned absolutely over the countries to the east of the Oxus. Ten years afterwards he crossed that river, invaded Khorassan and Georgia, and A. H. 790† he had traversed Persia as far as Schiraz, whence, however, he was recalled to defend his own capital, which was disturbed by insurrections, and at the same time attacked by foreign tribes, in pursuit of some of whom he advanced so far towards the north, that the sun did not set for forty days. Five years after his attack of Schiraz, he sent his son Miram Shah with a powerful army into Khorassan, and his grandson Pir Mahommed through Cabul and Ghazna to India, while he himself took the road to Baghdad, which he entirely ruined, and destroyed its inhabitants.   A. H. 800‡, Tamerlane turned his arms towards India; and having taken many

----

* A. D. 1353.   † A. D. 1387.   ‡ A. D. 1396.

of the mountain fortresses towards the North, while Pir Mahommed entered the country by the western provinces, he gave battle to Sultaun Mahommed in the following year, nearly in sight of Dehli, which was instantly seized and pillaged by the Tartars, who massacred its inhabitants, and left it in ashes, to proceed farther towards the East. Tamerlane led his victorious troops to the banks of the Ganges, at Toglipoor, where he crossed the river, and then marched northwards upon the left bank to the Straits of Kupele, where the flood bursts through the mountains upon the plains of Hindostan; and where, at that time, a multitude of pilgrims of all nations were assembled, in reverence to the holy stream. Mistaking the crowd of devotees for an army intending to oppose them, the Tartars fell upon them, and were for a short time vigorously repulsed; but the pilgrims were at length overcome, and Tamerlane, perhaps, ashamed of his victory, returned by the mountains to Samarkand, receiving on his way the homage of the king of Cashmere; and this was the only time he visited India, where Pir Mahommed continued, however, to make some conquests. It was only three years after this expedition that Tamerlane made the famous incursion into Syria and Natolia, took Aleppo and Damascus, and summoned Bajazet to abandon the siege of Constantinople; but that proud conqueror rejected his summons with disdain, and prepared to oppose his farther progress towards the West; but he was soon overcome, and taken prisoner by Tamerlane, who, according to some authors, treated him with generosity, and according to others with savage barbarity, shutting him up in an iron cage, and carrying him with his camp equipage in all his expeditions. But Bajazet did not long survive his capture; his death happened in the following year.

While Tamerlane was thus occupied, his grandson, Pir Mahommed, whom he had left to govern India, was assassinated*, and his son, sultan Sharoch, succeeded to the throne of Ghazna, on which he sat forty-two years. Tamerlane, however, beginning to feel the infirmities of age, resolved to close his career with a solemn festival. He, therefore, returned to Samarkand, and on an extensive plain near that city, he erected splendid pavillions, where there was feasting for sixty days. All classes and orders were assembled, the different artisans appeared with the insignia of their trades, and the royal armies passed in review before the monarch, whose court was crowded with ambassa-

---

* A. D. 1404.

dors, not only from the Asiatic sovereigns, but, according to some authors, those of Manuel Paleologus, and of Henry the Third, king of Castile, were present; and on the last day of this great festival, Tamerlane caused the marriages of all the princes and princesses of the royal house to be celebrated. This was the last public act of Timur, for, the next year, having marched towards the frontiers of China, he was taken ill at Otrar in Turkestan, where he died in his seventy-first year, A. H. 807.

Such is the outline of the history of Tamerlane, in whom all the qualities of a conqueror were united, and who, on many occasions, shewed that he possessed also a generosity and magnanimity worthy of his high situation. His written institutes concerning government and war, could be the production of no mean genius. But the barbarity of untamed nature rendered his brilliant course destructive as the wild tornado; and the only monuments that remained of his race, were ruined cities, surrounded by the whitening bones of their slaughtered inhabitants. Such, at least, were the traces of his rapid journey through the north of Hindostan, where his descendants were destined to feel every reverse of fortune, from the throne to the prison, and from the royal feast to the poisoned chalice.

The sovereign who reigned at Dehli when
Tamerlane invaded India, was, as I have already
mentioned, Sultan Mahmoud III. who had ascended the throne in his infancy, and whose
long and imbecile reign was filled with all the
disorders incident to a declining empire. Several sovereigns, supported by different parts of
the army, set themselves up in different provinces, and the ambition of the ministers gratified
itself at the expence of the interests of the state
and of its master. At length, the Seid Khizer
seized the reins of government, and seated himself on the Patan throne; and, after a turbulent reign of seven years, he died lamented
by his subjects. His son, Moaz o'dien Abul
Futteh sultan Mubarric Shah, succeeded him,
of whom Ferishta says, " he reigned thirteen
years: he was esteemed a man of parts, just,
and benevolent, and though no great warrior,
had he lived in a virtuous age, there is no
doubt but he possessed talents which might
render him worthy of the throne." His nephew, the murderer of Mahommed the Fifth,
with his son Alla II. occupied the throne,
the first during twelve, and the latter during
twenty-seven years, most unworthily, when Belloli, an Afghan of the commercial tribe of
Loudi, whose family had for some generations
distinguished itself, spread the royal umbrella

over his head, and marked his contempt for Alla by allowing him to govern a small district for twenty-eight years.

None ever deserved to wear the crown better than Belloli, both by his public and private virtues; and could any thing in those times of anarchy have restored Hindostan to a state either of dignity or prosperity, it would have been the reigns of such princes as himself and his son Secunder I. the first of which lasted thirty-eight years, and the latter but ten years less. But the son of Secunder disgraced his family; and during the twenty years that his weak and wicked administration lasted, all the horrors of civil war and assassination distracted the country, so that, at length, the nobles invited Baber Shah, of the house of Tamerlane, from Cabul, and placed him on the throne, so justly forfeited by Ibrahim Loudi. But the empire of Dehli was no longer the same that flourished under Balin or Nussur o'dien Mahommed. The province of Bengal was completely separated from it; the rich countries of the Deccan were the seat of another empire: Guzerat did not even nominally acknowledge the sovereigns of Dehli; and the mountain tribes of Patans were too turbulent to see tamely a Mogul dominion established, where they had for so many centuries borne the sway.

The provinces which Baber received were
those of Multan, Lahore, Dehli, Agra, Ajmere,
and Oude. A very small part of Bahar belonged even nominally to the kingdom of Dehli,
and the deserts of Ajmere contained few subjects, and those few it could scarcely support.
Still the empire was a prize worth contending
for; but it required the talents and the perse-
verance of Baber to establish even the shadow
of regal authority, where anarchy had so long
prevailed.

The family of Baber shall be the subject
of another letter: not that I mean it to be so
long as this; but I have been sometimes tempted
to dwell a little longer than I intended on the
reigns of some of the Patans, rather as a study
of human nature in a state of society, where
both the good and the bad appear in very high
relief, than because these reigns had any permanent influence on the state of India. Where
the system of government is so absolutely vicious, that its interior administration as well as
external policy, is dependent on the arbitrary
will of one man, whether weak and wicked, or
of a firm and virtuous character, the effects of
the longest and most beneficent reign, are
quickly obliterated; and the wisest institutions
and laws are subverted in a moment, by the
passions of a weak, or the cruelties of a tyranni-

cal prince. Thus the general tendency of such
governments is to decay; and it is only when
anarchy has risen to its height, and some vigorous genius who can be both a conqueror and a
legislator, enforces a temporary calm, that man
is allowed a little breathing time to recover
strength for new exertions, and but too certainly for new sufferings. Such, in few words,
has been the Mahommedan history of India.
Of the institutions which made its native monarchies more respectable and more stable, we
know too little; and of its present state, just
recovering from the horrors of long and cruel
wars, it is not fair to judge.

LETTER XII.

THERE is no prince whose life can be
better authenticated than that of Zeher o'dien
Mahommed Baber Shah, for he has written his
own memoirs in a style accounted elegant by
those most conversant in eastern literature, and
in a manner that shews him to have been a consummate general and an able politician at least
towards the latter part of his life. He was the
sixth in descent from the great Tamerlane, and
was born A. H. 888*. At the early age of

* A. D. 1472.

twelve years his father Seik Omar, king of
Firghana and Indija, part of the inheritance of
Timur, entrusted to him the government of Indija, depending entirely on his extraordinary
abilities, and Omar being accidentally killed
about the same time Baber, succeeded to the
whole kingdom. His uncles, jealous of his abilities, and thinking that the dominions of a child
would be easily seized, marched against him but
were repulsed, as were various other princes who
made the same attempts. When Baber had
reached the age of fifteen, having saved his own
dominions he thought of invading those of
others, and accordingly marched against the
king of Samarkand, and the same year took that
capital, but gave great offence to his army by
refusing to permit any plunder. This clemency
was at that time so detrimental to his interests,
that the greater part of his troops abandoned
him, and while he was possessing himself of
Samarkand, his own capital Indija was wrested
from him. On his march to regain Indija the
Samarkandians revolted, so that he found himself with a very small body of troops without a
kingdom, and retreating from place to place
without however losing courage or hope.

His fortune, which never remained long
either wholly good or bad, restored to him at
different times both Indija and Samarkand, but

his possession of either lasted but for a few months, so that at the age of twenty he found himself obliged to abandon his native country, and as the unsettled state of Cabul offered the fairest opening to his ambition, he marched thither, and two years afterwards established himself on the throne of that kingdom. This in all his future fortunes was the province most strongly attached to him, for he had won the hearts of the inhabitants by the patience and generosity with which he applied himself to relieve the miseries caused by a dreadful earthquake, which A. D. 1504 desolated that country.

It was in the year of the Hegira 925[*] that Baber first crossed the Indus, on the invitation of some of the nobles of Hindostan, who in the troubles of that unhappy time turned their eyes towards Baber for relief. But it was not until six years afterwards that he took possession of Lahore, and the next year marched to Dehli. Before he reached that capital Ibráhim met him with a large army, and a fierce engagement ensued, in which it is said that sixteen thousand Patans with Ibráhim himself were killed on the field. The Moguls immediately took possession of the capital, and the Kootba[†] was read in the

[*] A. D. 1517.

[†] The Kootba is the solemn declaration of the lineage and titles

chief mosque in the name of Baber.   He went
after the ceremony to visit the tombs of the
saints and heroes round the city, and thence to
Agra, which quietly opened its gates to the new
monarch, whose progress was marked by clemency and indulgence.

Thus Hindostan was subdued by a stranger
with a handful of men.   Ferishta says, " to what
then can we attribute this extraordinary conquest in a natural light but to the great abilities
and experience of Baber, and the bravery of his
few hardy troops, trained to war for their subsistence, and now fired with the hopes of glory
and gain?   But what contributed most to weigh
down the scale of conquest was the degeneracy
of the Patans, effeminated by luxury and wealth,
and dead to all principles of virtue and honour,
which their corrupt factions and civil discord
had wholly effaced; it being now no shame to
fly, no infamy to betray, no breach of honour
to murder, and no scandal to change parties.
When, therefore, the fear of shame and the love
of fame were gone, it was no wonder that a
herd without unanimity, order or discipline,
should fall into the hands of a few brave men."

titles of a monarch, after which the royal umbrella is spread
over their heads.   The emperors of Dehli were never crowned,
but on occasions of state the diadem was suspended over their
heads from the state canopy.

Such also was the end of the Roman empire, and such must be the termination of all despotic governments where there is wealth enough to corrupt the people, without laws to restrain the prince.

But the Patans did not tranquilly at once re-sign the empire; the reign of Baber was con-tinually harrassed by insurrections in different provinces, and at one period his fortune appear-ed so desperate that his chiefs advised him to retreat to Cabul. But his constancy overcame all obstacles; and his kingdom was beginning to enjoy a little more tranquillity, when in his fifty-first year he died*, leaving behind him the fame of a great warrior, unsullied with a single cruelty, and the reputation of being the wonder of the age in which he lived.

The character drawn of him by Ferishta is one of those which we contemplate with mingled respect and affection. " He so often pardoned ingratitude and treason that he seemed to make a principle of returning good for evil. He thus disarmed vice, and made the wicked the wor-shippers of his virtue. He was of the sect of the Haunafies†, in whose tenets and doctrines

* A. D. 1530. A. H. 937.

† A branch of the great sect of the Sunnies, who maintain the authority of the four first Kalifs. The Sheas respect only Ali.

he was perfectly versed; yielding more to the evidence of reason than to the marvellous legends of superstitious antiquity. He was not however forgetful of that rational worship which is due to the great creator, nor a despiser of those laws and ceremonies which are founded on sound policy for the benefit of the superficial judges of things. He was a master of the arts of poetry, writing, and music."

The historian adds that he was fond of pleasure, though moderate in its enjoyment; and that he was equally celebrated for his clemency, courage and justice. As an instance of the latter, he relates that a caravan from China having been buried in the snow in crossing the mountains of Indija, he caused the goods to be collected, and sent notice to China of what had happened, that the owners or heirs might claim their property, which he restored them, refusing even to be reimbursed for his expences.

Houmaioun, called also Nussur o'dien Mahommed, succeeded his father on the throne of India, but the Patans soon disturbed the tranquillity of his kingdom, and in this they were aided by the treachery and short-sighted policy of the brothers of Houmaioun. After twelve years of civil war, and encountering every reverse of fortune, sometimes a wanderer in the sandy desert, with scarcely an attendant, at

2

others at the head of a promising army, the son
of Baber was obliged to fly for protection and
safety to the court of Shah Thamasp, the second
of the Suffee dynasty of Persia. Of the sufferings of this prince and his little band of Moguls
the following incident may give an idea.
" On the fourth day of their retreat, they fell in
with another well which was so deep, that the
only bucket they had, took a great deal of time
in being wound up, and therefore a drum was
beat to give notice to the people when the
bucket appeared, that they might repair by
turns to drink. The unhappy men were so impatient for the water, that as soon as the first
bucket appeared ten or twelve threw themselves
upon it before it quite reached the brim of the
well, by which means the rope broke, the bucket
was lost, and several fell headlong after it.
When this fatal accident happened the screams
and lamentations of all became loud and dreadful, some, lolling out their tongues, rolled themselves in agony on the hot sand ; while others
precipitating themselves into the well met with
an immediate and consequently an easier death!"

Meantime Ferid an Afghan, commonly called
Shere, ascended the throne of Dehli. He appears to have been a man of extraordinary talents and a hardy warrior. But although capable
of the most generous actions, he was on many

occasions cruel and vindictive. He was one of the most treacherous politicians that history has recorded, but he maintained public justice throughout his kingdom, and punished all deceits but his own. The monuments of his magnificence and care of the public remain. He built caravanseras for travellers of every sect and religion, at every stage from Bengal to the Indus, a distance of three thousand miles; and planted rows of fruit trees along the road for the accommodation of the passengers. He was the first who established horse-posts in India, for the forwarding intelligence to government, and for the convenience of commerce; and in his reign the public safety was such that the traveller rested and slept with his goods on the high-road in perfect security. He was killed by the bursting of a shell at the seige of Chitore, after a reign of five years*, and his eldest son Adil succeeded him; but before the ceremony of inauguration took place, that timid prince gave up his title to Selim his younger brother, whose qualities though much inferior had a great resemblance to his father's. He died, after a turbulent reign of seven years, A. H. 960†.

The vices of his brother-in-law and successor Mahomed Adil soon distracted the kingdom

---

* A. D. 1545. A. H. 952.　　　† A. D. 1552.

anew; and several other sovereigns assumed the diadem, but Ibrahim the third is the only one regularly mentioned as emperor by the historians. Thus the Patan rulers again lost that credit which the vigorous reign of Shere had recovered for them, and Houmaioun, who had during the last thirteen years been residing a fugitive in the court of Persia, seized the opportunity of regaining the empire of Dehli, in which enterprise he was signally aided by Byram or Bahran, the tutor of his son Akbar.

Secunder, nephew of Shere, who had assumed the imperial titles at Agra, was now at the head of the Patans, and did all that prudence and valour could do to preserve the empire. But the battle of Serhind in which the troops of Houmaioun, with those of Byram and several Tartar and Mogul tribes were commanded by himself, assisted by the young prince Akbar and his tutor, was decisive of the fate of Dehli, and destroyed for ever the Patan power. This battle took place A. H. 962*, and by its success Houmaioun once more became emperor of India. But he did not long enjoy his crown, for in the following year he fell down the marble stairs of his library and died in his fifty-first year. He was a prince of great personal bravery,

* A. D. 1554.

and possessed many accomplishments and virtues; the characteristic mildness and humanity
of his family were most conspicuous in him, and
on some occasions were carried to an excess
that bordered upon weakness.

Shah Jumja, Abul Muzuffir, Jellal o'dien,
Mahommed Akbar Padshah Ghazi, commonly
called Akbar Shah, succeeded to his father,
A. H. 963 *. The unsettled state in which
Houmaioun had left the empire required all the
talents and resolution, and perhaps all the harsh-
ness of Byram, Akbar's tutor, and all the bravery
and gentleness of the young prince, to reduce
to any kind of order the discordant and turbulent members of which it was composed. The
first orders which were issued were in that spirit
which distinguished the reign of Akbar, and
rendered it a kind of golden age to the inhabitants of Hindostan. These orders prohibited
the exaction of the present-money on the accession of the new sovereign from the farmers, they
likewise prevented the pressing labourers for the
wars, and permitted all goods to pass from place
to place toll free.

But Akbar was soon called to less pacific
duties; the Patan chiefs still raised partial insurrections, some of which were quelled by the

* A. D. 1555.

timely severity of Byram, and others disarmed
by the clemency of Akbar. The minister, however, having tasted the sweets of power, knew
not how to resign it as his pupil advanced in
age, and being offended at the prince's endeavours to emancipate himself, he imprudently
took up arms against him, under pretence of
a pilgrimage to Mecca, but was soon overcome. Akbar invited him with kindness to return to him, and when the old man threw himself at the foot of the throne, he took him by
the hand, raised him and throwing a robe of
state over him, placed him in his former situation at the head of the nobles. " If" said Akbar, " the lord Byram loves a military life, he
shall have the government of Calpe and Chin-
deri, in which he may exercise his martial genius: if he rather chooses to remain at court,
our favour shall not be wanting to the great
benefactor of our family ; but should devotion
engage the soul of Byram to perform a pilgrimage to Mecca, he shall be escorted in a manner
suitable to his dignity." Byram chose the pilgrimage, and Akbar gave him a suitable retinue
and 50,000 rupees a year, or something more
than £6,000, to support him. He was unfortunately murdered, with his guard, by some of
the Afghans of the family of Loudi.

After this temporary storm, the interior of

Akbar's kingdom regained such a portion of tranquillity that agriculture, manufactures, and commerce, which had declined during the troubles that preceded and accompanied the downfall of the Patan monarchy, began to flourish. The emperor turned his thoughts to the improvement of his people; and while he employed the valour of his sons and the Patan and Hindû chiefs on the frontiers, sometimes as a guard against incursions from the north, and sometimes with a view to conquest towards the south, he, with his minister, the learned Abul Fazil, was employed in regulating the economy of the state; in procuring information concerning the different provinces, with their produce and revenue, and in framing regulations of public justice and utility. Schools were established in various parts of the empire, in which both the Indian and Arabic sciences were taught. Translations of works both of utility and elegance were made at the command of Akbar, and under the eye of Abul Fazel, whose brother Feizee was not only a great warrior, but one of the most learned men of Hindostan. In short, the government of Akbar shewed what advantage a virtuous prince may derive from despotic power, to do good; but, alas! all despots are not Akbars; and that excellent king died after a reign of fifty-one years, in the year of the Hegira 1014*, leaving his people in tears, for his kindness towards them had been as remarkable as his justice; and it is difficult to say whether he was most admired, loved, or respected.

His personal valour equalled that of the ancient heroes of the poets; his magnificence was suited to the greatness of his situation and the prejudices of his people; and his activity enabled him to see with his own eyes the state of his kingdom, and at the same time kept rebels in awe.

In a former letter I sent you Abu Fazel's account of the provinces which formed the empire of Akbar. His revenues received into the exchequer amounted to about thirty millions sterling; and from other accidental sources he derived anually about twenty millions more †. His armies consisted of about three hundred thousand horse, and as many foot. These immense resources account for his being able to defend, and even to enlarge, so extensive a frontier. At the same time, the constitution of those armies which were formed of detached tribes under independent chiefs rendered it difficult, if not impossible, to prevent rebellions, and afforded every facility for the factious or the ambitious.

* A. D. 1605.
† Dow's History of Hindostan, p. 2, vol. III.

The death of Akbar closes the history of Firishta : his successors have been less fortunate in the writers of their lives, but materials are not wanting for a modern history of Hindostan; and Dow, the translator of Ferishta, seems to have availed himself with ability of these resources.

On the death of Akbar, a faction at court endeavoured to place Khosru, the son of Selim, Akbar's only surviving son, on the throne; but their designs were defeated, and Selim, under the title of Jehanghire, or conqueror of the world, succeeded to the crown of Hindostan. The friends of Khosru, rather than his own dispositions, led him then into an open rebellion, which was soon suppressed, and the prince was imprisoned, and many years afterwards was murdered by his brother, Shah Jehan, who himself was more than once engaged in rebellions against his father. The person whose influence was most felt in this reign, was Mirh ul Nussur, afterwards Noor Mahl, the wife of Jehanghire. She was the daughter of Aiass, a Tartar, whose poverty obliged him to fly his country, and was born in the wilderness, under circumstances of peculiar misfortune. Aiass's talents and probity soon raised him into notice at the court of Akbar, and his daughter having been educated with the greatest care, became one of the most

R

accomplished women of her age, as well as the most beautiful. The young prince, Selim, became so enamoured of her, that he begged Akbar to demand her in marriage, but that monarch refused to commit so great an injustice, for she had been promised to Shere Afkhun, one of the bravest and most accomplished nobles of India. When Selim mounted the throne, his first care was to obtain Mirh ul Nussur, and for that purpose there was no meanness to which he did not descend, till at length the brave and prudent Shere Afkhun was assassinated, and his widow carried to the royal Zenana. It was some time, however, before Jehanghire saw her: but at length, when his conscience had a little forgotten the means by which he obtained her, her favour became unbounded, and her father and brothers were immediately raised to the first offices in the empire, and their relations from Tartary immediately flocked to the Mogul court to partake the fortune of the house of Aiass. That excellent man, under the name of Actemâd ul Dowlah, exercised the office of prime minister till his death, in such a manner that his name is to this day revered by the people of Hindostan; and his whole family, by their merits, seemed to have deserved their elevation. This reign was, as to the interior of the kingdom, most prosperous: forests were cut down, and towns and villages built; manufactures flourished, and agriculture was particularly encouraged. Provinces which had been desolated by war were repeopled and cultivated, and justice was done equally to the Hindû and Mussulman. The Mogul empire was so respected, that the court was crowded with ambassadors, among whom an English envoy from James I. who presented a coach to Jehanghire, was one of the most favoured; and in spite of the opposition of the prince royal, he obtained the object of his mission, which was leave to establish a factory at Surat.

But in the meantime, the martial habits of the nobles, whenever they were unemployed in foreign wars, broke out in rebellions, sometimes headed by Shah Jehan, the prince royal, at others by different nobles; but most of them were owing to the intrigues of Noor Mahl, whose active and overbearing spirit could brook no rival in the sultan's favour.

Jehanghire died A. H. 1037*, at Mutti, half way between Lahore and Cashmere, for which kingdom he had set out, to enjoy the beauty and coolness of its valley during the hot months, it being his custom to perform every year a journey to some part of his dominions.

* A. D. 1627.

This monarch had the reputation of being a deist, because he protected the followers of Brahma and Zoroaster, and even tolerated Christains as well as Mussulmans. He was most rigorous in administering justice, punishing even those he loved, without regard to greatness of situation or office. He was completely free from avarice, and his disposition was forgiving. In private, his temper was capricious, so much so, indeed, as to bear occasionally the character of insanity, with which malady his unfortunate son Khosru was certainly afflicted. He was naturally indolent, and indulged much in wine and opium; but he was fond of literature, and has left a well-written life of himself. So well known and so well beloved was he, that he frequently left his palace in a simple habit, and mixed with the evening parties of every rank; his person was too well known to be disguised, but he never had reason to repent of his familiarity with his people.

On the death of Jehanghire, several parties were formed, each with a different view, to prevent the accession of Shah Jehan; but, by the assistance of his father-in-law, Asiph Jah, who was brother to the favourite sultana of his father, that prince overcame them all, but unlike the merciful dispositions of the former sultans of the house of Timur, he put to death every one of the male descendants of Baber but himself and his four sons; and to make the people forget this cruelty, he held a festival, which surpassed in magnificence every thing of the kind that had ever been witnessed in the East. However, the virtues he displayed during a reign of thirty years formed the best veil he could throw over the crimes of his advancement. His justice and vigilance secured the happiness of his subjects, and his gratitude for services insured the lives and fortunes of those who grew great in the state.

It was Shah Jehan's peculiar fortune to have, in the beginning of his reign, the ablest vizier and the most consummate general that had flourished under the family of Timur. Asiph Jah, his father-in-law, inherited the virtues and abilities of Aiass, and ruled the empire almost despotically till his death, which happened in his seventy-second year. The general Mohabet, who had served Jehanghire, and his son Khan Ziman, were the military ornaments of the first years of Shah Jehan; but the death of the latter, shortly after that of his father, would have been a more serious loss to the empire, but for the rising geniuses of the four princes, sons of Shah Jehan, by his wife Mamtaza Zemânee. She was the daughter of Asiph Jah, and by her gentle disposition, her virtues, and her beauties, had acquired an almost unlimited influence over her husband, who, during her life, had no other wife, and after her death built that splendid monument to her memory, which has excited the wonder and admiration of all who have visited Agra, and where he himself was afterwards buried by his son Aurengzebe*.

The Mogul dominions were considerably enlarged during the reign of Shah Jehan. The whole of Bengal was entirely subdued; the states of Asem and Thibet were kept in awe. Under Aurengzebe, his third son, the frontier towards the Decan had been extended towards the north; Candahar was recovered; Cashmire was governed by a viceroy from Dehli; Guzerat was entirely reduced to obedience; and, with the exception of a famine which, A. H. 1043 †, desolated Hindostan, the interior of the kingdom enjoyed as perfect a state of prosperity as it is possible for human affairs to attain. But the time was approaching when this tranquillity was to be disturbed; and for the eventful period of the civil wars which terminated the reign of Shah Jehan, and preceded that of Aurengzebe, we have not only the testimony of native writers

* That beautiful tomb, constructed of fine marble, and inlaid with precious stones, is called the Taje Mahl; it cost £750,000.

† A. D. 1613.

but the recital of an eye-witness, the traveller Bernier, who, as physician to one of the Mogul nobles, resided twenty-two years at the court of Dehli.

The extraordinary qualities of the sons of Shah Jehan were the primary cause of those disturbances which terminated in the elevation of Aurengzebe and the murder of his brothers. Dara appears to have been one of the most accomplished of princes: although a Mussulman, he retained in his pay several Hindû Pundits, who instructed him in the ancient learning of the country; and from the Jesuits, whom he pensioned handsomely, and whose college was not among the meanest buildings at Agra, he became acquainted with European science. Like all the princes of the house of Baber, he was well versed in the literature of Persia and Arabia; and few men in his time surpassed him in the manly exercises, and in the qualities of a warrior or a courtier. At the same time he was frank and generous almost to imprudence; and the elegance of his address, and the beauty of his person, rendered him the favourite of the people. His eldest sister, Jehanara, partook of his qualities in an eminent degree; and those two were, of all Shah Jehan's children, the most remarkable for filial piety, and for affection towards each other.

Sultan Sujah, the second son of the king, had many of Dara's good qualities, and he was infinitely more prudent, but he was too fond of pleasure.

Aurengzebe was perhaps a greater warrior than either of his brothers; he certainly was more adapted for intrigue, but he possessed neither the beauty, the address, nor the sincerity of those princes. He was an excellent dissembler, and had a peculiar faculty of discovering the characters and dispositions of others, so as to bring them insensibly over to his own purposes. To cloak his ambition, which early aspired to the throne, he affected the habits of a Fakir or dervise, and used religion as a mask to all his designs. His sister, Roshenara Begum, resembled him in disposition, and what authority she possessed in the harem was employed for him.

Morâd was the fourth son of Shah Jehan. In his openness and sincerity he resembled Dara; in his courage he surpassed all his brothers; but he was impatient and passionate to excess. He was extremely beloved by the people, and for that reason he was for a time courted by Aurengzebe.

With four such sons, Shah Jehan felt an anxiety natural to one who, to secure his own throne, had murdered every male in his family, and was

therefore particularly careful to cause such respect to be paid to Dara, as he hoped would
smooth his way to the empire after his own
death*. To this end he associated him with
himself in the kingdom, and caused respect to
be paid to the signet of Dara equal to that paid
to his own. Sujah at the same time was made
governor of Bengal. Aurengzebe had the command of the southern provinces, and Morad,
with a powerful army, ruled in Guzerat.

In the year of the Hegira, 1067†, Shah Jehan was seized with a paralytic stroke, and continued for some time in such a state of weakness,
that the whole government was administered by
Dara. The three other princes being apprized
of this, and each expecting that ere they could
reach Delhi their father would have breathed his
last, determined to march towards the capital,
and contest the crown with Dara. Solimân
Shekoh, the son of Dara, immediately set out,
at the head of an imperial army, to oppose Sujah, who was rapidly advancing from Bengal,
and defeated him near Benares, when he fled

* On the birth of Dara's first son, Shah Jehan mounted
the famous peacock throne, valued at £1,000,000. On each
side was a peacock, whose spread tail was formed of coloured
jewels, and there was at the top a parroquet of the natural size,
cut out of a single emerald.

† A.D. 1657.

back to his government to raise new forces. Meantime Aurengzebe had marched from the Deccan, and was joined by Morad with his troops from Guzerat at Brampoor. Meer Jumla* was also, by the artifices of that crafty prince, brought over to his party; and these united forces soon overcame the resistance offered on the banks of the Nerbudda by the Maharaja Jeswunt Singh, and marched on towards Agra. There they were met by Dara, and victory seemed for some time doubtful, till Dara was forced to dismount from his elephant from different accidents. The soldiers, no longer seeing him in his station, fled, and Aurengzebe gained a decided victory.

Dara fled to Dehli, and Aurengzebe by a stratagem got possession of Agra, and consequently of the person of his father†, but it was not yet

---

* Meer Jumla was a man of low origin, who by his talents had raised himself to great power, and acquired immense wealth under the Kootub Shahee Kings of Golconda. While Aurengzebe commanded in the Deccan, Meer Jumla, upon some affront from his sovereign, fled with his treasures to Aurengzebe, who prized his abilities, and, at that time, still more his riches and forces. He died of a fever in Arracán, where he had remained on an expedition during the rainy season.

† Shah Jehan was imprisoned in the fortress of Agra, where his companions were his daughter Jehanara, and his grand-daughter, the child of Dara. He died A. H. 1076. A. D. 1666. He was the first who departed from the mild character of the house of Baber by the murder of his relations,

and

time to seize the throne. Dara still had re-sources; and Morad, whom he had deceived by his appearance of piety, and to whom he had promised to yield all pretensions to the crown, on condition of receiving a hermitage for him-self, was still the favourite of the army, and at the head of a powerful body of his own friends. He therefore marched in pursuit of Dara, but on the way he seized and murdered Morad in his own tent, where that unsuspicious prince had accepted of a sumptuous entertainment. After this crime Aurengzebe marched to Delhi, and there mounted the imperial throne, but con-trived to have it forced upon him by his friends, and assumed the title of Alûmghire, or Con-queror of the World, in the year of the Hegira, 1068*.

Meanwhile the most unprecedented misfor-tunes pursued the unfortunate Dara, nor was his heroic son, Soliman Shekoh, more prosperous. Sujah had again collected an immense army, and to oppose him Aurengzebe marched from Dehli, and defeated him in an obstinate and bloody battle at Kedgwa, about thirty miles from Allahabad. This was the last serious opposition to the ambition of Aurengzebe. Morâd was al-

and he perhaps suffered more than any other prince from the same crimes in his son.

* A. D. 1658.

ready murdered. Dara, with his family, was a fugitive, enduring incredible hardships in the same desert where Houmaioun had before suffered. In consequence of these hardships, his beloved wife, Nadira Banû, the daughter of his uncle Parviz*, died at the residence of Jihon, a petty chief in the province of Bichar, west of the Indus. Jihon then seized Dara, and sent him, with his son, to Dehli. There he was mounted on a sorry elephant, and after parading through the streets, where every eye wept for him, he was confined in a miserable hut a few miles from the town, and basely murdered in the night by the orders of Aurengzebe, who is reported to have wept when he received the bloody head. But the war with Sujah was not entirely at an end, and a peculiar circumstance rendered it more vexatious to his brother than any he had waged. Mahommed, son of Aurengzebe, was tenderly attached to one of the daughters of Sujah, and being wrought upon by a letter from her, he left the camp of his father's general, Meer Jumla, and joined his uncle. However, this desertion did not change the fortune of the new emperor: Sujah was again defeated at Tanda, and fled to the mountains of Tipperah, after having dismissed Mahommed

* Murdered by Shah Jehan.

with his wife and jewels to a large amount. An artful letter from Aurengzebe to his son had excited the suspicions of the unfortunate prince, who could no longer bear to live with a man he had ceased to trust; but Mahommed, on his return to his father, was immediately imprisoned in Gualior, where he remained till his death. Many years elapsed before the fate of Sujah was known with certainty in Hindostan; but at length it was discovered that the Rajah of Arracan had caused him to be treacherously drowned; his two sons and twenty attendants were murdered by a party of the Rajah's troops; his wife and her two eldest daughters escaped from ignominy by suicide, and the youngest died of a broken heart immediately after her forced marriage with the murderer of her family.

Thus every obstacle to the ambition of Aurengzebe was removed; and if a wise and just government of his people could atone for an imprisoned father and three murdered brothers, that monarch might hope for pardon. He is said to have exhibited signs of sensibility on the catastrophe of his last brother, and perhaps he was sincere; for now that he was seated on the throne, and no longer under the impressions of either fear or jealousy, he had leisure to look round on the havock he had made, and it would be strange indeed if he could have contemplated it unmoved. Aurengzebe reigned fifty-two years with a reputation which few princes have surpassed. The tranquillity of that period was only disturbed by a transitory inclination to rebel, rather than a real rebellion, in his son Shah Allum, and a suspicion of a plot formed by the Persian nobles, with his vizier at their head, to dethrone him. This suspicion had made him resolve for two days on a general assassination of the Persians, but the prudence of the Princess Jehanara saved him from that dangerous cruelty.

The magnificence of Aurengzebe's court has made the splendour of the Mogul throne proverbial. Bernier, in particular, has given us a high idea of it; and as under his successors the empire was in a state of continued and rapid decline, I will stop one moment, before I finish my list of emperors, to give you some idea of what the Mogul court once was,

> Where the gorgeous East, with richest hand,
> Show'r'd on her kings barbaric pearl and gold.

An idea may be formed of the riches of the royal treasury of Dehli, when we remember that after many years of weak government, and both public and private disturbances, Nadir Shah, when he invaded India, carried with him from its capital above eighty millions sterling in gold and jewels. Aurengzebe's manner of passing his day has been minutely described by different authors, and I give you an abridged account of it as a picture of his character, of the manners of his court, and of the riches he possessed. His dress was simple, except on days of festivals, when he wore cloth of gold and jewels; and his private life was that of an anchoret, although he encouraged magnificence in his nobles, and required it in the governors of his provinces.

He rose every morning at day-break, and having bathed, he spent half an hour in his chapel, and the same time in reading before he went to dress. At seven o'clock he went to the chamber of justice, to hear appeals and to overlook the last decisions of the judges, a practice of the house of Timur. At that time the people had free access to him; the necessitous were often relieved by the king himself, who had a large sum of money lying on a bench beside him, and he was always ready to listen to their petitions. If a well-grounded complaint appeared against the greatest noble, Aurengzebe, at his next audience, put into his hand a written paper, containing the nature of his fault, and a dismissal from all his offices: he deprived him of his estates, and thus degraded, he was obliged to appear daily at the hall of audience, till being sufficiently punished he was gradually restored if worthy; if otherwise, sent into banishment. At nine o'clock the emperor retired to breakfast, and spent an hour with his family, after which he appeared in a balcony facing the great square of the palace. There he sat to review his elephants richly caparisoned, his state horses, feats of horsemanship, and combats of wild beasts. At eleven o'clock he went to the hall of audience and mounted his jewelled throne, before which all the nobles were arranged in two rows, on rich carpets, according to their rank, when all ambassadors, viceroys, generals, and visitors were introduced. Each person presented made a nussur or offering; if he was in high favour, the king received it from his own hand. The ceremonies of introduction consisted of bowing three times, at three different intervals, in approaching the throne, and the same on retiring, which was always done backwards. When a new dignity was conferred on any omrah, a dress of state, two elephants, two horses, a camp bed, a sword, warlike instruments and ensigns, his patent, and a sum of money were conferred by the emperor.

The hall of audience, or *chehel sitoon**, opened

---

* Literally the forty pillars. The roof of this hall was of silver; the rails which divided it from the courts were of gold, and the other railings of silver. These were spared by Nadir Shah, but afterwards seized by the infamous Golaum Khadir Khan.

into a large square, where Aurengzebe reviewed and examined troops; a second square was occupied by the lower order of nobility; a third by artisans who came to exhibit their manufactures, and who received rewards according to their merits; and a fourth was filled by huntsmen, who presented wild animals and game. After spending two hours in the hall, he retired to his bathing chamber with the officers of state, and regulated ordinary affairs, after which he spent an hour at table, and in the hot season slept half an hour. At four he appeared in the balcony over the great gate of the palace, when a mob usually collected round him with petitions and complaints. From this noisy scene he retired to prayers, and thence to the bathing room, where the vizier and other ministers assembled, and the council frequently sate late, though the usual hour for the emperor's retiring was nine o'clock.

This was the usual manner in which Aurengzebe passed his time at Dehli or Agra; but the various occupations in which, during his long and active reign, he was engaged, necessarily occasioned a different disposal of his hours. However, when he was on a journey, the court of justice was held in the camp at the same hours as in the city; and those who were obliged to follow the king on account of their business, had each a sum allowed sufficient to defray their travelling expenses.

A minute attention to the comforts of his people distinguished the reign of Aurengzebe. On occasion of a scarcity, an inundation, or other pressing evil, the taxes were remitted in the suffering districts, and they were always lightened on those farms which, in the emperor's journies through his states, he saw the best cultivated. The frontier provinces, however, could not enjoy all the benefits of his administration, for in order to preserve the internal tranquillity of his empire, he kept up a constant warfare in the Deccan, and finally succeeded in re-uniting the whole of its Mahomedan kingdoms to the Mogul crown. But he had a more formidable opponent than any of the weak princes of those petty states, in the Mahratta chief Sevajee, whom he was accustomed to call the mountain rat, and who during nineteen years baffled all the emperor's efforts to destroy his power. But I have already in a former letter mentioned that singular man; and I shall now proceed to the successors of Aurengzebe.

He died A. H. 1119*, after a reign of fifty-two years. He began a reign which he owed to

* A. D. 1707.

hypocrisy, by the most unnatural murders. The splendor and beneficence of his rule taught his subjects to forget his early days. The piety he professed during his whole life, and especially in his last years, must not be ascribed wholly to dissimulation; conscience required an expiation of his crimes, and conscience also made him feel the necessity of a stronger protection than he could afford himself. Religion was his only refuge; and as he had learned to know it when he thought of it only as a means of gratifying his ambition, he probably ended by being a sincere believer, perhaps even an enthusiast, for his character allowed not of weak impressions.

His person was by no means remarkable, and his countenance had no beauty, but it was expressive, and sometimes agreeable. His manners were prepossessing and simple; his voice was harmonious, and he was a good orator and an elegant writer. He was well acquainted with the languages of Arabia and Persia, and he wrote the Mogul tongue, as well as the various dialects of India, with ease. He erected colleges in all the principal cities of Hindostan, and schools in the inferior towns; he proposed rewards for learning, and founded several public libraries. Hospitals, caravanseras, and bridges were built, and ferries established on all the public roads. The administration of justice was impartial, and capital punishments were nearly disused during his reign. Such were the atonements he endeavoured to make for his crimes; and he has found apologists in those who pretend that the nature of despotism bears " no brother near the throne."

Aurengzebe, or Alumghire, was succeeded by his second son Mahomed Mauzim, commonly called Bahadur Shah. It was this prince who, under the title of Shah Allum, had once been near disturbing the reign of his father by a civil war, and his own elevation to the throne was contested by his brothers, whose deaths in battle saved him from the crime of fratricide. He only enjoyed the crown four years and eleven months, when his son Jehander Shah, or Moaz o'dien succeeded to it, whose three brothers were sacrificed to his security. But his low and disgusting vices, together with the pride of his minister Zoolfeccar Khan, soon proved his destruction. The two brother seyds, Abdoolla Khan Bareah and Ali Khan, were soldiers of fortune, who had raised themselves to importance during the troubled times that succeeded the death of Aurengzebe. These two chiefs, with prince Ferokhsere, grandson of Bahadur Shah, raised a powerful army, attacked and killed Jehander Shah, and for some time deluged the capital with the blood of its nobles. To secure the throne to Ferokhsere, the princes of the blood, who might have aspired to the crown, were blinded with hot irons and imprisoned. The Seyds, however, grew tired of their emperor, whose private favourites often gave them great offence; and after a reign of six years they imprisoned him, and placed one of the royal family, whom they released from confinement, on the throne. The manner of Ferokhsere's death is differently related, but all agree that it was violent. It was during the reign of this prince that the East India Company obtained their fermân of free trade, in consequence of a successful operation performed on the emperor by Mr. Hamilton, the surgeon to the Company's embassy. That gentleman being offered any reward he chose, besought the grant of the Company's requests, which were instantly complied with; and the emperor, besides other valuable presents, gave him models of all his surgical instruments in pure gold.

Abu Berhaut Ruffeh ul Dirjât was the phantom that the seyds now placed on the throne, but dying of a consumption in four months, Ruffeh ul Dowlah was put into his place, where he died in three months more, and made way for Mahomed Shah*, grandson of Bahadur Shah, who, since the accession of Jehander Shah, had been in confinement.

* He began his reign A. D. 1720.

The chief event which makes this reign memorable in the annals of India, was the invasion of Nadir Shah. According to some accounts, he was called into Hindostan by the Nizam ul Moolk, who, about A.D. 1724, had begun to throw off the dominion of the emperor, and to make himself independent in the Deccan. But as the invasion did not take place till sixteen years after that period, it is probable that the love of conquest and the desire of plunder were sufficient to induce Nadir to invade so weak an empire as that of Dehli was become. Early in the reign of Mahomed a conspiracy of the nobles cut off the two seyds, who had made and unmade his predecessors at will. Shortly afterwards the Nizam withdrew all but a nominal allegiance for the states of the Deccan. The Mahrattas had seized Guzerat and Mulwa, and even scoured the country within sight of Agra. Nadir had possessed himself of Candahar, and Cabul was but feebly guarded. Under these circumstances, the imprudence of Mahomed offended the Persian ambassador, and thus afforded an immediate pretext for the invasion of his master. A kind of infatuation seems to have prevailed in the Mogul councils; the army was not half assembled; and Mahomed had only marched four days' journey from Dehli into the plain of Karnal, when Nadir, fresh from the conquest of Lahore, defeated him, with the loss of his best and bravest minister. At first the strictest discipline had prevailed among the Persians: no one was molested; and the emperor, after having been kept a state prisoner with his family for a few days, was permitted to return quietly to his palace.

But this tranquillity did not last. On the night of the 10th March a quarrel in the Bazar raised a tumult, and one of those engaged suddenly called out that " Nadir Shah was dead, and now was the time to free Dehli from the Persians." A massacre instantly began, and during the whole night the city was a scene of confusion and murder. But the morning saw it revenged. Nadir Shah at daylight marched to the musjid of Roshen ul Dowlah, situated in the principal street, and there gave orders for a general massacre of the inhabitants, without distinction of age or sex. The havock lasted from sunrise to mid-day, when the emperor and his nobles appeared before Nadir Shah, and, for the sake of Mahomed, he pronounced the words, " *I forgive.*" Instantly the carnage stopped, but not its effects. Many Hindoos and Moguls, to save their women from pollution, set fire to their houses, and burned their families and effects. These fires spread, and the city became incumbered with ruins. The dead bodies

soon caused a pestilential disorder among the
surviving inhabitants. Private murders, in order
to extort confessions of treasures, filled the houses
with tears and groans. A famine was added to
these calamities, and some hundreds of honourable persons committed suicide, to escape at
once from such accumulated distresses.

It was not till the fifteenth of April that Nadir
and his Persians left the city. A treaty had
been concluded, by which he confirmed Mahomed on the throne of all the provinces east of
the Indus, and reserved those to the west for
himself. He carried with him three millions
and a half sterling in money from the royal treasury, one million and a half in plate, fifteen
millions in jewels, the celebrated peacock
throne, valued at a million, other thrones of
inferior value, and the canopy for the royal elephant, estimated at eleven millions; besides five
hundred elephants, a number of horses, and the
imperial camp equipage. Nor was this all: five
millions at least were collected by way of fine
from the nobles and other inhabitants, besides
the private plunder of the soldiers, which probably amounted to as much more.

The historian whom Scott translates, remarks
on the miseries of these dreadful times, that
they were produced by the selfishness of all ranks
of people. I should be tempted to change the

cause for the effect. Despair had rendered them indifferent to the future, and to each other; none had hopes of better times, and consequently present enjoyment was all that could be attained; to betray another afforded a chance for favour, and therefore for safety; but to trust even a brother, was to arm him against you for the day of adversity.

After the departure of Nadir Shah, a mournful tranquillity took possession of the court of Dehli, but it was soon disturbed by those private intrigues which rendered the Nizam wholly independent, and by the invasions of the Mahrattas on one side, and those of Ahmed Shah Abdalla on the other. This Ahmed Shah was a soldier of fortune, raised to high rank by Nadir Shah, and who, after his death, had made himself independent in Candahar and Cabul. In the year of his first invasion of India, A. D. 1747, died Mahomed Shah, who, though not fitted for the turbulent times in which he lived, was a humane and respectable prince.

Ahmed Shah, the son of Mahomed, succeeded him; but though he had before his accession shown marks of spirit and bravery, he disappointed his subjects by giving himself up entirely to pleasure after he mounted the throne. His reign was a scene of confusion, owing to the turbulence of the nobles and the incursions of the Mahrattas and Ahmed Abdulla, nor was that of his successor, Alumghire II. more tranquil. Ahmed's eyes were put out, and he was consigned to a state of tranquil oblivion in 1753, and his cousin, Alumghire, placed on the throne. The principal event in his reign was the total overthrow of the Mahrattas at the battle of Paniput, A. D. 1761, by Ahmed Abdulla, commonly called the Durannee Shah; but that did not secure greater tranquillity. The wretched monarch was alternately the prisoner of his open foes and of his ministers, till he was murdered by his vizier, in the year in which the Mahrattas were defeated. During this calamitous reign the French general, M. Bussy, had rendered himself almost absolute at the court of the Nizam who had granted the northern Sircars in Jaghire to his nation; but the English had become so powerful by their union with the nawab of Arcot, that Bussy and his countrymen found it necessary to oppose them. A long struggle between the two nations terminated in the taking of Pondicherry by the British, which ruined the French in that part of India; and the Nizam bestowed great part of the Jaghire they had formerly possessed on the conquerors.

The singularly miserable reign of Shah Allum the Second began A. D. 1761. The battle of Plassey Plain, which had been won by Colonel,

afterwards Lord Clive, A. D. 1756, and its consequences, had rendered the interference of the
English of great importance to the contending
parties in Hindostan. Accordingly, the ac-
knowledgment of Shah Allum, then a fugitive at
Patna, by the English and the nawab of Bengal,
Meer Casim, whom they had raised to that station, put an end to all other competitors. The
depredations of the Mahrattas, and of the Jauts
under Rajah Mul, rendered it impossible for the
emperor to attempt to get to Dehli without the
assistance of an armed force; and as the English were too fully occupied with their own affairs in Bengal to afford him assistance, he requested and obtained the escort of Scindia, the
Mahratta chief, and in the tenth year of his
reign removed from Allahabad, where he had
been pensioned and protected by the English, to
Dehli, the ancient capital of his empire, and
where his coming diffused a general joy. But
the emperor was now obliged to accompany, if
not to head the Mahratta armies; and it was
with difficulty that he prevented them from falling on the forces of his own vizier Sujah ul
Dowlah, and the English. As soon as the royal
treasury was drained, the Mahratta allies seized
all Shah Allum's estates except the ruined city
of Dehli, and treated him with personal indig-
nity. The small remains of his own force, con-

sisting of only four battalions of Sepoys, were easily overcome by Bissajee and Holkar. The city was plundered, and a famine added to the misery of the people. From that time, to the year 1787, the unhappy Shah Allum was alternately the pageant of every successful party that could seize his person, whether Mahratta or Mogul. At that period Scindia afforded him the means of daily subsistence, and Mahratta troops garrisoned his citadel. But he was destined to drain the cup of misery to the dregs. Gholaum Khadir Khan, a Rohilla chief, marched suddenly from his residence of Gooseghur, and seized Dehli and the persons of the whole royal family. Nature shudders at the recital of the monstrous cruelties committed by that wretch, who deposed Shah Allum, and raised another of the royal family to the mock dignity of emperor.

On the twenty-sixth of July, 1788, the royal family was confined; and between that time and the fourteenth of September their sufferings exceeded any thing that the wildest imagination can frame. To extort confessions of treasures, they were frequently kept many days without food; and for the crime of conveying fourteen cakes and some water to Shah Allum, a noble was condemned to be beaten with clubs. The women of the harem were tied up and beaten;

many of the princes were brutally struck; the king's uncle, and other respectable persons, were so severely flogged as to faint away; two infants and twelve women died of hunger; and four more, in despair, threw themselves out of the window into the river! But the masterpiece of cruelty was executed in Gholaum's presence. Before Shah Allum's face, he caused several of his sons to be lifted up and dashed against the ground, and then throwing down the unfortunate emperor, his eyes were stabbed out with a dagger.

But the approach of the Mahrattas alarmed Gholaum, who fled from Dehli; Scindia replaced Shah Allum on his throne; and, soon after, seizing the Rohilla chief, he cut off his ears, nose, arms, and legs, and sent him as a present to the emperor, but he died on the road unpitied and unrespected.

Meantime the English, partly by arms, and partly by negotiation, had obtained the real possession of Bengal and Bahar; and their nawab, Casim, having proved refractory to their orders, they, after a considerable struggle, in which the nawab was aided by the vizier Suja ul Dowlah, completely subdued all their enemies; and the battle of Buxar gave them a reputation in war, which, aided by their policy, placed the whole of Hindostan Proper at their disposal.

The province of Allahabad was settled on the emperor, but he unfortunately left it for Dehli, which occasioned all his subsequent sufferings. The vizarut was confirmed in the family of Suja ul Dowlah. The son of Jaffier Khan, who himself had been both the predecessor and successor of Casim Khan, was, on the death of his father, appointed nawab of Bengal under his mother Munny Begum. Every principal city admitted an English resident; and the predominance of British influence was felt both in the cabinet and the field. Such was the state of Hindostan when Mr. Hastings became governor-general on the part of the Company: and as, since that time, the history of India belongs properly to that of Britain, I shall conclude this rapid sketch of the rise and decline of the Mussulman power in India.

The state of that country, from the death of Aurengzebe, was so disastrous both to the nations and individuals who compose it, that not a momentary doubt can exist of the advantages of its present government over the past, whatever be the opinion as to the merits of the government itself. Every man may now repose under his own plantain tree; and if in the early and unsettled period of our first possession of the country, some injustice was committed, and some enormous fortunes unfairly amassed, the present purity of the Company's servants is best attested by the unfeigned respect in which most of them are held by the natives, and by the very moderate fortunes which, after long and arduous service, they can now attain to.

LETTER XIII.

MY DEAR SIR,

AFTER so long a digression to the Mussulmans, I intend to go back to the Hindûs; and though I know no more of their history than I have already sent you, their customs, and manners, and the division of castes, which so peculiarly distinguish them from every other nation, may perhaps be interesting.

The division of the different classes of society into separate tribes, forbidden to intermarry or hold communion with each other, seems anciently to have been by no means confined to the Hindûs. The perpetuity of trades and professions in ancient Egypt, the setting aside the tribe of Levi and house of Aaron for the priesthood among the Israelites, attest this; and though, in the latter instance, it was by the peculiar disposition of heaven, we may well suppose it to have been in conformity with the

wants of that people, and with the customs of
the surrounding nations, whose ignorance and
grossness required a visible pomp as the external
sign of religion and devotion. So, in compas-
sion to their weakness, the ark of the covenant
was permitted to be built, which, like the
moving temples of even the modern Hindûs,
accompanied the nation in its wanderings, whether in warlike expeditions or peaceful ceremonies, the brazen serpent was erected in the
wilderness, and the tent of the tabernacle was
watched and guarded by a consecrated tribe, as
the family of Koreish served the sacred Caaba.

With the exception, however, of the customs
of the small remnant of the Jewish nation, and
perhaps of the Chinese hereditary trades, the
Hindûs are the only people which now presents
a complete model of the system of castes. The
number of distinct classes at present acknowledged among the Hindûs, is infinitely greater
than it was at first, if we may believe the ancient books in which they are enumerated.
But as this very artificial system must have been
formed long after the wants of society had produced difference of professions to supply those
wants, it is most probable that, in order to introduce with more authority a division so extremely oppressive to certain orders, the lawgivers referred it to more ancient times, and thus

3

added the sanction which respect for ancestry never fails to give, to their own institutions. If one wished to illustrate the doctrine that knowledge is power, it would be scarcely possible to find a history more apposite than that of the subordination of castes in India. Nothing but superior knowledge could have procured for the Brahmins a sufficient ascendancy over the minds of their countrymen, to allow them to take to themselves the first rank in society, to enjoy without labour the conveniences and even luxuries which others must toil to gain, and without taking on themselves the burdens of either government or war, to reap the advantages of both, and to enjoy the privileges without incurring the dangers of dominion. Such, however, is the highly endowed Brahmin, who, in the solitude of his caverned mountains, or consecrated groves, studied the various powers and passions of the human mind, in order to bend and wind it the more surely to his purpose, while he investigated those laws of nature, the application of which, among a simple people, might make him alternately the prophet of blessings or the denouncer of woes. Nor were these the only means by which they virtually governed their fellow-citizens. Those religious feelings which are inherent in every human breast, and which sanctify every association with which they are

T

combined, are of all others the most easily
wrought upon.

The Brahmins feigned to hold immediate intercourse with the deity : they personified his
attributes, and held them up as objects of worship to the people ; they multiplied ceremonies
and expiations, in which themselves were the
officiating ministers, and thus placed themselves
in the awful situation of mediators between the
gods and men.   Thus powerfully armed and ar-
rayed, the first bold step towards the securing
for ever such transcendant advantages, was the
positive prohibition against the study of any of
the sciences which had founded and maintained
their empire of opinion, by any one who should
either bear arms or exercise any profession separate from the priesthood; and this would
probably not be difficult, for the natural disposition of man inclines him to lean on others for
that knowledge and that protection which singly
he feels so necessary, and at the same time so
incapable of affording to himself.   Even the monarchs of the earth were below the Brahmins in
dignity.   Caressed and flattered, or reviled and
anathematized by the subtle Brahmins, the
greatest sovereigns moved but as they willed ;
and if, provoked by their insolence, he called
upon his warriors for revenge, he had no
sooner extirpated the race within his own do-

minions, than all the horrors of conscience seized upon him; and expiations, the recital of which make the blood run cold, or sometimes suicide, were resorted to, in order to propitiate the gods, or rather the priests, who styled themselves gods upon earth. Nor did these always suffice : the Brahmin was at liberty to adopt any of the professions of the other castes ; and they not unfrequently seized the sword of extermination and revenge, and more than one record remains among the actions of their deified heroes, of whole nations of warriors utterly exterminated even to the babe at its mother's breast.

The four great tribes into which the Brahmins feign mankind to have been originally divided, are, first, the *Brahmanas,* who proceeded with the Vedas from the mouth of Brahma the Creator, and they were made superior to the other classes. The protector from ill, who sprung from the arms of Brahma, was named *Cshatriya.* He whose profession was commerce and husbandry, and attendance on cattle, was named *Vaissya,* and was produced from the body of Brahma, while his feet gave being to the fourth or *Sudra* class, whose business was voluntarily to serve for hire *.

* For this, and whatever concerns the castes, see Mr. Colebrooke's Paper on the Enumeration of Indian Classes, Art. III. Asi. Res. vol. V. p. 53. Calcutta edition.

The Brahmins are divided into ten great classes, named from the nations whence they came, which are, with the exception of Casmira or Cashmere, the same with the ten ancient nations of India, which I formerly mentioned. Their names are the Saraswata, Canyacubja, Gaura, Mit'hila, Utcala, Dravira, Maharastra, Telingana, Gujjera, and Cashmira Brahmins. These ten classes are farther subdivided, according to the districts they are born in, and the families whence they spring; and their usages and professions of faith differ in almost every tribe. While some hold it unlawful to destroy animal life, and abstain even from eating eggs; others make no scruple of feeding on fish or fowl.

Brahmins of different nations and families do not usually eat with each other, and under many circumstances, priests even of the same tribe refuse to eat together.

The most important function of the Cshatrya or Xetrie class, is that of government. That caste, alone, ought to furnish monarchs, and a Brahmin is forbidden to accept of any gift from a king not born a Xetrie. At the same time, while the sceptre is thus placed in the hands of the military class, there are strong injunctions to leave the civil administration to the sacerdotal tribe, and Menu abounds with texts favourable to that nation, where the seats of justice are filled by holy Brahmins.

Although the intermarriage of different classes be now unlawful, it was formerly permitted, or at least those who framed the present arbitrary system of castes feigned it to have been so, in times anterior to the written law, in order to account for the extraordinary number of intermediate classes sprung from the four original divisions of mankind. These intermediate classes are reckoned by some to be thirty-six, although other authors count more than double that number, many of which, according to them, are of doubtful origin. Those which rank higher are such whose fathers are of the first class, and the mothers of the second, the third, and the fourth; then those whose fathers are of the second caste, and the mothers inferior; afterwards the children of a man of the third class, by a woman of the last; and these afford six divisions. As many proceed from the marriages of women of high caste with men inferior to themselves, and innumerable others are derived from the intermarriages of these mixed divisions, both among themselves and the pure families. These form the regular respected castes; but there are several classes of outcasts, called chandelas, pariahs, &c. who are not permitted to live in towns or villages, or to draw water from the same wells as other Hindûs; but they pay a small sum to the patel or head-man of the township, for permission to fix their hamlets near the market, and other conveniences, and are in some places bound to carry luggage for travellers, to cleanse the streets of the town or village they belong to, and to perform other mean offices.

The profession of astrology, and the task of making almanacks, belong to degraded Brahmins, and the occupations of teaching military exercises and physic, as well as the trades of potters, weavers, braziers, fishermen, and workers in shells, belong also to the descendants of Brahmins.

Bards, musicians, herds, barbers, and confectioners, descend immediately from the Xetrics.

Attendants on princes and secretaries are sometimes said to spring from the Vyassa and Sudra, but they are also sometimes considered as unmixed Sudras. These derive their rank from their fathers, but the classes most degraded are such as belong to the high castes by the mother's side only, for a man exalts or degrades his wife to his own station. Those who keep cows or horses, or drive cars, florists, pedlars, hawkers, attendants on women, catchers of animals who live in holes, are all of this lower class, but the most wretched of all, the chandela, sprung from a Brahmin mother by a Soodra, has the office of executioner, carries out dead bodies, and is in all respects a Pariah. The

Natas and Naticas, who are players, dancers,
and singers, are also distinct classes of the very
lowest kind *.   Such are the general divisions of
the Hindû castes; with regard to the strictness
with which each is obliged to follow its peculiar
trade, there are a variety of opinions.   The
most commendable method by which a Brahmin can gain a subsistence, is by teaching the
Vedas, assisting at sacrifices, of which, as among
the Jews, a stated portion is reserved for the
priests, and receiving gifts from great men.   A
Xetrie should bear arms; a Vaissya's proper
avocations are merchandise, agriculture, and
pasturage; and that of a Sudra, servile attendance.   But a Brahmin who cannot subsist
by his proper functions, may bear arms, till the
ground, or tend cattle, and, in common with the
Xetrie, practise medicine, painting, and other
arts, besides accepting of menial service, receiving alms, and lending money for usury.   A
Vaissya may perform the duties of a Sudra, and
I believe he may bear arms; and a Sudra may
live by any handicraft, painting, writing, trad-
ing, and husbandry.   The mixed classes may
practise the trades peculiar to the mother's

---

* Grellman was, I believe, the first who suspected that the
Gypsies of Europe were a tribe of the Nats of Hindostan.
Richardson's paper, in the 7th volume of the Asiatic Researches, on the Bazeeghurs, seems to leave no doubt on the
subject.

caste, with one exception in favour of the Brahmins, for none but one of that holy order may
teach or expound the Veda, or officiate in religious ceremonies. Thus you see that the numerous exceptions to the general precepts concerning the inviolability of the castes, render
those precepts less vexatious in their operation
than they must otherwise have become.

The distinctions between the castes and sects
of Hindûs are known at first sight, by certain
marks made on the forehead, cheeks, or other
parts of the body, with a variety of pigments;
and that this practice was not in ancient times
peculiar to the Hindûs, may I think be inferred
from the XIXth Chapter of Leviticus, where the
Israelites are forbidden not only to make cuttings
in their flesh for the dead, but to *print any
marks upon them*. This is, indeed, far from
being a singular instance, which might be taken
from the scriptures, of the truth with which the
modern Hindûs have preserved to us the customs of the antique families of the world. I do
not know if you will allow me to compare the
ceremonies practised by the *Nazarites*, or those
Israelites who wished to dedicate themselves to
the Lord as Levites, in order to obtain the holi-
ness of the tribe of Aaron, with the austerities
of the Sanyassees, who, from motives of a similar
nature, aspire to perform the functions, and attain to the sanctity of the holy and recluse Brah-

min, although born in a lower class. But I
think you would find it interesting to read the
books of Moses attentively, while you are study-
ing the Hindûs, either in your closet here or in
their own country. One would throw light on
the other, and you know I have often said that
I thought that one reason why our countrymen
have distinguished themselves so much in oriental literature and research, is, that from their
infancy they are accustomed to the richness of
oriental imagery, and the sublime wildness
of oriental poetry, and initiated into oriental
manners, by the common translation of the
Bible, which, fortunately for us, was made at
the time when our language was polishing into
beauty, while it retained enough of its ancient
simplicity to follow the divine original in its
boldest flights, as well as through its tenderest
passages, and thus the very phrase and manners
of the cradle of all religions has been handed down
to us with the pure doctrines of our own divine
Apostle. But the ceremonial institutions of the
Jews have passed away, and the learning of their
taskmasters, the Egyptians, has perished! Hindostan alone presents the picture of former
times in its priesthood, its laws, and its people.
To inquire into the causes of that stability is
beyond my powers, even if I possessed all the
facts which would be necessary to form any

theory concerning it : at the same time I cannot
but attribute something to the system of castes.
The climate of India, where but little clothing and
shelter are necessary, and where food is plentiful,
in proportion to the wants of its inhabitants, is
productive of that indolence which deadens ambition and palsies exertion, in the generality of
mankind. The little wants of a Hindû are so
easily supplied, that he has scarcely any spur to
his industry for the sake of procuring necessaries
or comforts ; and his ambition is checked by the
reflection that if a wish to ameliorate his condition should arise, no virtue, no talent, no ac-
quirement, can raise him to a higher rank in
society than that enjoyed by his forefathers ;
and this reflection is embittered too by the consideration, that the crime of another may, un-
countenanced by him, and in some cases unknown to him, deprive him of the station he
enjoys, and render him and his family outcasts
for ever*. Thus, by a moral action and reac-
tion, the castes have been preserved inviolate ;
and if in some spots where European settlements have encouraged industry, and by hold-

* The 12000 Brahmins of the coast of Malabar, who perished
in consequence of the cruelty of Tippoo Saheb, in forcing
them to swallow beef-broth, by which they *lost caste*, or became outcasts, many being starved to death, and many committing suicide in despair, is an instance of this.

ing out a high premium to ingenuity and labour, have induced some individuals of the
lower orders to exert themselves, so as to acquire at least the external circumstances of
rank; the jealousy of the Brahmins is always
on the watch to repel such encroachments, and
to render uuavailing the slow but certain progress that the spirit of commerce is making
towards raising the lower orders to a certain degree of importance*.

When we see the poor Hindû covered with
disease, scarcely sheltered from the monsoon
storm, and scantily fed, leaning on his mat
without a hope, and perhaps without a wish, to
better his condition, but with the tranquillity
of despair saying it is the *poor man's custom*, who
can abstain from execrating the fetters with
which his forefathers have shackled his heart and
understanding? And who that sees the wealthy
and useful merchant standing with joined hands
at a respectful distance from the begging and

* In Bombay, the merchant Suncurset Bapooset built, at
the expense of upwards of £12,000, a very beautiful temple
to Maha Deo. The Brahmins, who had patiently watched the
building, and had consecrated the ground and the materials,
discovered, on its completion, that poor Suncurset was of too
low a caste to make an offering to the gods, and that, consequently, he must make a deed of gift to the priests, who then
sanctified it as the holy place of Maha Deo.

profligate Sanyassee, but feels indignant at the
abuse of some of the best and strongest feelings
of our nature? I am not, as you know, among
those who either extravagantly praise or extravagantly condemn the Hindûs or their religion.
It is enough that the latter is false, to wish it exchanged for a better ; but the Hindûs are men,
and moved by human motives and by human
passions, and never, never will a conversion be
wrought among them by the present system of
the missionaries. They must be bad judges
indeed of human nature, who can suppose, that
millions of men are, without a miracle, to be
converted by a few hundreds of preachers, who
go among them, ignorant of their language and
philosophy, and even the religion they would
combat. Moses, the lawgiver of the Jews, was
learned in all the wisdom of the Egyptians, and
consequently could sooth or elude the prejudices
of the people who were born in the land of Mis-
raim. St. Paul, the Apostle of the Gentiles, was
versed in the philosophy of Rome and of Athens,
and wielded against their superstitions, the very
doctrines and forms of their own sages. But we,
with ample means of learning, send inexpe-
rienced youths, virtuous indeed in their own
lives, and skilled in their own doctrines, but ignorant of the science of the East, and above all,
ignorant of the motives and passions of human

nature, and the art of leading men's minds.—
" Whom ye ignorantly worship, him declare I
unto you," were the words of St. Paul to the
people of Athens. He turned not to the temples crowded with images to expose the follies
and vices of Jupiter, or to falsify the predictions
of Apollo, but he seized upon the simple altar
of the wisest of men, *to the unknown God*, and
thence beginning his exposition of divine truths,
he, without irritating the passions of his hearers
by open defiance calling on them to defend
their deities, announced the pure faith of Christ,
" That they should seek the Lord, if haply they
might feel after him, and find him, though he
be not far from every one of us : For in him we
live, and move, and have our being; as certain
also of your own poets have said, For we are
also his offspring. Forasmuch, then, as we are
the offspring of God, we ought not to think that
the Godhead is like unto gold, or silver, or
stone, graven by art and man's device. And
the times of this ignorance God winked at;
but now commandeth all men everywhere to
repent."

Such were the arguments of the model of
preachers before the most enlightened people of
ancient times. Why, then, are we harshly to
denounce to the Hindû condemnation and contempt? Should not his greater ignorance de-

mand greater tenderness? And if his poets, too, abound with precepts of piety and morality, why should they not also be called in aid of the doctrine we wish to preach? But the enthusiasm and the courage which are requisite to carry men through great undertakings, the learning which should baffle error, and the calmness which should refute it, are so seldom joined with that deep insight into human character, necessary to produce important moral changes, under the existing circumstances of the world, that it is vain to expect much from the exertions of individuals who can be paid for those exertions, and still less could be hoped from the interference of the legislature, as it would only excite that tenacity of opinion which all men feel when their belief is rudely attacked, and that spirit of resistance which now lies happily dormant. Perhaps were the church establishment in India better supported, and the English residents more disposed to shew respect to it both by purity of morals and decorum of manners, the natives of India might respect it also, at least they could not despise it. And if, in process of time, by the encouragement of native schools, the widening of the circle of commerce, and the consequently increasing intercourse between the natives and the Europeans, some few respectable Hindûs should be induced

to join the Christian community, they would
escape the contempt into which proselytes now
fall, and perhaps might attract new converts,
instead of, as now, standing a melancholy warn-
ing against a change of faith, which in this
world renders them miserable and ridiculous.
Far be it from me to oppose the conversion of
the Hindûs; but I cannot but grieve that the
means employed are so inadequate to the end
proposed, and whether, as happens in the physical world, doing little and unskilfully in a deep-
rooted disorder, be worse than leaving nature
to her own quiet operations, is to me not doubtful.
Sooner or later these will take effect: once excite the hopes of gain, the desire of advancement, place knowledge within the reach of those
not unwilling to know, they will conquer difficul-
ties to attain their wishes, they will feel, with the
conscious superiority which a vanquished obstacle inspires, courage and ambition to overcome
anew, the fetters of opinion will be broken, and'
the Hindû, as he rises in the scale of beings,
will shake off the superstitions, with the lethargy
of slavery, and the long desired object of good
men will be obtained by a creature worthy of
enjoying it.

All this you will say is visionary: alas! I am
compelled to acknowledge, that without some of
those extraordinary occurrences that have oc-

7

casionally changed the belief with the destiny
of nations, centuries must elapse before these
things can come to pass; and I can only excuse
myself by saying, that certain as I am of the
impossibility of the present and sudden conversion of the Hindûs, I have no resource but to
build my hopes on the silent operation of ages,
and the certain though remote effects of moral
causes on the mind of man.

LETTER XIV.

MY DEAR SIR,

    I FANCY I shall exercise your patience
as much in the Letter I am now beginning as I
have ever done in any I have written on the same
subject, for I have to speak much of ceremonies,
which to us are tedious and unmeaning, but
they influence greatly the private life of the
Hindûs, which passes among the higher castes
in complete indolence, when not engaged in superstitious observances. The existence of the
lower classes is an alternation of the greatest
bodily labours, with perfect idleness; but among
all, there is discernible a portion of that ingenuity which, in times of remote antiquity, rendered India the nurse if not the mother of arts

and science, and of that spirit which in all times has made the Hindûs a warlike people.

The manners of the Hindûs are proverbially mild and gentle, and among the higher orders especially it is extremely rare to see any one allow himself to be transported by passion into the slightest intemperance of word or gesture. The higher classes of women are now almost as much recluses as those of the Mussulmans, who have introduced their jealousy of the sex into India; but we have abundant proofs in the ancient poets that they formerly enjoyed perfect freedom, or at least were only subject to the restraints which among a civilized people are imposed by the laws of society and decorum. Sacontala, the adopted daughter of a holy Brahmin, received his guests and exercised all the rites of hospitality, and appears to have been restrained by no ties but those of religion and virtue. The mother of Dushmanta governed his people during his absence from his capital; women were competent witnesses in a court of justice: indeed, Menu says, that in a case concerning a woman, women are the proper witnesses. But it is needless to multiply examples, for every Hindû tale confirms the fact of the ancient polished state of India, when its splendid courts presented all the charms of literature, and all the chivalrous gallantry, which in raising

U

women perhaps a little higher than nature intended them in some respects to stand, polished the manners of the men, and produced that gentleness and suavity which the refined yet easy intercourse of the sexes can alone secure among a warlike people.

The lower castes of Hindû women are employed in a manner analogous to the professions of their husbands; and it is by no means uncommon to see them carrying burdens, working in mortar and lime, tilling the ground, and other laborious occupations.

The daily life of a Hindû admits of little variety, almost every action being prescribed by law *. The Puranas contain rules for diet, and for the manner and time of eating; two meals, one in the forenoon, the other in the evening, being allowed. They also enumerate the places, such as a boat, where a Hindû must not take his repast, and the persons with whom it is permitted to partake of food, among whom are his sons and other inmates, excepting his wife. The posture in which it is enjoined to sit, and the quarter to which the face must be turned while eating, with the precautions requisite to insulate the person, lest it be touched by the impure, are particularly insisted on. After washing his

* Mr. Colebrooke.

hands and feet, and sipping water, the Hindû must sit down on a stool or cushion before his plate, which is placed on a plain spot of ground, wiped and smoothed, in a quadrangular form if he be a Brahmin, a triangle is required for a Xetrie, a circle for a Vaissya, and a crescent for a Sudra. When the food is brought in, he must bow to it, and raising both hands to his forehead, say—" May this be always ours." When he sits down, he must lift the plate of food with his left hand, and bless it. If the food be handed to him, he must say " May Heaven give thee," and on taking it, " Earth accepts thee." Before he begins to eat, he must move his hand round his plate, or rather his own person, to insulate himself; he then offers five lumps of food to Yama (the Hindû Pluto), sips water, and offers five other lumps to the five senses, when wetting his eyes, he eats his repast in silence, with all the fingers of his right hand. At the end of his meal, he again sips water, saying, " Ambrosial fluid, thou art the couch of Vishnu and of food!"

The sipping of water is necessary in all ceremonies and religious acts. When a Brahmin rises from sleep, he must rub his teeth with a twig of the banian or racemiferous fig-tree, under penalty of losing the benefit of any other rites performed by him, excepting on the days of the

conjunction, and the 1st, 6th, and 9th of each
lunar fortnight; he then utters a short prayer,
sips water, and sprinkles some of the same element before him, preparatory to his morning
bath, which consists in ablutions, followed by
worship, and the inaudible repetition of the
Gayatrie *, with the names of the worlds, after
which he sits down to worship the rising sun.
This ceremony is begun by tying the lock of
hair on the crown of the head, while he again
recites the Gayatrie.   Then holding cusa-grass†
in his left hand, and three blades of the same
in his right, he sips water three times, then rubs
his hands, and touches with water his eyes, nose,
ears, feet, head, and navel‡, and sipping thrice
again, he meditates on the holiest of texts during
three suppressions of the breath.   A suppression
of the breath implies the following meditation—
" Air! earth! sky! heaven! middle region!
place of births! mansion of the blessed! abode
of truth! we meditate on the adorable light of

---

* *Gayatrie,* the most holy text of the Hindû Scriptures,
contained in the last chapter of the Rigveda; for the Gayatrie
and its context, see the 5th Letter.

† Poa Cynosuroides.

‡ The Jewish ritual required the tip of the right ears, toes,
and thumbs, of the priests to be touched with the blood of the
burnt offering, Lev. viii. 23. Touching the tip of the right
ear is also used as a purification by the Brahmins.

the resplendent generator which governs our intellects, which is water, lustre, savour, immortal faculty of thought, Brahma, earth, sky, and heaven*!" Then follows sipping of water, with renewed ablutions and prayers, when the Brah-

* The triliteral syllable Om or Aûm, is thus explained, together with the rest of the text, by *Yajnyawalcya.*—" The Parent of all beings produced all states of existence, for he generates and preserves all creatures, therefore he is called the Generator; because he shines, and sports, and irradiates, therefore is he called resplendent or divine, and is praised by all deities. We meditate on the light which, existing in our minds, continually governs our intellects in the pursuit of virtue, wealth, love, and beatitude; because the being who shines with seven rays, assuming the form of time and of fire, matures productions, is resplendent, illumines all, and finally destroys the universe; therefore, he who naturally shines with seven rays, is called Light, or the effulgent power. The first syllable denotes, that he illumines worlds; the second consonant implies, that he colours all creatures; the last syllable signifies, that he moves without ceasing. From his cherishing all, he is called the irradiating power." Of the numerous other commentaries or glosses on the Gayatrie, the following is the only specimen I shall copy—" On that effulgent power, which is BRAHME himself, and is called the light of the radiant sun, do I meditate; governed by the mysterious light which resides within me, for the purpose of thought, that very light is the earth, the subtle æther, and all which exists within the created sphere; it is the threefold world, containing all which is fixed or moveable; it exists internally in my heart, externally in the orb of the sun; being one and the same with that effulgent power, I myself am an irradiated manifestation of the supreme BRAHME."

min, standing on one foot with his face towards the East, and holding his hands before him, worships the sun with the following ejaculations. 1st, " The rays of light announce the splendid fiery sun, beautifully rising to illumine the universe : 2d, He rises, wonderful, the eye of the sun, of water, and of fire, collective power of gods ; he fills heaven, earth, and sky, with his luminous net : he is the soul of all which is fixed or locomotive : 3d, That eye supremely beneficial rises pure from the East ; may we see him a hundred years—may we live, may we hear him a hundred years : 4th, May we, preserved by the divine power, contemplating heaven above the region of darkness, approach the Deity, the most splendid of luminaries."

After this and some other similar prayers, an oblation, called Arg'ha, is offered to the sun ; it consists of tila * flowers, barley, water, and red sanders-wood, in a clean copper vessel, shaped like a boat, and is presented with an ejaculation, signifying that the sun is a manifestation of the Supreme Being, present everywhere, produced everywhere, and pervading every place and thing. Then the Gayatrie is particularly invoked, for the Hindús have personified, or rather deified, this their favourite text, and after pro-

* Sesamum Indicum.

nouncing the sacred triliteral word Om, the Gayatrie is repeated a hundred or a thousand times, according to the sins to be expiated, and the times counted on a rosary, composed of gems set in gold, or of wild seeds, and sometimes even of flowers. The poet, in describing Gun-carri, one of the consorts of the pensive Ma-lava, the musical genius of Melancholy, says—

> On a shrunk chaplet of neglected flowers
> In pensive grief she counts the weary hours.

But the Hindû, accustomed to repeat his Gayatrie by rote, is as little serious or attentive to the words he utters, as the poor Catholic, who re-peats his paternosters and aves without under-standing them ; so that the text may be re-peated backwards or forward, or the words in-differently placed, without diminishing its holi-ness. The ceremony of counting the beads being over, a few more texts are repeated, and the Brahmin is at liberty to attend to his worldly concerns. Preparatory to every act of religion, ablutions must be performed, for which all water is proper, but that which has lain above ground is to be preferred, as is running water to a stand-ing pool, a river to a brook, a sacred before a common stream, and above all, the water of the Ganges. The superstitious veneration for par-ticular rivers is among the most natural into

4

which men have fallen: when the Egyptian
worshipped the Nile, he adored the visible pro-
ducer of fertility and abundance in his fields; if
the Jews paid the highest respect to Jordan,
consistent with their purer religion, it was
through that stream that they had entered the
promised land; and in the burning climate of
India, the mighty Ganges, with its tributary
streams, became almost necessarily an object of
devotion among a nation whose vivid imagination peopled all nature with divinities. The
typified purity of mind, by ablution of the body,
is in all its forms native to the East. The Hindû
temples are all provided with tanks for that
purpose, when they are not on the bank of a
stream; the mosque of the Mussulman is never
without its well or bath.   The brazen sea with
which Solomon adorned his temple, and the
lavers for the sacred utensils, and the laver of
brass that stood at the door of the tabernacle,
with all the different forms of Christian baptism,
are derived from a common source, and may be
compared with those primitive sounds which
philologers say have the same signification in
all languages.

But the Hindûs have figuratively varied their
ablutions. Those sacred to fire are made by rub-
bing the body with ashes; others sacred to wind,
consist in standing in dust raised by the treading

of cows; and some are consecrated to the sky by standing in a shower of rain. All these ablutions are performed with ceremonies nearly similar to those I have described, and with divers holy texts first invoking the rivers, the gods, and water. These formalities must be repeated before reading the vedas, vedangas, sacred poems, mythological histories, law, and other branches, of sacred literature; and after such study, the priest should offer barley, tila, and water to the Manes, sitting with his face towards the East with cusa-grass spread before him, and touching the offering with the tips of his fingers only, as they are parts sacred to the gods. The Manes to whom these oblations are offered, are those of the progenitors of mankind, the Brahmin's own father, paternal grandfather, and great grandfather, to his mother, and both paternal and maternal grandmothers, and great grandmothers, paternal uncle, son, grandson, daughter's son, son-in-law, and other relations and the ceremony is concluded by three voluntary oblations, one presented like those to the gods, looking East, another like those to the Manes looking South, and the third is an oblation of water to the sun.

The reading of the vedas, and oblation to the Manes are two of the five *sacraments* which form part of the daily duty of a Brahmin; the others

7

are separate sacrifices to the deities and the spirits, and the rites of hospitality.

The consecrating the sacrificial fire, and hallowing the sacred utensils are the groundwork of all religious acts, and they are consequently performed with peculiar care. First, the priest smears with cow-dung a level piece of ground, four cubits square, free from impurities and sheltered by a shed; then he describes different lines of various lengths and colours sacred to various deities, and having cast away the first embers from the vessel containing the fire, in order to exorcise its hurtful qualities, he places the rest on the hearth, when he names the fire according to the use he means to make of it, and silently burns a piece of wood a span long, smeared with clarified butter*. He next places the Brahmana or superintending priest, who, except on very solemn occasions, is represented by a bundle of fifty blades of cusa-grass, and after many ceremonies, such as walking round the fire, following the course of the sun, pouring out water, and exorcising whatever is evil, all which formalities are accompanied by prayers and ejaculations, the ladle, and other implements of sacrifice, are consecrated by touching

* The fuel used at sacrifices should be wood of the racemiferous fig-tree, the leafy Butea, or the Catechu mimosa: but the Mango or the prickly Adenanthera may be used.

and describing figures on them with the tips of the fore-finger and thumb. Oblations to fire precede all other offerings; and the *nine* planets, that is, the Sun, the Moon, Mars, Mercury, Jupiter, Venus, Saturn, the ascending node, and the descending node are also peculiarly adored at the beginning of the sacrifices, and oblations of clarified butter with prayers are offered to each.

Brahmanas who maintain a perpetual fire, as all who devote themselves to the priesthood ought to do, daily perform the sacred ceremonies in full detail; but the greater number comprise them all in one, called *Vaiswadeva*, consisting of oblations to the gods, to the Manes, and to the spirits, out of the food prepared for the daily meal, and complete the sacrifice by presenting a part of that meal to some guests. The religious rites intermixed with acts of courtesy which are practised by way of formal hospitality are nearly the same, whether it be high rank, a venerable profession, or cordial friendship, which entitles the guest to distinction; they consist chiefly, in offering him a stool to sit on, water for ablutions, and honey mixed with other food for refreshment*. Anciently it

---

* See Genesis, Chap. xviii. verses 2, 3, 4, 5, 6, 7, 8, for the manner in which Abraham received the three angels.

See

appears that a cow was killed on such occasions, but at present, and probably ever since the great reformation of the Brahminical religion which put an end to the sanguinary sacrifices, the host contents himself either with releasing a cow who has been bound for the purpose, or repeating the ancient formulary which accompanied that ceremony. This last formality is especially practised on receiving a son-in-law on the day of his marriage, after the performance of oblations to the ancestors of both parties. The cow in this case is tied up on the northern side of the apartment, where also, a stool with the jewels and bridal ornaments are arranged, and on the approach of the bridegroom the prayer of consecration is uttered, when he sits down and receives water for ablution. An Arghya or offering, in a boat-shaped vessel, is then made to him, after which he accepts of food, which he eats while prayers are recited over him; an interchange of presents suitable to the rank of the parties is then made, the bride is formally presented by her father to the bridegroom, and the cow is at that moment let loose, when a barber, who attends for the purpose, exclaims, The cow! the cow!—

See also the reception of Telemachus by Nestor, in the 3d book of the Odyssey.

In the mean time, the bride bathes while texts are recited over her, and both the hands of the bride and bridegroom are smeared with turmeric, or some other auspicious drug, when a matron binds them together with cusa-grass, to the sound of cheerful music. The priests then begin joyful acclamations, while the bride's father pours water and grain on their hands, blesses them, and proclaiming their names solemnly gives them to each other. Being thus affianced, they walk out, and the bridegroom addresses her with the following and similar sentences, " May the regents of space, air, sun, and fire dispel the anxiety thou feelest, and turn thy heart unto me! Be gentle in thy aspect, loyal to thy husband, amiable in thy mind, and beautiful in thy person!" He then presents her with a waistcloth and mantle; and when she has put them on, the father ties the skirts of his daughter and her husband together, saying, " Ye must be inseparably united in matters of duty, wealth, and love!" After this, the bridegroom goes to the principal chamber and prepares a sacrificial fire, and hallows the sacred utensils, while two of his friends walk round his fire with jars of water, and place themselves on the South. He then puts four double handfuls of rice mixed with sami-leaves* into a flat basket, near which he

* Adenanthera aculeata.

places a stone and mullar*, and causing the
bride to be new clothed, he leads her to the sacred fire, where, with many ceremonies, texts,
and prayers, upwards of fifty oblations, chiefly
of rice and butter, are offered up.

The most material part of the ceremony is
the bride's taking seven steps, for after the seventh, and no sooner, the marriage is completed
and the guests dismissed. In the evening the
young couple are seated on a red·bull's hide,
and the bridegroom points out to his bride the
polar star, as an emblem of stability; they then
partake of a meal, and the young man remains
three days in the house of his father-in-law, after
which he conducts his bride home in procession, when she is welcomed by his kindred, and
the ceremony ends with an oblation to fire.

This is now the most usual mode of marriage
in India. Menu mentions seven others as having been anciently practised, and we read in
Sacontala, that on some occasions at least, a
great part of the ceremony was dispensed with.
The law censures the delaying to marry a daughter after her tenth year, because the father is
bound to provide for her a suitable match, and
the restrictions on marriages are so numerous as
to render this no easy task. Besides the obstacles arising from difference of caste, the pro-

---

* For grinding curry-stuff, &c.

hibited degrees of relationship extend to the sixth of affinity, and the bearing the same family name is a sufficient cause of impediment.

The custom of the widows burning themselves with the dead bodies of their husbands, which has excited so much compassionate indignation in Europe, although decidedly encouraged by the Hindû legislators, has, according to Mr. Colebrooke, never been frequent, and he grounds this consoling opinion on the excessive spiritual rewards, promised even to the spectators of the holy ceremony; for it is said by grave authors that even those who join the procession shall be rewarded as for an *Aswamedha* or other great sacrifice, and that those who throw butter or wood on the pile, shall acquire merit ten million-fold that of an Aswamedha.

Although it be the duty of a widow to burn herself with her husband, she has the alternative either to live after his death as a Brahmachari or to commit herself to the flames*. Should she resolve to live, she must pass her life in chastity, piety, and mortifications. She must eat but one meal a day, and never sleep upon a bed, under pain of causing her husband to fall

* The custom is not unexampled in ancient Greece. Evadne, the wife of Capaneus who perished in the Theban war, burnt herself on her husband's funeral pile.

from a state of bliss. She must abstain from ornamenting her person, or eating out of magnificent vessels, or of delicious food, and she must daily offer oblations for the Manes of ancestors. In some cases, as where a woman has a young infant, or is pregnant, she is positively forbidden to burn herself, and the widow of a Brahmin who dies in a foreign country is also prohibited from giving this proof of affection for her absent lord; but the widows of other castes may if they please burn themselves, on the news of the death of their husbands.

A widow who recedes after having declared her resolution to burn with her husband, is now compelled by her relations to complete the sacrifice; hence some of the shocking scenes which those of our countrymen who have been eye-witnesses, have described; but in general what is thus courageously undertaken, is as courageously carried through.

The ceremonies attending this sacrifice are as follows: " Having first bathed, the widow, dressed in two clean garments and holding some cusa-grass, sips water from the palm of her hand. Bearing cusa and tila in her hand, she looks towards the East or North while the Brahmana utters the mystic word Om." Then after bowing to Narayuna* she repeats the *Sancalpa*,

* The Hindû Neptune.

which contains a declaration of her name and
family, with the day and month in which she
performs the sacrifice, and the motives which
induce her to do so, and concluding with the
following adjuration : " I call on you, ye guardians of the eight regions of the world ! sun, and
moon, air, fire, ether, earth, and water ! My own
soul ! Yama ! Day, night, and twilight ! And
thou conscience, bear witness.   I follow my husband's corpse on the funeral pile."   She then
walks thrice round the pile, while the Brahmin
utters the following Muntras, " Om ! Let these
women, not to be widowed, good wives, adorned
with collyrium, holding clarified butter, con-
sign themselves to the fire, immortal, not child-
less, nor husbandless ! excellent, let them pass
into fire whose original element is water."

" Om ! let these wives, pure, beautiful, commit themselves to the fire with their husband's
corpse."

After this benediction and repeating the mystic *Namò Namàh,* she ascends the pile, and her
son, or other near kinsman of her husband
applies the funeral torch with the ceremonies
prescribed by the *Grihya* or ritual of his tribe.

The efficacy ascribed to this affectionate sacrifice is wonderful, not less than purifying the
husband from all his crimes and insuring him
an existence of bliss during the reign of four-

x

teen Indras, which she is to participate, being praised by the choirs of heaven. This sacrifice also, though certainly an act of suicide, is in the Rigveda expressly exempted from the punishment attached to that crime, namely, that of the privation of obsequies, and the faithful widow is honoured, by having the same chief mourner with her husband.

It is plain from the benedictory texts used on the burning of a widow with her husband, that a plurality of wives was common when those texts were composed, although it is now more rare among the Hindûs, especially of the lower classes, and probably it was formerly rare also in the sacerdotal caste, as we find none of the gods provided with more than one consort, and they were, it is most likely, the images of their priests. The military caste, however, indulged themselves in a plurality. In the Ramáyuna we see not only the fact of the three wives of Dasarathra, the father of Rama, and mention made of the many consorts of other monarchs, but the ill effects which the rivalship between the ladies was apt to produce; for it was the promise obtained from the king by the artful Kikeya, in favour of her son Bharata, that caused the separation of the family of Dasarathra, and the subsequent wanderings and wars of Rama.

Indeed the Ramayuna, at least that part of it which is translated, would give you a more explicit account of the private and public life of the ancient heroes than any thing I can write to you; but then I could scarcely insure your patience to read much more than the first section, and I believe nothing but the desire of variety during a long voyage would have carried me through so much of it as I have read. Hereafter I must refer to it again, but at present I shall return to my constant guide, Mr. Colebrooke, for the account of the funeral rites of the Hindûs, or at least of the greater part of them, for some castes bury their dead, and I believe all bury very young infants; other tribes throw their dead into rivers; but I think no Hindûs expose them to the air, in the manner now practised by the few remaining disciples of Zoroaster.

As soon as a sick Hindû loses all hope of recovery, his relations begin to perform the appointed ceremonies necessary to secure his salvation; and some of these are in many cases so severe, that the patient must be endued with no common strength, if he escape the perils of his *extreme unction*. In truth, it is scarcely desirable that he should, for after having gone through the proper ceremonies it is accounted unholy to live, and consequently the patient

loses caste and becomes a pariah, than which
it is impossible to imagine a more wretched
fate. You may suppose that a greedy heir may
take advantage of this absurdity to get rid of an
old relation before the appointed time, and I
was told in Calcutta, that a Hindû whose father had for some time been ill, appeared one
day in the greatest agitation at the house of an
English gentleman, whom he intreated to come
and save his father, of whom he was very fond,
for that the Brahmins and near relations had
already seized him to convey him to the river
whence he could never return. The English-
man immediately accompanied the pious son,
and had the satisfaction of rescuing the old man
from a premature death, and for aught I know
he still lives to bless his preserver.

A dying Hindû must be laid in the open
air on a bed of cusa-grass; if it be practi-
cable he is brought to the banks of the Ganges
or other sacred stream, where he first makes
donations to the priests of cattle, land, gold,
silver, or whatever he may possess. His head
must be sprinkled with water from the Ganges
and smeared with mud from the same river, a
Sálágrámá stone* must be placed by him,

* The Sálágrámás are black stones (calcareous I believe)
found in a part of the Gandari river, within the limits of
Nepaul. They are mostly round, and are commonly perforated

strains from the Vedas or other sacred poems
must be sounded in his ears, and leaves of holy
basil scattered on his head. When he dies, his
body must be washed, perfumed, and decked
with golden ornaments, a piece of which metal
is also put in the mouth of the deceased, a cloth
perfumed with fragrant oil is then thrown over
the body, which is carried by the nearest relations to some holy spot on a forest, or near water, preceded by fire and by food borne in un-
baked earthen vessels, and followed by various
musical instruments. The body of a Brahmin
must be conveyed out of a town by the western
gate, that of a Xetrie by the northern, a Vaissya
is carried out by the east, and a Sudra by the
south. A corpse may not pass through an inhabited place, and it is required to rest once by
the way to the pile. If the deceased be a priest
who maintained a consecrated fire, the place
whereon the funeral pile is erected, must be

in one or more places by worms; or, as the Hindûs believe,
by Vishnu in the shape of a reptile. According to the number of perforations and of spiral curves in each, the stone is
supposed to contain Vishnu in various characters. For example, such a stone perforated in one place only, with four
spiral curves and with marks resembling a cow's foot and a
long wreath of flowers, contains Lacshmi Narayana. In like
manner stones are found in the Nermada, near Oncar Man-
datta, which are considered as types of Siva, and are called
Bân-ling.

hallowed in the same manner as for the sacrificial fire, and the pile lighted by a brand from his own consecrated hearth; but in other cases the hallowing the spot is omitted, and any unpolluted fire may be used. Those fires peculiarly forbidden are those from another funeral pile, the dwelling of a pariah, or that of an unclean person.

On its arrival at the place appointed for the funeral, the body is laid with its head to the south on a bed of cusa grass while the relations wash and prepare themselves for the ceremony; they then, after adorning it with flowers, place it on the funeral pile with its head towards the north (if it be a woman the face is placed downwards), and butter and perfumes are thrown upon the wood, after which the nearest relation taking up a brand and walking thrice round the pile invoking the gods, sets fire to it near the head; the burning must be so managed that some bones may remain for the ceremony of gathering the ashes; and to cover the spot where the funeral pile stood, a tree should be planted, or a mound of earth or masonry raised, or a pond be dug, or a standard be erected. This formality is in modern times generally neglected excepting where a widow has burnt herself with her husband. You will I am sure on reading this recollect the 11th Æneis where the Trojans and ancient Italians conclude a truce for the purpose of celebrating the obsequies of their fellow-soldiers slain in battle.

> The Trojan king and Tuscan chief command,
> To raise the piles along the winding strand,
> Their friends convey the dead to fun'ral fires,
> Black smould'ring smoke from the green wood expires;
> The light of heaven is choak'd and the new day retires.
> Then *thrice around the kindled piles they go,*
> For ancient custom had ordained it so,
> Thrice horse and foot about the fires are led,
> And thrice with loud laments they hail the dead.
> * * * * * * * * * * *
>
> * * * * * * * * * * *
>
> Now had the morning thrice renew'd the light,
> And thrice dispell'd the shadows of the night,
> When those who round the wasted fires remain,
> Perform the last sad offering to the slain.
> They rake the yet warm ashes from below;
> These and the bones unburn'd, in earth bestow;
> These reliques with their country rites they grace,
> *And raise a mount of turf to mark the place.*
>
> *Dryden's Virgil.*

I might also beg you to look at the twenty-third book of the Iliad for the burning of Patroclus, where Achilles performs the part of the nearest relation and of officiating priest, invoking the guardian deities of the winds, and other gods in conformity with the Hindú practice*.

* That funeral games in honour of deceased heroes were sometimes performed in India, as well as by the Greeks, we

have

After the burning, all who have touched or followed the dead must repair to a river or other water, and perform various oblations and washings, after which they sit down on the turf, and refraining from tears alleviate their sorrows by the recital of such sentences as the following.

" Foolish is he, who seeks permanence in the human state, unsolid like the stem of the plantain tree, transient like the foam of the sea."

" When a body formed of five elements, to receive the reward of deeds done in its own proper person, reverts to its five original principles, what room is there for regret?"

" The earth is perishable; the ocean, the gods themselves pass away; how should not that bubble, mortal man, meet destruction?"

" All that is low must finally perish; all that is elevated must ultimately fall; all compound bodies must end in dissolution; and life is concluded with death."

" Unwillingly do the Manes of the deceased taste the tears and rheum shed by their kinsmen: then do not wail, but diligently perform the obsequies of the dead."

At night, if the funeral was performed by day, or in the day time, if the ceremony was

have the authority of Major Wilford, who mentions such to have been instituted in honour of the hero Jara Sandha, slain in the wars of the Mahabharat.

not completed until night, the nearest relation takes water in a new earthen vessel, and returns home preceded by a person bearing a staff to scare evil spirits, and attended by all the relations, the youngest leading the way. An oblation of a funeral cake, boiled rice, tila, sugar, roots, pot-herbs, fruit, honey, milk, and butter, is then made; the funeral cake being crowned with flowers, and on it a lamp, resin, and betel leaves are offered. Some food is placed on a leaf apart for the birds of prey, and in the evening jars of water and of milk are suspended from the door, and the spirit of the deceased is invited to bathe and drink. The relations then engage for ten days, three days, or only one day, according to circumstances, in a multitude of ceremonies, such as touching holy plants, sipping water, sucking sugar, making libations, and repeating prayers and texts, during which time, whether it be the longest or the shortest period, ten cakes must be offered to the Manes.

While the mourning lasts the kinsmen to the sixth degree are only permitted to eat one meal a day, and that purchased ready dressed; flesh meat is forbidden, and all dishes dressed with factitious salt; and the three first days and nights, or at least one, a rigid fast is observed. Till the ashes are gathered, the kinsmen may not sleep on a bedstead, or adorn or perfume their persons, and it is only on the third, fifth, seventh, and ninth days that they assemble in the open air to bathe, and take a repast, after which they place lamps in the cross roads, and at their own doors, as if to guide the wandering spirit, which, till after the second ceremony or Sradd´ha, rambles melancholy between earth and heaven*. The time of mourning having expired, the Sradd´ha is performed : it consists of offerings, prayers, and texts from the Vedas, besides a kind of exorcism to drive away evil spirits. On offering food one of the formularies is extremely curious, alluding to the mystical sacrifice of Brahme by the immortals by which this world was created ; thus signifying that the elements of which bodies are composed are not annihilated by death, but their forms changed to revive in others; and there is another text, which out of the multitude I select for its beauty. " May the winds blow sweet, the rivers flow

* " Let my pale corse the rites of burial know,
  And give me entrance in the realms below ;
  Till then the spirit finds no resting place."

Iliad, xxiii.

All men feel some anxiety concerning the disposal of their bodies after death ; and most nations, in early times, have supposed that the happiness of the soul depended on it. This anxiety for what may come after death would alone distinguish man from " the beasts that perish."

sweet, and salutary herbs be sweet unto us;
may night be sweet, may the mornings pass
sweetly; may the soil of the earth, and heaven
parent (of all productions) be sweet unto us;
may (Sóma) king of herbs and trees, be sweet;
may the sun be sweet, may kine be sweet, unto
us."

After the food has been offered to the Manes,
the Brahmins are fed, and the officiating priest
receives his fee before the ashes are collected*.
When that is to be done, the nearest relation with
his kinsmen carries into the cemetery eight vessels as offerings to Siva and other deities, and presents an Argha with other offerings, after which
he walks round the place where the funeral pile
stood, and places two vessels at each of the car-
dinal points, and shifting the sacerdotal thread
to the right shoulder, he sprinkles the bones
with cow's milk†, and beginning with the skull
he draws them from the ashes with a branch
of sami and another of palasa. They are then
put into an earthen jar lined with yellow cloth
and leaves of the palasa, and covered with a lid,

* The Brahmins who officiate at funerals are not much esteemed. The priests of Egypt who performed the funeral
rites were held in abhorrence.

† Achilles quenched the ashes of the pile of Patroclus with
sable wine, and the urn containing the hero's bones was
lined with fat.

which, being wrapped in mud and thorns mixed with moss, is buried, and a tree or other memorial erected on the place. The ashes are thrown into the water, the spot where the pile stood is cleansed, and the deities convoked are dismissed with an oblation, which is thrown into the water, and thus the ceremony of gathering the ashes is completed.

On the last day of mourning, the heir puts on neat apparel, has his head and beard shaved and his nails cut, when he gives the barber the clothes worn during the performance of the obsequies, after which he anoints himself with oil of sesamum, and rubs his body with meal of the same, mixed with white mustard seed, bathes, sips water, touches auspicious things, and returns purified to his house, which concludes the first obsequy.

The Hindús are not the only people who consider the touching or approaching a dead body as a defilement. The Jews, both ancient and modern, have the same superstition, (see the 21st chapter of Leviticus,) and the Egyptians, who were so anxious to embalm and preserve the dead, held those who touched them in abomination.

The next obsequy is the consolatory oblation, after which a bull is consecrated and let loose in honour of the deceased; I should be curious to ascertain whether this part of the ceremony is of the nature of turning the scape-goat loosed into the wilderness as loaded with the sins of the people among the Jews.

Various Sradd'has are performed monthly for the first year after the death of a relation, but those at the end of the third fortnight, the sixth month, and the first anniversary are peculiarly holy. The first series of obsequies is intended to effect the re-embodying of the soul, and the second to raise the shade from this world to a place of happiness, for otherwise, like Homer's unburied heroes, it would wander

A naked, helpless, melancholy ghost.

To perpetuate the felicity of progenitors ninety-six formal obsequies are performed in the course of the year, besides the daily oblations to the Manes, which I mentioned before. And now having fed, married, and buried my Hindû, I shall take leave of him and you for the present, satisfied if I have made you better acquainted, and shewed you at the same time that he is not very unlike some of the heroes of other times whom he has had the fortune, whether good or bad I will not say, to outlive.

LETTER XV.

YOUR questions, my dear sir, concerning the barrows found in some parts of the interior of India, are in part answered by the injunction to plant a tree, or raise a mound of earth or masonry on the spot where a funeral pile has stood, or where a sepulchral urn is buried. Some of the artificial hillocks you mention, contain urns, in which bones, coins, and ornaments have been found, and others are heaped over rude stone tombs, in which similar vases are deposited.

Barrrows, ⸜from

——————— " The mound
Of him who felt the Dardan's arrow,
That mighty heap of gathered ground,
Which Ammon's son ran proudly round,
By nations rais'd, by monarchs crown'd,"

to those on which the shepherd of Mona lies to see the green-clad fairies of his isle, while his flock feeds on its short herbage, are found in every part of the globe. The pile of stones in the African desert which hides the entrance to the sepulchral chamber of the Copt, the grassy hillock which breaks the horizon of the vast plains of Tartary, and the tomb of the Cacique which arrests the steps of the Lama

5

driver as he ascends the ridges of the Andes, all attest the desire of man to be after death. All when opened discover the signs of mortality, but all contain likewise some memorial for the future. In one it is the armour which helped to earn the warrior's fame, in another the simple implements which supplied the savage with his food, the pitcher from which he drank, or the axe which opened his path through the forests.

In India the wife, the object of affection, perhaps of that delicate jealousy which dreads the change of sentiment even after death, accompanies the Hindû to his funeral pile. In America the savage

> Thinks that transported to a better sky
> His faithful dog shall bear him company.

The Scaldic warrior carried his armour to his tomb, that in the hall of Odin he might join the joyous battle of the Immortals, and as his manners softened and his creed improved, he still cherished the hope of living in the memory of those he left behind; hence the sword, the spur, and the banner were transferred from the Gothic cairn, to the Christian shrine, and the deep rooted principle of immortality connected man with his progenitors, through all the variations of time, of climate, and of religion.

We may leave to professed antiquarians the task of tracing the individual resemblances and

possible connection between these widely scattered tombs; our present business is with those
of Hindostan, many of which are of unpolished
stones, of a very large size erected on the
plain, and not at all covered; and it is not
uncommon on the road side, or in a grove, or
other public place, to see a simple stone erected
as a memorial of a Hindú soldier fallen in battle,
near the spot where his rude monument stands.
To the memory of kings and warriors, ceno-
taphs were sometimes erected; but the Hindú
tombs which most attracted my attention, were
some of very beautiful forms, which adorn a
low point at the junction of the rivers Moot'ha
and Moolha, near Poonah, raised to the memory
of those pious widows who had ascended the funeral piles of their deceased lords.

A cemetery in the East is generally planted
and adorned with flowers and sweet shrubs, in
affectionate memory of departed friends; and I
have often seen the shrub which marked the
place of a grave, adorned before sunrise with
chaplets of sweet mogree and half blown roses.
Where a holy person has been interred, a little
temple is not unfrequently erected, which, like
the shrine of a Romish saint, is hung with votive
offerings, and crowded with suppliants. Such
are the tombs of the Deos at Chimchore, a
particular account of which I long ago sent
you.

The Mussulmans have contributed greatly to adorn the cities of India with tombs, whose magnificence has never been surpassed, and though all superstitious reverence for the dead be strictly forbidden by the Koran, they have borrowed from their Hindû subjects much of that kind of devotion; and a *Pir's kubber*, or tomb of a Mussulman saint, might pass for the shrine of St. Frideswide or St. Agnes. These buildings, in the parts of India I saw, are of very various sizes and degrees of beauty; they have all domes, under which is the tomb, generally unadorned, however rich the superstructure may be. Two of them at Bombay, one on the point of Love-grove, and the other on the rocks close to the sea-shore, have an interesting story attached to them. Two lovers were together in a pleasure-boat, enjoying the cool breezes of the ocean, when their little bark struck on a concealed rock and sunk; the youth easily got on shore, but finding that his beloved was still struggling in the waves, he returned to save her, but in vain: the bodies of both were afterwards drifted to the land, where they were buried on the different spots on which they were found. Peculiar reverence is paid to these kubbers both by Mussulmans and Hindûs; and I believe that the priest in whose guardianship they are, makes no small profit of the offer-

Y

ings made to the Mánes of the unfortunate lovers.

A stranger in India will not fail to be struck with the indiscriminate respect which the lower classes of Hindûs pay to the objects worshipped by all other sects. I have seen them making their little offerings, and joining the processions at the Mussulman feasts of Hassan and Hossein, and as frequently appearing at the doors of the Romish Portuguese chapels, with presents of candles to burn before the saints, and flowers to adorn the shrines; in short, whatever is regarded as holy by others, they approach with reverence, so much are uncultivated men the creatures of imitation and of habit.

Among the singular coincidences between the usages of the Hindûs and the Christian nations of Europe, I was surprised to find the custom of making April fools, which is equally a practice of the Mussulmans and Indians, and was probably derived to the Western churches by the first importers of Christianity, or at least its forms and ceremonies, from the East, together with some others, as the tonsure, vows of poverty and celibacy, and possibly the chanting of the ritual, although that and the burning of incense be more immediately taken from the Jewish practice.

It is possible that the Mussulmans in India may only join in the *Huli*, for that is the name

of the festival during which the Hindûs amuse
themselves with making what we should call
April fools, from the disposition all men feel
to rejoice with those who rejoice; but it is singular that a custom which some even suppose a
relic of ancient British usages before the introduction of Christianity should prevail to this
day in a country at the distance of half the
globe. The Huli is held in the month of March,
and seems a natural rejoicing for the return of
spring, especially if the theory which derives
the people and religion of Hindostan from a
more northern climate be true. Indra, who
is the lord of showers, or the *Jupiter pluvius* of
the East, is also the god of illusions and deceits
of every kind; now the showery season commences nearly at the time of this festival, and
this mirthful deception may not improperly be
considered as a popular homage to the king of
deceits. Remember, this is only a conjecture
of my own; for I am not learned enough in the
antiquities of Britain or India to pronounce in
any question concerning either. But as I am
mentioning the Huli fools, I must take notice
that on one of the festivals of Bhavani, whom
we may compare to Tellus or Ceres, which happens about the beginning of May, the cow-
keepers and others of that class, erect a pole
adorned with flowers in the gardens with great

Y 2

ceremony and rejoicings, similar to those still made in some parts of England on the erection of the may-pole.

The Hindûs, from what I have seen of them, I should consider as a cheerful people, fond of shews and amusements, although custom prevents them from joining in many of those which enliven the populace of other nations.

Dancing is a diversion of which they never partake, as it is the trade of a peculiar caste, who are hired at all feasts; and that dancing consists more in pantomime than what we call dancing in Europe. The dancers are adorned with jewels and flowing robes, and hung with little bells, which as they move in cadence give an agreeable sound, and men and women are both occasionally employed, although the men chiefly confine themselves to pantomime in the strictest sense of the word. The dancing girls are generally of agreeable persons and countenances, and their motions extremely graceful, to which advantages they frequently add a good voice, and they are taught to sing with sufficient care. Next to exhibitions of dancers, those of tumblers and jugglers, whose feats surpass any thing I have seen in this country, are the favourite diversions of the Hindû populace; the latter have indeed, by their importation into England, made it unnecessary to speak of their feats; and you must be content to believe me when I tell you, that the tumblers are not less excellent in their own line. The exhibiters of *dancing snakes*, as they call themselves, are also peculiar favourites; for it appears a kind of miracle that man should handle unhurt the most noxious of all reptiles, but I never could distinctly ascertain, or make up my mind to believe without ascertaining, what influence may reasonably be ascribed to the music made use of, on these occasions, and more especially on the first catching the snakes, which is certainly accomplished with safety by these men, while others dread to approach their haunts.

Shews of wild beasts are also favourites with the Hindús, and although the drama and the arts depending on it have almost disappeared, representations of a more rude nature are eagerly run after by the idlers that crowd the streets of an Indian town towards the evening. But though these shews and exhibitions, with religious processions and feasts, make a tolerable catalogue of popular amusements, it would be incomplete without that one which every Hindû, from the prince to the peasant, delights to indulge in; I mean the recital of poems or histories, either simply told or sung in a kind of recitative. For this a Hindû will forego his sleep and his food, and sit for hours motionless in the circle formed round the bard or story-teller; and I think I may fairly say that no inducement would tempt him to forego that enjoyment, excepting the stronger passion for play, which rages with unlimited power in Hindostan.

Among the lower classes, it is very common to see a man who was loaded with jewels of gold and silver on his hands, feet, waist, neck, ears, and nose in the morning, come home at night without a single bracelet left, and frequently also without his turban and his cloak. Cock-fighting and other similar diversions are the principal enjoyments of this class; quails, and even still smaller birds, are trained in the same manner, according as the master can afford to rear them; and happy, indeed, is he who is possessed of a fighting ram. These animals are very easily trained to combat, and a battle between two of acknowledged reputation, is a feast to the villages for miles round. The courts of Hindostan are equally fond of this kind of spectacle; but their shews consisted formerly of combats between elephants, often previously made drunk with wine or spirits, and sometimes also of tigers with other animals.

As to the sedentary games of the Hindûs, their well established claim to the original invention of chess, proves them to have been long

addicted to that kind of amusement. The Chinese have endeavoured to appropriate the invention; but as they acknowledge their acquaintance with it to be so recent as only 174
years before Christ, and as the Hindûs unques-
tionably played it before that time, their claim
falls to the ground. The game played in Persia and modern Hindostan is so exactly similar
to that known in Europe, that you can be at no
loss to understand it; only you will have to
unlearn all the names of the pieces except those
of the king and the pawns or peons. The
queen being the *vizier* or *ferz*, minister or
general; the bishop *fil* or *hust*, elephant; the
knight *asp* or *ghora*, horse; and the castle *rookh*
or *rat'h*, war chariot, though it is sometimes
called *naucà*, a boat. The game, however, as
described by ancient Hindû writers, cited by
Sir William Jones, is more complicated, and
according to him more modern than the simple
game as we know it. It is played by four persons, each of whom has only half the number
of pieces which our game gives to each army,
and these are ranged on each side of the board,
composed like ours of sixty-four squares, the
black army being to the north, the red to the
east, the green to the south, and the yellow to
the west; two of the kings become allies, and
the moves are determined by dice; if a cinque

is thrown, the king or a pawn must be moved; if quatre, the elephant; if trois, the horse; if a deux, the boat. The king may seat himself on the throne of his ally, if he be skilful enough, and take the command of the two armies; and his object is always to get the thrones of his opponents, and if at the same time he takes his enemy, it is a complete victory. The mixture of chance and skill in this game renders it inferior to the game of chess as now generally used; but it is not less an image of war, as its name Chaturanga or Chaturanji denotes. It signifies the *four members* of an army, elephants, horses, chariots, and foot-soldiers; and through its corruptions by the Persians, Arabs, and Europeans, Sir W. Jones most ingeniously derives the name of chess.

The Hindû legends ascribe the invention of this game to the wife of Ravana, king of Lanka, or Ceylon, to amuse her husband with an image of field war, while he was closely besieged in his capital by Rama and his army of mountaineers from the continent, called not unaptly monkeys, baboons, and satyrs; whence the fables concerning the divine ape Hanumân. The varieties of this game are almost as numerous as the nations who play it in the East. The Chinese have, in the centre of their board, a river or moated ditch, over which the elephant never passes; and the king and his two sons never leave a diagram marked out for them, and called a fort, in the centre of their respective dominions. They have besides a rocketeer or *pao*, who can only take one adversary when he leaps over the head of another. The Burmahs have, like us, only two armies; but the places for the pieces, excepting the pawns, are arbitrary, and may be varied according to skill or caprice. Some of the games limit the honours of the pawns who reach the last squares of their enemies; others allow them no privileges at all; but they are all evidently the same game and founded on the same principles. The common people in India are very fond of a game, which is to their chaturanga, what our draughts is to chess: they either use as a board, a piece of cloth on which squares and diagrams of different colours are wrought, or they chalk the ground, or draw lines on the sand, to answer the same purpose; the game is played with different coloured seeds, or stones, or shells, or even balls of cotton; to fix the moves, a shell is thrown up as in playing at pitch-farthing, and the side on which it descends determines the play. There are a number of other popular games, but I am ashamed to say that I did not sufficiently attend to them while I was on the spot, to be able to give an intelligible account of them. However, as we are assured by grave authors, that the Greek babies amused themselves with playing at what every Scotch child would call *chuckies*, and moreover that they were not ignorant of hot-cockles, some traces of which I think I discovered, with other symptoms of *practical wit*, among my Eastern friends; I dare say that in many of our nursery games, we might find the identical diversions of the deified Rama, as well as the childish sports of Achilles and his Myrmidons. But although these games, as they now are the chief recreations of the Hindûs, were also formerly the delight of their kings and heroes, who carried them to such lengths as sometimes even to lose their kingdoms at a game, witness the story of the sons of Pandoo, they were still more famous for martial and manly exercises. The tribe of Jhattries, which was divided into ten families, and descended from the Brahminical caste, had, like the ancient Athletæ, no other profession than that of teaching the arts of boxing, wrestling, running, and managing the discus and other warlike instruments, of which they reckon ten peculiar to their tribe. I am told by gentlemen who have seen them exercise, which they do naked in an arena covered with red sand, or fine earth, and with their bodies rubbed with oil, that their feats of strength and agility are wonderful, and that nothing can exceed the beauty of their attitudes. But they are not now either so numerous, or in such high repute, as in the days of Hindû splendor. The Ayeen Akbery mentions a tribe of wrestlers from Iran and Touran long settled in India, and called in the days of Akbar *Pehlawan*, from the name of their native country. The Hindû wrestlers consider Crishna as their patron, but their tutelary deity is Bhawanee, as that of the wrestler Antæus was his mother *Earth*, who, as I have already remarked, is the same; and although the reformed Hindû religion forbids sanguinary sacrifices, they by no means conform to the bloodless rites of their modern Hindû brethren, for they eat meat in large quantities, and twice a year offer up a ram or a goat to their goddess.

The Jhattries are thus among the very few remains of the Hindûs who still persevere in the ancient sanguinary sacrifices. Some of the others even go so far as, on very great occasions, to choose a human victim; but the sects of this description are so rare, and so little numerous or powerful, that they conceal themselves with the greatest care, and content themselves with poisoning a poor beggar now and then, as an offering to Kali, another form of Bhawanee, in which she may be compared to Hecate, or the Infernal

5

Diana. The instances of suicide in honour of the divinities, can scarcely be ranked among the sacrifices ordained by the ancient worship, as they are merely acts of momentary enthusiasm or despondency, inflicted on a man's own person.

The following sketch from Mr. Blaquiere's translation of the Rudhirádhyáyá, or sanguinary chapter of the Cálicá Purana, you may compare, if you have leisure, with the bloodstained rites of the ancient Greeks, Syrians, and even our own Druids. The goddess Cáli or Bhairava, is the proper consort of Siva, the destroying principle, in his character of Rudra the terrible; and to her, all sanguinary sacrifices are acceptable, from a tortoise to a human victim; and the pleasure which she receives from each, is proportioned to their supposed importance in the scale of existence. That arising from the blood of a fish or tortoise, only lasts for one month; while that from the sweet savour of a human being is extended to a thousand years, and an offering of three men delights the goddess for a hundred thousand years. The sacrifice is most dignified when performed with an axe; less so, when a hatchet, knife, or saw, is used; and the least worthy, is when the victim is slain with a hoe or spade. The *formulæ* employed on these occasions are savage and blood-thirsty, as the sacrifice is commonly offered in order to obtain revenge on enemies; and whether it be the blood of a victim, or the supplicant's own blood, which he presents, the rites are nearly the same. Human blood must be offered in vessels of gold, silver, copper, brass, or earth; but that of other sacrifices may be presented in vessels made of leaves or of wood.

The sacrifice of human victims, or indeed of animals, especially the horse, cow, and elephant, if I understand rightly, is reserved for monarchs; unless in cases of war, when it may be performed by princes or their ministers at pleasure, to insure the success of a battle. If a human offering be made, he must be a man of twenty-five, without taint or blemish, and what is still a harder condition, he must be a voluntary victim. Being led to the place of sacrifice which is a cemetery*, he is rubbed with the dust of sandal wood, adorned with chaplets of flowers, and fed with the consecrated food which has for two days previously been his diet. The sacrificer then worships him, and prays to him, as having already become like the deity; and standing with his face

---

* See the account of Malati Madhava in a former letter.

to the north, and averting his eyes, while the victim looks eastward, he severs his head from his body; and according to the quarter in which it falls, omens, good or bad, for the sacrificer, are drawn. The head and blood, mingled with salt, which are particularly sweet to the goddess, are then presented on her right side; and portions of the flesh are offered as burnt oblations.

It is allowed to substitute images for the real victims; and I believe it would be impossible to trace for years, perhaps for centuries past, any instance among respectable Hindus of this shocking outrage of nature. The few obscure murders which I before mentioned, must be regarded in the same light with the offerings of the wild mountain tribes near Chitagong, who, to avert a war or a pestilence from their horde, descend from their hills, and falling on the first traveller, carry off his head in triumph, as an acceptable present to their gods.

The sacrifice of animals was expressly substituted by the Jewish law in the room of the first-born of the children of Israel; so that it is natural to infer from this circumstance, as well as the intended offering up of Isaac, to say nothing of Jephtha's daughter, that such rites were common in Syria, if not in Egypt, the birthplace and the cradle of the Hebrew nation. Their ritual also required victims without spot or blemish, and they were slain with an axe, and the blood sprinkled on and round the altar, while the touching it purified the sacrificer. (*See Leviticus, of the different offerings.*) The cutting of the flesh, however, and the offering one's own blood, were strictly forbidden; neither was the burning of one's own flesh, or any other such superstition, practised or permitted.

Joyless I view the pillars vast and rude,
Where erst the fool of superstition trod,
In smoking blood imbru'd,
And raising from the tomb
Mistaken homage to an unknown God.
* * * * * * * * * *
* * * * * * * * * *
Ye dreary altars, by whose side
The Druid priest in crimson dy'd,
The solemn dirges sung,
And drove the golden knife
Into the palpitating seat of life,
When rent with horrid shouts the distant vallies rung.
The bleeding body bends,
The glowing purple stream descends,
Whilst the troubled spirit near,
Hovers in the steamy air.
Again the sacred dirge they sing,
Again the distant hill and coppice valley ring.
Chatterton.

Bulls and goats appear to have been the appointed offerings of the Jews. Goats were the most common sacrifices in India; but for these it was permitted to substitute spirits or fermented liquors. But the great sacrifice which monarchs performed to obtain their dearest wishes, and which indeed required a monarch's revenue to accomplish, was the *Aswamedha,* or sacrifice of a horse. The steed intended for that purpose was to be young, unbroke, pure, and free from blemish, and he was allowed to ramble unconfined for twelve months previous to the ceremony; but if during that time any one laid his hand upon him, he was rendered unfit for the purpose, and the preparations which were both expensive and tedious were to begin anew. The Ramayuna begins the history of Rama with the description of the Aswamedha performed by Dasaratha to obtain a son; and it appears that on this solemn occasion all the neighbouring monarchs were invited, and the Brahmins from every surrounding nation assembled; artificers from every country were employed in erecting the wood-work for the ceremony, and, it is to be supposed, the temporary shelter for the immense multitude that assembled to share the largesses distributed by the monarch. The poet says, that during the whole time, the words, Give! Eat! were everywhere heard, and serving-men in sumptuous apparel

3

distributed food. The voice of the holy Brahmins repeating the sacred texts, was heard amidst the songs of gladness in the streets, and at length, when the horse returned from his journey of a year, he was sacrificed with transports of joy. Pits lined with bricks had been prepared for the altars, that the blood and the water of oblations might flow round them; these pits were arranged in the form of Garoora the divine eagle, and those of the wings were lined with bricks of gold; three hundred other animals, birds, beasts, and fishes, were sacrificed at the same time, by the sixteen officiating priests, appointed by Dasaratha; and the chief priest then took out their hearts, and dressed them according to the law of sacrifices, carefully observing the omens, which promised happiness and the accomplishment of his wishes to the King. The most ancient Greek and Tuscan ceremonies appear to have resembled these in many, if not most particulars; but the heroes of Homer were too impetuous to wait so long for the fulfilment of their vows, as the great Aswamedha required. They no sooner reached the destined place of worship, but they

" Their hecatomb prepar'd;
" Between their horns the *salted barley* threw,
" And with their heads to heaven the victim slew."

Pope's Homer, b. i.

z

But I dare say you will think this enough of sanguinary sacrifices. Of other offerings I have spoken in describing the ceremonies of hospitality, marriages, and funerals. They consist of milk, water, honey, fruit, seeds, and flowers, besides butter and curds, with which on many occasions the barley and other seeds are moistened.

These simple acknowledgments of the goodness of the Deity are certainly more pleasing than the former sacrifices. But the universal belief in the fall of man from a state of happiness and innocence, and the consequent necessity for a means of propitiating the offended Deity, has over the whole of the ancient world produced the same effects; and feeble man, eager to avert punishment from himself, or to draw it down upon his enemies, has often been led to the commission of crimes revolting to nature, under the idea, that a great and painful sacrifice was alone meritorious in the eyes of the God of mercy and forgiveness!

Happily those days of darkness have passed away; and that there is not now a spot upon the earth, where a human victim is deliberately sacrificed, and scarcely any where even an animal bleeds upon the altar, is a sufficient answer to the cant of those who are daily lamenting the deterioration of mankind, and the corruption of the world in general.

LETTER XVI.

MY DEAR SIR,

I AM not surprised that you find it difficult to reconcile the enormous absurdity and horrible superstitions I mentioned in my last letter, with those sublime notions of the Deity implied in the account of the creation of the world, by the simple *thought* of the Self-existent Intelligence. But you must remember that the one is the belief of the philosopher, the other that of the multitude, and that even Lycurgus could do no more when he reformed Sparta, than to change the human victims offered to Diana upon its altars, into those severe flagellations, which often proved real sacrifices, and which were regarded as honourable in proportion to the blood spilt in the sight of the goddess.

I am not fond of the Hindû mythology, but I do not on the whole think worse of it than of that of the West, excepting indeed that its fictions have employed less elegant pens. When Apollo, crowned with light and surrounded by the Muses, wakes the golden lyre, and harmonizes heaven and earth; or Love and the Graces move in magic dance on the delicious shores of Pa-

phos, we Westerns feel, as Akenside expresses
it,

" The form of beauty smiling at our heart."

But the graceful Crishna with his attendant
nymphs moving in mystic unison with the Seasons, and the youthful Camdeo, tipping his
arrows with the budding floweret, are images
scarcely inferior in beauty, and have waked
the poet's song as sweetly on the banks of Sona
or Godavery as the triumphs of the ocean-born
goddess on those of " smooth sliding Mincius." -

However this be, I will endeavour to give
you an intelligible account of the deities of Hindostan, premising that there are parts of their
mythology over which the veil of mystery is,
and ought to be spread.

The creation of the gods is supposed to be
coeval with that of the world, and when the
Supreme Intelligence called the universe into
being, he delegated to the gods the creation of
mankind, and the formation and government of
all mundane objects. Brahma, the creating
energy, with Vishnu the preserver, and Siva,
the destroyer, were the greatest of the deities;
and there is a mysterious fable concerning a
great sacrifice offered up by the immortals in
which Brahma was the oblation, and from his
different members the different classes of mankind are said to have sprung. But leaving the

mysterious part of the mythology, which might perhaps be traced to an allegorical description of the operations of nature, I will name the principal gods whose images are now worshipped in India, from the mountains of Cashmeer to Cape Comorin; and as Brahma is usually named first, and the priesthood and religion are called after him, I shall begin with him accordingly.

Since the creation, Brahma, according to the vulgar mythology, has little concern with the affairs of men. But identified with Savitri, the sun, he is worshipped by the Brahmins in the Gayatri, which you are already acquainted with, as the most holy of texts, and indeed as itself deified and receiving oblations. One of the most important of Brahma's characters is that of the father of legislators, his ten sons being the promulgators of laws and science upon earth, and from himself the Vedas are supposed to have originally proceeded, although in later times, i. e. about 1400 years before Christ, they were collected and arranged by the philosopher and poet Vyasa. The laws bearing the name of Menu, sometimes called the son of Brahma, and the works of the other Rishis or holy persons, have also been re-written, or perhaps collected from oral tradition, long after the ages in which the sons of Brahma are said to have revealed them; but still they are all ascribed to the immediate offspring of the Creating Power. This character of Brahma agrees with what the Grecian poets say of Jupiter the father of Minos; whose wise and celebrated laws were promulgated in the same century in which Vyasa collected the Vedas.

Jupiter also, under the name of Anxur or Axur, was worshipped as the sun, and Brahma is identified with that deity. The common form under which Brahma is represented is that of a man with four heads*, when he is called *Chaturmooki*, and four hands, and it is remarkable that Jupiter with four heads was worshipped by the Lacedemonians; and the title of father of gods and men is equally applicable to Brahma and to Jupiter.

The wife or *sacti* of Brahma is Saraswatee; she is the patroness of learning and the arts, and is frequently invoked with Genesa at the beginning of books. She is sometimes considered as the daughter, sometimes as the sister of Brahma; and, under her name of Brahmanee, is worshipped among the primeval mothers of the earth, of which there are eight, who are the wives of the eight regents of the world †. One

---

* There is a mystical story of his having had five heads, one of which was cut off by Siva.

† Indra, lord of the East; 2. Agni, of the South-East; 3. Yama, of the South; 4. Nyruta, of the South-West; 5. Varnna, of the West; 6. Voyoova, god of wind, of the North-West; 7. Cuvera, of the North; 8. Iswara, of the North-East.

of the names of Seraswatee is Sach or Speech, and in one of the sacred books she is introduced describing herself, nearly in the words of the famous inscription on the statue of Isis—" I am all that has been, or shall be, &c." A goose, the emblem of watchfulness, is consecrated to Se-raswatee, and she is often represented in paint-ing and sculpture, borne by that bird, and play-ing on the vina or Indian lyre, of which the in-vention is ascribed to her. She is sometimes seen attendant upon Brahma, while he, seated on a lotus, is engaged in holy ceremonies, and holding in one hand the vedas, while with the other three he consecrates the sacrificial utensils.

Siva is the deity who appears to have been most extensively worshipped. In his attributes he sometimes agrees with Brahma, sometimes with Vishnu, and often with the Sun. His own double character of destroyer and reproducer, refers to the operations of nature, who annihi-lates nothing, but, in the apparent destruction of bodies, only changes the form under which their elements appear. His names are too numerous to be recounted at length, but his principal cha-racters are Rudra, Iswara, and Mahadeo. As Rudra he is cruel, and delights in sanguinary sacrifices; under the character of Iswara, he is absolute lord of all; but, by the name of Maha

Deo, or great god, he is worshipped over all the mountainous parts of India, and has even many votaries in the plains. He is adored with the same pomp as that by which the Egyptians consecrated to Osiris, and the Athenians to Dionysius or the Indian Bacchus; and it is remarkable that one of the incarnations of Siva was Deo Naush, and one of his names Baghis. I know not if Iswara and Osiris have the same signification, but the similarity of their attributes and worship renders it probable that they are one and the same. The bull commonly called Nundi, is the animal sacred to Mahadeo, who frequently is mounted on him, and Apis in Egypt was a type of Osiris, divine honours were paid to him, and, as in India, to every animal of the ox kind.

In the character of Rudra, Siva corresponds with the Stygian Jove or Pluto, and there is a curious coincidence between him and Jupiter, namely that the titles of Triophthalmos and Trilochan have the same signification, the first being applied to the Grecian god whose statue was found about the time of the Trojan war, with a third eye in his forehead, and the second is a common name of Siva when he is depicted with the same feature. As Cala or Time he also agrees with Chronos or Saturn, who like him delighted in human sacrifices.

SIVA and PARVATI attended by VISHNU
and BRAHMA CHOTURMOOKHEE.
Mahabalipur.

Among the Hindûs, Siva is one of the greatest of the deities, and there are some sects who contend that all others are subordinate to him, or only his attributes; he is a particular favourite with the common people and with the Sanyassees who claim him as their peculiar patron, under the name of Dhoorghati, or with twisted locks. He is often represented with several heads, but generally he is contented with one. The number of his hands differs from four to thirty-two, and there is a peculiar weapon appropriated to each. He sits upon a tyger's or an elephant's hide, and he wears round his neck a chaplet of human skulls; the river Ganges is seen descending from his head, where she rested on her way from heaven to earth, and the moon adorns his forehead.

Thus decorated, his residence is on Mount Kailassa, where he is surrounded by celestial forms, and is amused with songs and dances, while his wife Parvati, the mountain-born goddess, sits by his side and partakes his banquets.

This Deity is one of the most celebrated in Hindû legends. She is Maha Cali or the great goddess of time: as such she demands victims of every kind from man to the tortoise. She is the punisher of all evil doers: in this character she corresponds with Proserpine, Diana Taurica, and the three-formed Hecate, as well as in that of patroness of enchantments. The Diana of Ephesus who was represented with a number of breasts, was considered by the ancients as the same with Cybele and Terra; Parvati is also Bhawance, or female nature upon earth, when she appears like the Ephesian Diana. The appropriate name, however, of the goddess Earth is Prit'hivi, an inferior deity, but not on all occasions distinguishable from Bhawanee, whose attendant animal or vahan, *vehicle*, is like that of Cybele a lion, though as the wife of Siva, she is often seen with the Bull. Diana, Ceres, and Cybele are all supposed to be the same with Isis the wife of Osiris, and one of the names of Parvati is Isa, as the wife of Mahesa or Iswara.

Besides these characters in common with the deities of Greece, she is Doorga, or active virtue, in which character she fought and overcame Maissassoor the demon of vice, and this battle is celebrated by all sects in poems and songs. She is represented as Maha Cali, extremely ugly with long teeth and nails, sometimes dancing on a dead body, with weapons of destruction and punishment in her eight hands, and a chaplet of skulls round her neck. As Bhawanee she is more comely, and is worshipped with feasts in the spring. But Doorga is her favourite character, and her worship is performed in the autumn with excessive rejoicing and splendor.

One of the appellations of Doorga is Maha moordanee, and by this name her figure which is sculptured at Mahaballi pooram, and is one of the best sculptures I saw in India, is distinguished. On the festival of Doorga Pooja her statues are carried in procession to the nearest river or lake, and there plunged into the water. But all these characters of the goddess are either obsolete or eclipsed by that of Padmala and Camala, or the lotus-born. Here she is decidedly the Venus of the western mythologists; she sprung from the churning of the ocean on a flower, and was received as the goddess of beauty by the celestials who bestowed her in marriage on Siva. With him she partakes of the charms of Kailassa, and she is the mother of Camdeo or Depac, the Indian Cupid, and of Cartakeya, the Indian Mars, whose vahan, the peacock, is often placed by her side. Ganesa, the god of wisdom, is also reckoned among her sons, and she is regarded not less than Seraswattee, as the patroness of science. She is also the guardian of those who work in mines, and is the inventress of musical instruments whose sounds are produced by wires. Here she resembles Minerva, and from her being equally skilled in arms and arts, she may be regarded as one with that goddess. The statues which were placed in public roads of Mercury and Minerva joined, had, possibly, the same origin with those of Siva and Parvati, which are extremely common in India. Parvati is peculiarly the goddess of the women of the lower class, by whom she is invoked on all occasions, and she has also a sect of worshippers who call themselves Sactis, and who own no other deity. The temples of Siva and of Parvati have always a bull placed at the entrance, and at his feet is usually depicted a tortoise: the Greeks, in adopting the forms and accompaniments of the more ancient mythologies, at a loss for the mystical meaning of this attendant on Jupiter, invented the fable of Chelone, to account for the presence of that animal in the temples of Jove.

My favourite among the Hindû deities of the higher order is Vishnu, not only as he is the preserving power, but as he is a much more gentlemanlike personage; for we never read of his flying into those outrageous passions which derogate from the dignity of Siva, or find him using unworthy stratagems, like Indra, for the accomplishment of his purposes. He is always ready to take upon him the evils of humanity in order to relieve the distrest. He it is who, by his benign influence, counteracts the rage of Mahadeo, and preserves the present order of creation; but when his sleep commences, destruction will prevail, and after the night of Brahma, who for a season is absorbed in Vishnu, a new effort of the Almighty must be made for a new creation.

Jupiter, in his best character of conservator, is the western prototype of Vishnu. They both preside over the rites of hospitality and protect strangers, and the constant attendant of both is a celestial eagle.

But Vishnu is also Varoona armed with a trisool, or three-toothed sceptre, and rules the ocean; thus he is Neptune, or Oceanus *. Sir William Jones calls Varoona a form of Siva, but I believe he will be found to be Vishnu, who is constantly called Narayana, and is in that character always represented floating on the ocean, sometimes on a leaf, and sometimes on Maha Shesha the great serpent, who is also Ananta, or Endless. It is true that the attributes, and even weapons, of Siva and Vishnu are interchangeable; hence the former is occasionally armed with the trisool of the latter.

When Vishnu is not seen sleeping on the ocean, he is represented with four or more arms, of an agreeable aspect and graceful figure. His colour is dark blue; hence he is called Nielkont, and he holds a lotus, the emblem of water; the

* There is besides Varoona, Samudra, who is to Varoona as Oceanus to Neptune.

chakra, or ornamented discus ; and the chank or
conch, the large buccimun, on which the note
of victory is sounded. Besides these, he has
sometimes the Agniastra or fiery dart, perhaps
the thunderbolt, and often the trisool. His
head is sometimes ornamented with a three-
plaited lock, symbolic of Ganges, who is said to
fall from his foot upon the head of Siva, and who
is often called Triveni, or of three locks or divisions, which name refers to the three great
streams Ganges, Jumna, and Sareswata, the last
of which, the Brahmins affirm, joins the other
two by a subterraneous passage. Vishnu is often
borne on the wings of Garura or Garuda, who is
not unfrequently depicted with a human body,
but the beak and wings of a hawk. Jupiter's
eagle and attendant Ganymede seem here to be
blended. The paradise of the preserving power
is Vaikont'ha, where he enjoys the company of
his beloved Sree, or Lukshmce, the goddess of
fortune and of plenty. She is one of the most
beautiful of the goddesses, and is often considered as Camala, the lotus-born, and the mother of Camdeo, and consequently the same with
Parvati. Indeed the whole of the goddesses,
like the gods, seem resolvable into one divinity,
and the fables invented concerning the different
attributes have given rise to the idea of their
being actually different persons. The names of

7

the three great divinities, however various, are
all resolvable into those of the sun, fire and air;
and these again into that of one great deity, who
is visibly represented in the creation by the sun.
But in the vulgar mythology, Surya, the regent
of that planet, is a person of much less importance than either of those who compose the great
triad. He has, however, a numerous sect of
worshippers, who call themselves after his name
Sanras. The splendid sun is, according to the
Gayatri, one with truth, and with the supreme
intelligence who creates, directs, and animates
the whole universe. He is invoked with peculiar reverence by the learned, but the people
only see his image drawn in a chariot by a many-
headed horse, who represents the hours, and attended by a favourite charioteer, Arun, whom
we may call the dawn, and followed by the
twelve Aditis or seasons. When we come to
speak of the Awatars, or incarnations of Vishnu,
I shall have further occasion to mention Surya
under the form of Crishna; till then I will go
on with the other popular deities. Chandra, the
Moon, is, like the Deus Lunus of the ancient
Italians, a male, contrary to all our western notions. This personage has been chiefly introduced into the mythology by his place in the
astronomical sastras. The twenty-eight lunar
stations into which the heavens are divided by the

Hindûs, are fabled to contain each a wife of Chandra, whom he visits in turn. Hᴖ is invoked with Surya and the other planets in   sacrifices, and is drawn in a car by an antelope, as Diana frequently is by a stag.   All animals with horns, and the hare and rabbit are especially under the protection of Chandra.

Yama, the God of Death and Sovereign of Patala or Hell, is also judge of departed souls, who at stated periods travel in great numbers to his dreary abode, which was fabled to be situated far to the north-west, for the purpose of being judged.   The track of the souls in passing to the place of reward or punishment is fabled to be the milky way.   Yama is nearly akin to Pluto, or perhaps still more nearly to Minos: one of his titles is Dherma Raja, or king of justice; another Petripeti, or lord of patriarchs; and a third Sraddhadéva, or god of funeral offerings. He is also Cala, or Time, though Siva is sometimes worshipped under that name.

Plutus has been sometimes confounded with Pluto by the western mythologists; but the Hindû god of riches has nothing in common with Yama, unless we suppose the Golden, Silver, and Iron Islands, which constitute part of the dominions of the latter, to give the former a title to share his kingdom.   But Cuvera is rather the presiding genius of riches or metals than a god him-

8

self; he has no altars, and prayers for wealth are addressed to Lakshemi, the goddess of Fortune. His splendid residence is in the palace of Alaca, in the forest of Chitraruthra, and he is drawn in a splendid chariot, and surrounded by numerous beautiful attendants called Yacshas.

Agni, the god of fire, is one of the most singular in his form of all the many-limbed tribe of Indian divinities. He has usually three legs and four arms, and is represented breathing fire and riding on a ram: he has various names, but he is best known by that of Agni. Viswacarma, the artificer of the gods, is annually worshipped by the Hindû mechanics, and all tools of carpenters, masons, and other artificers, are consecrated to him.

Aswini and Kumara are the regents of medicine. Kartekeya is the son of Parvati; he is the leader of the celestial armies, and being born with six heads he was committed to the six Kritikas * to nurse, who each fed one mouth. These nurses were placed among the stars at a distance from their husbands the Rishis†, whom they had betrayed, and only the seventh, the

* The Kritikas are the stars which form the constellation of the Pleiades.

† The Rishis are the seven stars of the Great Bear. The small star which makes one of these a double star is Arundati.

A A

faithful Arundati, was permitted to remain with her spouse, and to attend him in his nocturnal revolution. Kartekeya is also called Scanda and Swamykartic; he is represented riding on or attended by a peacock, with weapons in his eight hands. His temper is irascible, like that of his brother Mars, but his power is very limited. Camdeo, the god of love, is called Kundurpa, Muddun, and Ununga or the bodyless. He is the son of Parvati, and besides his bow and shafts he carries a banner on which a fish is depicted, and he sometimes also rides on a fish. His bow is of sugar-cane, with a string of bees, and his darts are tipped with the new buds of the sweetest flowers. It happened one day, that while Siva with uplifted arm was performing sacred austerities, the thoughtless Camdeo wounded the terrible god, who instantly with a flash from his eye consumed his body; hence Kundurpa is the only one of the Indian deities who is incorporeal.

Pavana, the deity of the winds, is the father of Hanumân, the monkey-formed god, whose adventures are closely connected with those of the Awatara Rama Chandra, but his character nearly resembles that of Pan; and the whole race of divine monkeys, whose birth is recorded in the Ramayuna, may be said to be of the same family with the satyrs and fauns of the west.

Like Pan, Hanumân was the patron if not the inventor of a particular mode of music, and like him also he inhabited the woods and forests, and was the chief of the sylvan deities.

Nareda, a son of Brahma, was the peculiar patron of music in general, but his principal character is that of a lawgiver. Of the Ragas and Raginis, or male and female genii of music, I formerly gave you an account, and I only mention them now as the companions of Nareda.

Indra is a deity who ranks next to the three great divinities, and in most of his attributes he resembles the Jupiter of Europe. He is particularly the god of the atmosphere, and his will directs all its changes. He is also the deity of delusions; and being in his moral character no better than Jove himself, his changes of form served him for the same purposes as those of the Grecian father of gods and men. His body, from the shoulders to the waist, is spotted with eyes, to mark his constant vigilance, hence he is said to resemble Argus. He is the chief of the celestial spirits who are innumerable, and who inhabit Swerga, the Hindû Paradise, and the abode of virtuous souls; he also presides over the spirits of the earth and sea. His favourite palace is in the forest Nundana, where his pleasures are participated by his wife Indranee, who partakes also of his power, and is usually seen seated by his side on their beautiful three-trunked elephant, surrounded by attendant Dewtas.

High in a mountain vale, retired from the painful task of guiding either gods or men, resides Casyapa, the priest of the gods, and sometimes called their father; his life and retirement resemble that of Saturn while he reigned over Latium in the golden age. He and his respectable consort are attended by holy nymphs, fair as the Houris of Mahomet and pure as the maidens of Vesta. In their court the innocent and oppressed on earth find repose and protection, and a holy calm breathes eternal peace through their beneficent shades, where Ganesa, the god of wisdom, is the most frequent and most welcome guest.

Ganesa, whom I have placed last among the Hindû gods, is invoked the first by the Brahmins in all sacrifices and in all trials by ordeal. His name, sometimes accompanied by that of Seraswati, begins every book and writing, and even grants of lands and transfers of estates. His statues are placed on roads and at the boundaries of townships and villages, like those of the god Terminus, and he is worshipped, like Hanumân and Pan, under trees and in sylvan places. On the Coromandel coast he is peculiarly honoured under his name of Polear; at Chimchore the incarnation of Ganesa in the Deo of that

Drawn by M.G.   Etched by S.D.G.

GANESA
the Hindoo God of Letters.

place receives divine honours, and he is univer-sally respected throughout India.

A statue of Ganesa is always placed on the ground where it is intended to erect any build-ing, after the spot has been sanctified by smear-ing it with cow-dung and ashes; and in short, the god of wisdom, or rather prudence and foresight, is of all the Indian deities the most familiar, and the most resembling the Lares of the ancients; though Hanumân, among the lower classes of Hindûs, partakes of this character.

Sir William Jones has so carefully and elo-quently compared the Indian Ganesa with the Roman Janus that we can scarcely doubt of their identity. They both presided over the begin-nings of things and actions, they had both two faces, and occasionally four, to denote that pru-dence sees around and contemplates the past and present as well as the future, and they were equally invoked the first in all sacrifices.

One character of Ganesa, that of patron of letters, he has in common with the Grecian Apollo, although the Delphian deity is better represented by Crishna, one of the Awatars of Vishnu, of whom we shall have to speak in his proper place. Ganesa is represented of a large size, with the head of an elephant, usually four-handed and often four-faced; his common at-tendant is the rat, the emblem of foresight. He

4

is frequently seen attending on Siva and Parvati in the bowers of Kaylassa, when his employment is to fan his parent deities with a chamara of feathers, while Nareda plays before them on his vina, accompanied by the heavenly choirs.

Thus I have given you a short list of the principal deities of Hindostan, which will be sufficient for the understanding of such ceremonies as you are most likely to see performed in India; but you must expect to find a different name, or at least a different pronunciation of the name, in every district for the same divinity. The self-torturers, who as fakirs, sanyassees, &c. will sometimes shock your sight, are commonly votaries of Siva or of Parvati, under some one of their various names. The celebrated temple of Jaggernaut or Jagganat'h,* which at its annual feast presents, perhaps, the greatest abuses that ever disgraced a religious institution, has received its full measure of reprobation. The charitable feast, where, contrary to the laws concerning caste, all Hindûs are not only permitted but commanded to eat together, is, perhaps, the only pure remnant of the ancient institutions of the temple. And if the frenzy of superstition casts the votaries of the god under the wheels of his carriage to meet a glorious death, it is to the fanaticism consequent on the persecutions which the long wars that brought about the change of religion in India produced, that it must be attributed. Crishna, who is the same with Jagganat'h, abolished the sanguinary sacrifices required by Rudra and Cali. He in his turn was deified, and the enthusiastic self-devotion of the poor Hindû who prostrated himself before the car of the merciful power who had arrested the sacrifice of his children, may account, on principles not totally unworthy of our nature, for actions which seem to be at war with that nature itself. I am aware that the account I now send you of the Indian mythology may deserve the censure which one of the ablest oriental critics pronounced on a certain elaborate work, that it is but a "Bazar account of the Hindû theology." But I could not, if I would, have given you a deeper insight into it without entering upon topics which would have led me far beyond the limits I had prescribed to myself, and which, as they would have been useless to you, would have been disagreeable to me.

There is one portion, however, of this mythology which is blended with the history of India, and which I will enlarge upon. It may be compared to that of the heroic ages of Greece, namely, that of the several Awatars of Vishnu, or his incarnations and descents upon earth. The first of these Awatars refers to that universal deluge, of which the tradition is preserved by all nations. Here the preserving deity in the form of a large fish (Matsya Avatara) is fabled to have watched over and preserved the boat of the Menu Satyavrata, during the deluge occasioned by the wickedness which degraded all mankind after they had lost the holy books of laws given them by Brahma.

The second Awatar is that of Koorma, or the Tortoise, which has also a reference to the deluge. The good things of the creation having perished in the waters, the immortals wished to renovate the earth, and for this purpose Vishnu became a tortoise, and supported on his firm back the Mount Meru, or the north pole, while the deities placing round it the great serpent of eternity, gave it a rotatory motion so as to agitate the milky ocean, whence sprang innumerable good things, but seven were pre-eminent: the moon, the elephant *, the horse †, a physician, a beautiful woman ‡, a precious gem, and Amrita, or the water of life, which was drunk immediately by the spirits, so that man still

* Mythologically this elephant had three trunks, and is the favourite of Indra.

† This was the seven-headed horse of Surya or the Sun.

‡ This woman is often said to be Lacshemi, or Camala, when she is like the popular Venus, and is the chief of the Apsaras or graces, who, however, are more akin to the inhabitants of Mahomet's paradise.

VARAHA AWATAR.

remains subject to death. The third Awatar has
likewise reference to the drowning of the world,
for in it Vishnu is feigned to have heard the
complaints of Prit'hivi, the goddess of Earth,
who was nearly overpowered by the genius of the
waters, and taking pity on her, he descended
from heaven in the form of a man with a boar's
head, and seating Prit'hivi firmly on his tusks,
he combated the water demon and restored the
earth to her place. The fourth and fifth descents of Vishnu are probably connected with the
ancient lost history of India, and appear to have
reference to religious wars. The legend of the
fourth is, that an impious monarch having de-
nied the existence of the Deity, was so enraged
against his son for holding a contrary opinion,
that he was about to put him to death, when
Vishnu, in the shape of Narasinha or the Man-
lion, burst from a pillar of the palace and slew
the atheistical king. The fifth is Vámuna, or
the dwarf Brahmin, called also Trivikera, or the
Three Stepper. The famous Bali, who is now
one of the judges and monarchs of Hell, or Patala, had, by his meritorious austerities, obtained
the sovereignty of the three worlds, earth, sea,
and sky; but he so misused his power, that the
spirits and Dewtahs were afraid of losing their
celestial mansions, and therefore petitioned
Brahme and the assembly of the immortals to

free them from the tyranny of Bali. But as the
celestial and irrevocable promise had been passed
that no being should have power to dispossess
the tyrant, Vishnu undertook by artifice to render him his own undoer, and therefore appeared
before him as a mendicant dwarf, begging a
boon from the mighty Bali. This boon the king
bound himself to grant, and immediately the
crafty deity claimed the space he could compass
in three strides, and dilating his form, he strode
over the earth with the first, over the ocean
with the second, and with the third he mounted
to heaven, leaving the astonished Bali only his
portion of Patala to rule.

The sixth Awatar, or Parasu Rama, is distinctly stated to have been a Brahmin, who, in
revenge for severities practised by the military
caste upon the sacerdotal class, assembled an
army, and completely exterminated the soldiers
of his country, which appears to have been that
of the Mahrattas, and to have substituted individuals of the inferior castes in their places. The
same country was at no very distant period, the
scene of a counter-tragedy; for the Brahmins
being slain, the fishermen and other low persons
were raised to that dignity, and hence the small
esteem in which the Mahratta and Kokun Brahmins are still held.

The seventh Awatar was Rama-Chandra, the

VAMUNA AWATAR

hero of Valmiki's great poem, and of whose adventures I gave you a sketch in a former letter. A numerous sect of religionists, calling themselves Ramanuj, worship Rama-Chandra as the only real descent of the Deity upon earth. Most Hindûs regard him as the most auspicious of heavenly personages, and the common salutation of peaceful travellers in passing is Râm Râm.

Crishna, or Krishen, the eighth Awatar, was the son of Vasudeva by Devaci, sister of the tyrant Cansa, who, jealous of the young Crishna, caused all the young children in his dominions to be massacred ; but the child had been sent to Yasoda, the wife of Ananda, a herd in Mat'hura, who brought him up as her own son, and gave him for playmates and attendants the Gopas or herds, and Gopis or milkmaids, from whom he selected nine as his principal favourites, and the poets and painters seldom represent him without these attendants. None of the Awatars are so celebrated as that of Crishna. In his youth he slew the serpent Caluja, besides other giants and monsters: he also protected his favourites the herdsmen of Mat'hura from the wrath of Indra, by raising the mountain Goverd'hana on the tip of a single finger to shield them from the showers of stones which the incensed Dewtah was pouring on them. He afterwards put to death his enemy Cansa, and having taken his cousins the

Pandus under his protection, he conducted the cruel war which I mentioned in speaking of the kings of Magadha. The private adventures of this god have furnished the pastoral and lyric poets of India with their most fruitful subjects. The beauty and affection of his consort Rad'ha, the friendship of his attendant Nanda *, the demigod's various and numerous amours and wanderings, are all celebrated with enthusiasm by his votaries, a considerable sect of whom, the Goclast'has, acknowledge no deity superior to him.

Great part of the history of Crishna bears a resemblance to that of Hercules †; the persecutions of his youth, his triumphs over different monsters, and the wars in which he was engaged, may all be compared to the adventures of the Grecian hero, while the pastoral life of Crishna Govind'ha resembles that of Apollo Nomius, and his appellation of Cesava, the beautiful-haired, comes sufficiently near to that of the

---

* Some say that as Crishna was an incarnation of Vishnu, Rad'ha was a form of Lacshemi, and Nanda was the great serpent Ananta Naga in a human shape.

† The wars of Crishna changed the religion of part of India, and substituted for the sanguinary sacrifices required by Maha Deo and Kali, offerings of images in lieu of human victims, and milk for blood. Hercules also substituted images of clay for the human victims offered on the altars of Saturn.

golden-haired Phœbus. But like Apollo, Crishna was the patron of music and song; he is often represented playing on a reed, while the nine Gopis dance round him in a circle on the Mount Goverd'hana, the Hindû Parnassus; and sometimes he appears surrounded with twelve pairs of dancers, representing the twelve months, the youths being the dark and the maidens the light fortnights, while he himself designates the Sun or Surya, like Apollo in his character of Phœbus.

Like Vishnu and all his Awatars, Crishna is represented of a dark blue colour, with the large bee of the same hue hovering over his head, splendidly dressed, adorned with chaplets of flowers and jewels, and holding a lotus, or sometimes seated on a throne shaped like that flower. When he is not depicted in his human character, his numerous hands hold the weapons consecrated to Vishnu himself, and in short he has all the attributes of that deity.

Bhûd, the ninth Awatar, appears rather an adopted than a legitimate Brahminical divinity; unlike most of the other descents of the gods, he was not a warrior but a contemplative sage, and introduced many novelties into religion, especially holding the destruction of life in abhorrence, either for the purposes of sacrifice or food. His life so exactly resembles that of the founder of the Bauddha religion, that he is generally considered as one and the same with that lawgiver.

The tenth Awatar Kalkee is to come. But Campbell must announce him and his purpose.

" But hark! as bow'd to earth the Brahmin kneels,
From heav'nly climes propitious thunder peals!
Of India's fate her guardian spirits tell,
Prophetic murmurs breathing on the shell,
And solemn sounds that awe the list'ning mind,
Roll on the azure paths of ev'ry wind.
  " Foes of mankind! (her guardian spirits say)
Revolving ages bring the bitter day,
When heav'n's unerring arm shall fall on you,
And blood for blood these Indian plains bedew;
Nine times have Brahma's * wheels of light'ning hurl'd,
His awful presence o'er th' alarmed world;
Nine times hath Guilt through all his giant frame
Convulsive trembled as the mighty came;
Nine times hath suffering mercy spar'd in vain,
But heav'n shall burst her starry gates again.
He comes! dread Brahma shakes the sunless sky
With murmuring wrath, and thunders from on high;
Heav'n's fiery horse, beneath his warrior form,
Paws the light clouds and gallops on the storm!
Wide waves his flickering sword; his bright arms glow,
Like summer suns, and light the world below!
Earth and her trembling isles in Ocean's bed
Are shook, and Nature rocks beneath his tread!
  " To pour redress on India's injur'd realm,
The oppressor to dethrone, the proud to whelm,
To chase destruction from her plunder'd shore,
With arts and arms that triumph'd once before,

* The poet is not incorrect; Brahma and Vishnu are one under different forms.

The tenth Awatar comes ! At Heaven's command,
Shall Seraswati wave her hallow'd wand !
And Camdeo bright and Ganesa sublime,
Shall bless with joy their own propitious clime !
Come, heav'nly powers ! primeval peace restore,
Love ! Mercy ! Wisdom ! rule for evermore !"

LETTER XVII.

MY DEAR SIR,

THE time of your sailing is now so
near at hand, that this will be the last letter I
shall have leisure to address to you in England,
and I have pretty well exhausted my store of
notes concerning the Hindûs properly so called.
But you must be aware that the inhabitants of
the peninsula of India, consist of many various
sects and tribes, and that when we have enumerated the Hindûs and the different European
nations who have settled on their coasts, we are
far from having completed the list of the inhabitants of Hindostan. We may divide them
into the Christian, Jewish, Mussulman, and
Parsee tribes, besides those sects derived from
the Brahminical faith.

From the time that the spirit of navigation
and commerce began to revive in Europe, some
faint reports of a Christian empire in the East,
which some placed in Abyssinia, others in In-

5

dia, and all agreed to call the country of Prester John, had excited the curiosity of the
Western states; and many missions were sent
to discover that desirable country, supposing it
to contain, if not the garden of Eden, at least,
that happy place where Enoch, Moses, and St.
John awaited in their earthly bodies the day of
judgment. Its riches were imagined to be as
admirable as its government, and all together
to realize the fables of the Happy Islands.

Accordingly when the Portuguese found on
the western coast of India a few villages inhabited by the remains of a settlement of Nes-
torian Christians, they were persuaded that they
were soon to fall in with the country of Prester
John, and it was only when they discovered
that these poor creatures were heretics who did
not acknowledge the Bishop of Rome, that they
remanded Prester John to Abyssinia, and set to
work to convert the new Christians, by the gentle modes of the inquisitions established at Goa
and elsewhere, to the true Roman Catholic
faith. They have succeeded; and at the time
I was in India, I confess, that the ceremonies
I saw performed in the Catholic churches, appeared to me scarcely less contemptible, than
those of the neighbouring pagodas. It is impossible to conceive a more degraded form of
Christianity than that commonly professed by

the black Portuguese of India. The greater
part of the priests are of their own complexion,
and if the revenues of a church should be tempt-
ing enough to attract a white pastor from Goa,
a sermon delivered in barbarous Latin, is not
very likely to produce much effect on ears, per-
vious to no sounds but those of the *lingua
Franca* of the East, under the name of Portuguese, but which contains nearly as much of
every native tongue as of that language. This
class of inhabitants is extremely numerous,
though, as you may infer from what I have
said of them, not very respectable in India.
The richest Christian merchants, always excepting the Honourable Company's servants,
are the Armenians, who are settled on various
parts of the coast, and in some of the largest
towns in the interior. And these are the only
two denominations of Christians I shall mention, for it is needless to say how very Christian
all the European settlers are.

The Jews have larger settlements and more
permanent abodes in India than they have any
where in Europe. Bombay has several thousand useful Israelite subjects, who do not refuse
to communicate with the Mussulmans, or to
bear arms. Cashmire contains a large colony,
supposed by Bernier, who was among them a
hundred and sixty years ago, to be part of the

ten tribes who migrated thither during the Ba-
bylonish captivity; but I refer you to himself
for his reasons for that opinion, and to the second vol. of the Asiatic Researches, for the
authority on which the Afghans, Patans, or
Rohillas, are considered as descendants of Saul,
king of Israel, and for their conversion to Ma-
homedanism during the life of the prophet.

Of the two great Mahomedan sects the Shiahs
and the Sunnis, the Shiahs are now most numerous in Hindostan*; but they are subdivided
into a variety of minor sectaries, who throw
upon each other the reproach of impiety, or at
least that of heresy. One of those which you
will most frequently meet with, is that of the
Borahs from Guzerat, who were converted near
six centuries ago; and among whom are a few
individuals of the Sunni sect. They are merchants, or perhaps I should more correctly say
pedlars, and are in general an inoffensive race
consisting of from three to four thousand families in the neighbourhood of Ahmedabad, and
probably many more, dispersed over the rest
of India.

* The subdivisions of these, compose the seventy-two sects
of the Faithful, to whom may now be added the Wahabis,
those reformers, who to break the Mussulmans of their superstitious veneration for the tombs of departed saints, have
levelled the temple of Mecca to the ground.

The Sadikyahs or *the pure* are also Shiahs, fifty or sixty thousand of whom are settled in Multan, Lahore, Dehli, and Guzerat; they chiefly subsist by commerce, but complain of persecution from other more powerful sects.

The Hazarehs of Cabul, and the Baloch of Sinde are also Shiahs. A singular race of heretical Shiahs exists in the Nizam's territories; its members believe in the metempsychosis, abstain from flesh, hold it lawful to worship the image of Ali, in whom they believe that God was actually manifest; and they consider the Koran as it now exists, to be a forgery of Abubecr, Omar, and Othman.

Such is the progress the Shiah sect has made that it has nearly superseded the Soonis, who were the orthodox Mussulmans during the reigns of the family of Babershah; but at present as there is no persecution on either side, they are likely to settle quietly into good neighbours and friends, and probably in a short time the Sunnis may be nearly forgotten, for the stranger Mussulmans, who come from Persia to settle in Hindostan, are continually increasing the number of the Shiahs, while that of the Sunnis in its branches of Hunafi and Shafei is, I have been informed, on the decline.

The Parsees, of whom you will find a great

number in Guzerat, and in Bombay, are the descendants of the followers of Zoroaster, who fled before the Mahomedan arms under the Calif Omar. They are the most enterprising traders of India, and seem rapidly increasing in numbers and riches. Their present internal police is the same with that of the Hindû townships, by whose laws and customs they abide, in strict conformity with the conditions on which they first obtained their settlement in Guzerat. They are a hardy race of men, more robust and vulgar than the Hindûs or the Mussulmans, but incomparably more spirited than either.

Of the different sects which have sprung from the Brahminical Hindûs, that of the Sikhs is the most remarkable*. Its founder Nanac, a Hindû, who was born in the middle of the fifteenth century of the Christian æra, appears to have been a man of singular virtue and benevolence, who, willing to end the bloody wars then carried on by the Mussulmans against his own nation, attempted to reconcile the Vedas and the Koran, by showing that the Hindûs really acknowledged but one supreme God, and calling upon them to abandon the idolatry

* See Sketch of the Sikhs by Sir John Malcolm.

which had crept in among them, and to abide by the pure faith of their ancestors. The consequence was, that instead of conciliating the contending parties, he formed a third, which, though it long continued harmless and peaceable, was destined one day to carry on the most cruel wars in the very heart of that country, which the benevolent founder wished to save from all dissensions. After the death of Nanac, his followers, who were composed of people of all ranks and of all religions, in their zeal to celebrate their prophet, ascribed to him the power of working miracles ; so widely did they stray from his principles.

The Sikhs continued to increase in numbers, and as it should seem in consequence, for we find that their fourth Guru or spiritual leader built the town of Ramdaspoor now called Amritsar, which is the holy city of the Sikhs. But their tranquillity was soon to be disturbed, and the peaceable religious sectary, urged by Mussulman persecution, changed his character for that of an intrepid warrior before an hundred and fifty years since the death of Nanac had elapsed ; and in half a century more the repeated cruelties of the Mahomedans, especially the murder of the leader of the Sikhs, Tegh Bahader, raised a new champion and legislator in the person of Guru Govind, his son, who carried every religious innovation on both the Mussulman and Hindû creeds, far beyond the boundaries Nanac had prescribed, abolished the distinctions of caste, and engrafted the military devotion to *steel* on the religious faith of Nanac, and thus formed that singular combination of Monotheism with worship distinctly paid to the sword, by which he purchased and preserved his political existence, which so long excited the curiosity of Europeans.

Guru Govind's first step in his new legislation was to make all his subjects equal in civil rights, and to inspire them all with pride and military ardour he caused them to take the name of Singh or Lion, and constantly to wear *steel* in some shape about them*. He also enjoined them to let their hair grow and to wear blue clothes, customs which are still regarded by the Acalis or never dying, a tribe of mendicant devotees, who surround the pool of Amritsar, and who, at once insolent and powerful, have a singular influence in the state. These distinctions were part of Govind's policy to

---

* " The protection of the infinite lord is over us: thou art " the lord, the cutlass, the knife, and the dagger. The pro- " tection of the immortal being is over us, the protection of " ALL STEEL is over us: the protection of ALL TIME is over " us: the protection of ALL STEEL is constantly over us."

Verses of Guru Govind from Sir J. Malcolm.

separate his people from those by whom they were surrounded. His courage, his policy, his intellect, were all applied to revenge his father's death, and to make his people formidable to the Mahomedans; but his power was unequal to the mightiness of his views, and after a race of glory suitable to his wishes for some years, fortune turned and favoured his enemies, and he died A. D. 1708, of wounds received in the Deccan at Nader, a town on the Godavery. After his death the Sikhs seized the opportunity afforded by the distractions of the Mogul empire under Aurengzebe's immediate successors to revenge their priest; they seized Serhind and ravaged the greatest part of the northern provinces of Hindostan. But they were too few long to contend with the Moguls, and they were persecuted and put to death wherever they could be found, a high reward being offered for the head of every Sikh. The troubles, however, caused by the Mahratta incursions, the inroads of Ahmed Shah, and the cruel fate of some of the last sovereigns of Dehli gave a breathing time to the Sikhs whom persecution had hardened, and they again assembled at Amritsar, whence they began those inroads into the Panjab, which finally put them in possession of the whole province.

The sacred books of the Sikhs contain both

3

their history and their laws. The first or Adi Granth was composed by Nanac and his four immediate successors. The other is the Dasama Padshah ka Granth or book of the tenth ruler, written by Guru Govind. These books are read in the religious assemblies of the people, who on meeting eat together, and then proceed to their devotions. The form of government which prevailed among the Sikhs under their ten Gurus, was that of a commonwealth, acknowledging a spiritual chief, who took upon himself the military command, when the people changed their character of peaceful devotees, for that of martial enthusiasts.

But from the death of Guru Govind, they have scarcely acknowledged a chief, even in battle; and were it not for the authority exercised over them by the mendicant Acalis, who arrogate to themselves the right of guarding Amritsar, and of convening the national council, they might be regarded as the freest people upon earth. Their internal police and civil law is the same as that of the Hindûs, with whose customs and even religion their own is intimately blended, although they profess to despise their superstitions.

The next division of the inhabitants of India which I shall mention, is the sect of the Baudd'has. As the proportion of these sectaries in British India is small, although they form the greater part if not the entire population of Ceylon, Siam, Cochinchina, the Burman Empire, Cambodia, Japan, Tonkin, and China, differently modified, however, in each, I shall content myself with little more than naming them.

Their principal deity, or perhaps I should say prophet, is Gautama or Bhûd, who is evidently the same person whom the Brahmins have adopted into the family of the Awataras of Vishnu, whence we might, perhaps, suspect that the Baudd'ha religion was derived from that of the Brahmins. That it once prevailed over great part of the continent of India is undeniable, but that it preceded the Brahminical faith in that country, though it has been vehemently asserted, appears not to be proved. The intimate resemblance which the laws, customs, sciences, and language of the Baudd'has bear to those of the Brahmins afford a strong presumption that one people has borrowed largely from the other; but in my feeble judgment, the Brahmins bear the most antique stamp.

However, we will, if you please, leave this discussion to the antiquarians, who are not wanting in plausible arguments on each side, and the Baud'hists I believe can even prove that

s

Bhûd, or Boden, is Fo in China, and Woden in Scandinavia. So far has his worship extended. The Baud'hists in our India are mere sectaries, scarcely more numerous than the Jines, whose tenets have so remarkable a similarity with theirs, that they have often been confounded. The character of their philosophy and politics, their laws, their notions of the universe, have the same family air as those of the Brahmins; their mythology is the chief point of difference, and as it is more free from superstition, and, above all, contains no traces of the barbarous and sanguinary traits which once disgraced the Hindû faith, I should humbly conceive it to have been reformed from it.

The Bhaudd'ha priests do not marry while they continue in the priesthood; consequently there are no castes among them. The Jines, on the contrary, adhere to the system of castes, and they differ in their chronology and upon various other points, although they both acknowledge Bhûd as their legislator. The few establishments still belonging to them in Hindostan have been carefully concealed from the dread of persecution; but the indefatigable researches of Col. Mackenzie, whom I trust you will be so fortunate as to meet at Madras, has discovered that the Jines have still considerable colleges at Pen-

naconda, Conjeveram, Dehli, and Collapoore.
The principal seat of Bauddhism is in Siam,
but you will meet with it as a national faith in
Ceylon. There it is remarkable that some
monuments whose origin is unknown to the
Baudd'has, have a relation to the Brahminical
creed. The religion of the court of Candy is
also Brahminical; but as that has an accidental
and modern cause, it cannot have any connexion
with these ancient monuments.

Besides these sects, undoubtedly of great antiquity, there are a few mountain tribes who
seem to practise rites different from any of those
I have named, and these inhabit the hilly
countries surrounding Bengal. But I cannot
help suspecting, by the few accounts I have
heard of them, that they are Hindûs, who have
preserved the sanguinary sacrifice and its attendant barbarisms, or as some intelligent
writers have supposed, that they may be the
remnants of the aboriginal inhabitants of India.
Of these, however, you will meet very few:
their history is one of the many desiderata in
our knowledge of the East.

Before you return, I trust you will have thrown
some new light on these subjects, and I entreat
you to remember that nothing is beneath the
attention of a philosopher, or of one who

wishes to enlarge his views of human nature, to study that most wonderful of the works of God, the mind of man, or to be that most respectable of beings, the benefactor of his fellow-creatures.

THE END.

G. WOODFALL, Printer,
Angel Court, Skinner Street, London.

OBSERVATIONS ON THE PLATES.

THE Plate containing the specimen of sculpture is composed of two very different subjects. The upper one was drawn by Mr. Glennie, from a green steatite tortoise, in the care of Dr. Fleming, of Gloucester Place. It had been found in digging for a well in a bed of clay, at a very great depth on the banks of the Jumna, not far from Dehli.

The chisseling of this tortoise is most delicate, and its polish the highest that stone is capable of, it is in the highest preservation, and is, altogether, an exquisite specimen of the excellence of the ancient Hindû artists in the minor subjects of art.

The lower subject is from the skreen in the front of Carli Cave, it is rather a favourable specimen, as far as the writer is acquainted with Hindû sculpture. There is, however, one figure on the same skreen, which greatly surpasses it in lightness and ease ; but the drawing was unfortunately lost.

The large centre column of the second plate, or specimens of architecture, stands in the area in front of the Cave of Carli. The others are detached pieces from Canara in Salsette, and the Seven Pagodas or Mahabalipooram.

The Muntapum is an open temple in which Vishnu is placed by the priests of Mahabalipooram on days of festivals, each pillar is of a single stone, the unfinished building on the right is part of a royal Goparum or triumphal arch, and the colonnade in the back ground is part of the Choultry or place of rest for travellers.

Vicramaditya at the feet of Kali, is taken from the sculptured rocks at the Seven Pagodas. I have given it this name because the subject accords with the legend, but I may be wrong.

Siva and Parvati with their attendants were sketched from a large tablet in a ruined temple at Mahabalipooram. The sea washes into its courts and it is surrounded by fragments, the remains of former grandeur. A singular circumstance concerning this temple is, that it is evidently constructed from the ruins of an older fabric, its latest deity was Siva, whose symbols occupy the remaining apartments. A colossal figure of Vishnu Narayn, however, lies in a corner of one of the remaining virandas.

Ganesa, whose uncouth figure is given in the plate, is the God of Wisdom. This sketch was copied from one in the possession of Col. E——, taken from a town south of Madras, where Ganesa under the name of Polear is peculiarly worshipped.

The Vamuna and Varaha Awatars are from the sculptured rocks at Mahabalipooram, the height of the principal figure in each exceeds six feet. The chisseling in some places is very fresh as the rock is remarkably hard, appearing to me to be a grey granite.

ERRATA.

DIRECTIONS TO THE BINDER.

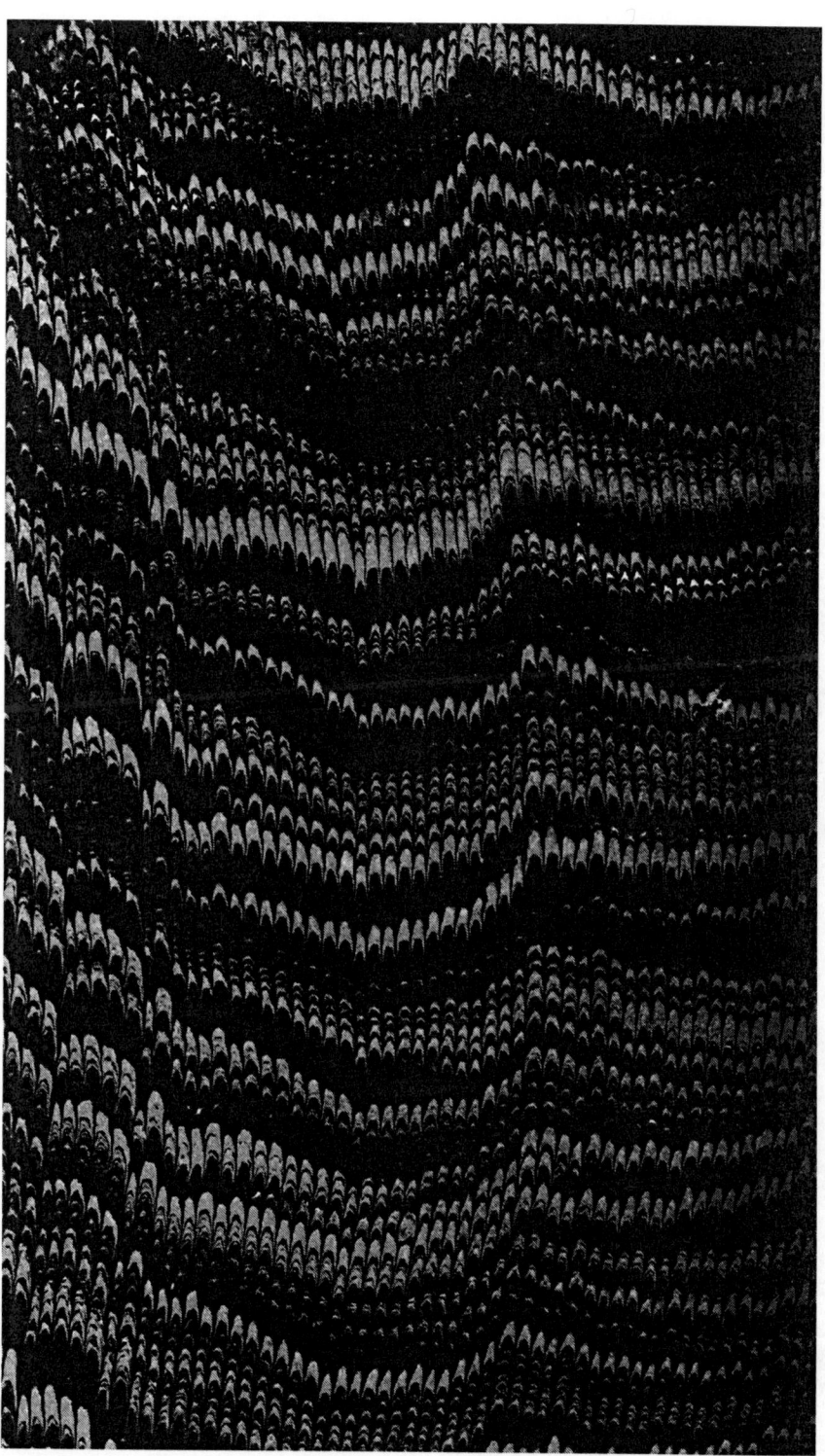

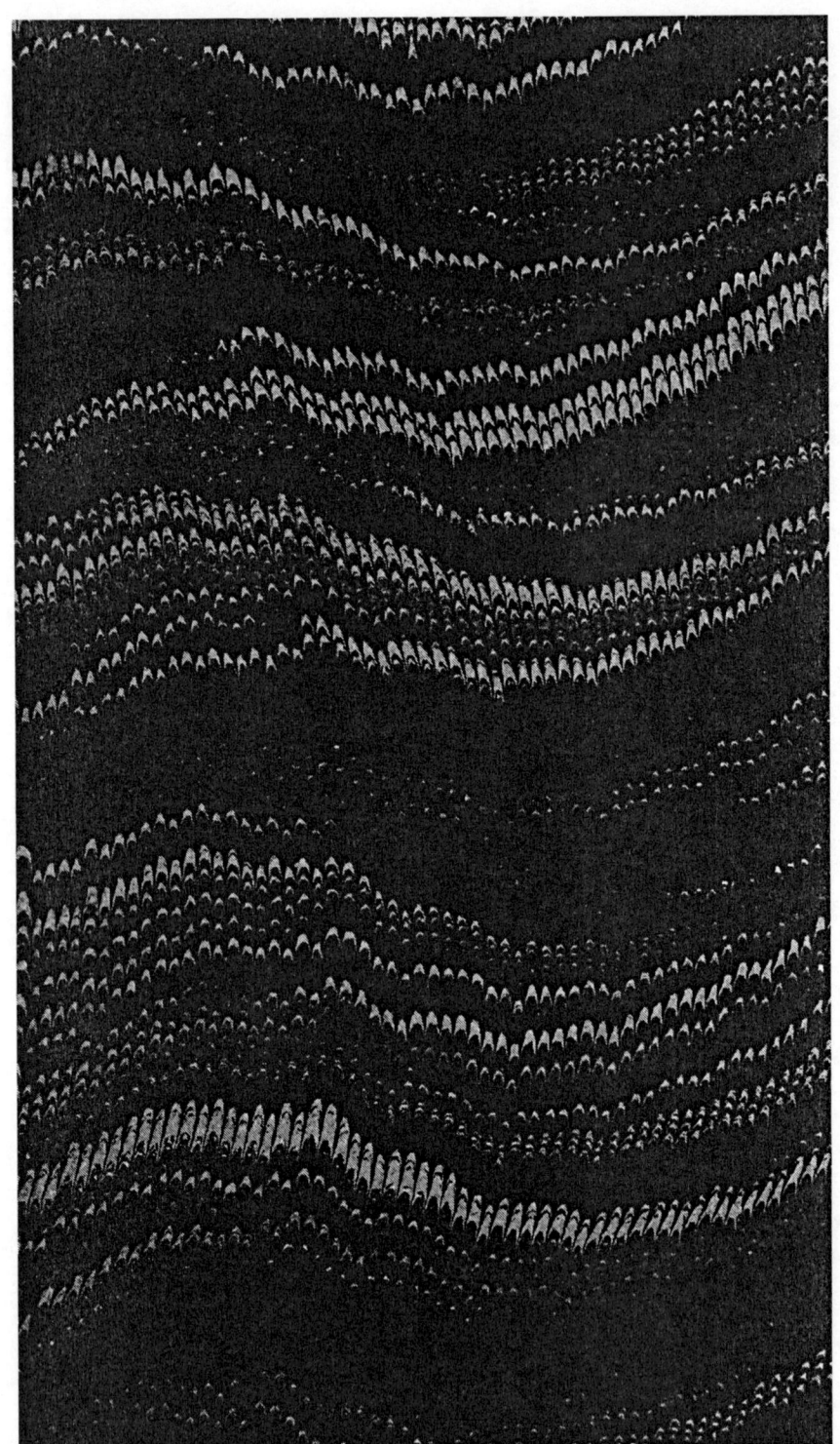

Lightning Source UK Ltd.
Milton Keynes UK
UKOW041924170212

187485UK00006B/38/P